Robes

A Book of Coming Changes

BY
PENNY KELLY

Robes
A Book of Coming Changes
by
Penny Kelly

All rights reserved © 1999, 2005 by Penny Kelly

Published by:
Lily Hill Publishing
32260 - 88th Avenue
Lawton, MI. 49065
USA

ISBN 0-9632934-2-7
Robes: A Book of Coming Changes / Penny Kelly.—2nd ed.
Includes index
1. New Age   2. Spirituality   3. Future/Forecasting   4. Prophecy

This book is dedicated to
the little men in brown robes
and the cheery, gentle, patient way
they went about teaching
a very resistant student.

It is also dedicated to
all the peoples of Earth,
especially those who
wish the world was
different, but don't really have
a vision of what we could
create, or re-create,
if we set our minds to it.

Other Books By Penny Kelly:

The Evolving Human

The Elves of Lily Hill Farm

From The Soil To The Stomach

Table of Contents

INTRODUCTION

I have written this book to share some of the experiences and changes that occurred in my worldview as I worked my way through a serious transformation of consciousness known as a "full, spontaneous awakening of kundalini." The awakening triggers arousal of the full powers of consciousness, including, but not limited to, visions, voices, numerous psychic abilities, and alterations in perception that introduce one to the surprising number of time-space realities that co-exist with our own.

Although it sounds dramatic, during my long struggle with kundalini, a group of about seven little men began appearing in my home. They were dressed in long brown robes and looked like monks. Although the first few visits did not accomplish much, the little men continued to show up at irregular intervals over the next year and half, always asking if they could show me some "pictures."

At first, I had great difficulty with their visits. Their pictures concerned the future, and I never really thought about the future in any organized way. To me, this dim, hazy topic was the territory of gypsy fortune-tellers. Believing the future to be an amalgam of luck, accident, and fate that smoldered in one murky cauldron, I held long and tightly to the notion that the future could not be seen or known.

However, the approach of these little men was that it was easy to see the future. They insisted that it wasn't set in stone, and needed to be created carefully, chosen wisely from among a host of possibilities.

Their approach carted me unceremoniously outside my comfort zone and dumped me there, kicking and squealing. At the time, I was a classic example of immaturity. I did not really care about the world and believed that what happened "out there" was of no concern to me. If something serious did happen, I was sure that I would be spared any real difficulty, or would somehow get around or beyond the problem.

One of the strongholds of my psyche was a generalized attitude that fit under the label "I am not responsible for stuff that happens." Whatever happened just happened; it was God or the other guy that controlled things. We had very limited choice, which was never really a choice at all; it was more of a calculated gamble. Common gambling went on with one's future, for instance, in the act of going to school to get an education, deciding on a career, or choosing a husband. There were no guarantees that we would get what we wanted from these choices, and we were all subject to the whims of Fate and the fortunes she brought.

The visits of the little men began in early 1980. When they stopped in the latter part of 1981, I was relieved and tried to forget about them. As time went on, however, what I'd seen and learned began to have more and more influence in my life. When they returned for one last visit eleven years later, they encouraged me to write down what they had shown me. With many misgivings, I finally decided to do so.

Although any observer or media fanatic of the past few years could easily look at what I've written and declare that all I've done is catalog the ongoing worldly events of the last seventeen years, the things the little men showed me were truly a revelation to my narrow self in 1981. If there is a value in what is written here, my hope is that it will be in the unique combination of practical appraisal, common sense, deep insight, and creative vision they constantly urged.

One of the greatest barriers to accepting the information they showed me was their insistence that what *I* thought about where we were headed as a people was relevant at all. I couldn't see this, and when I did get glimpses of it, was overcome with feelings that ran the gamut from helplessness, to superiority, to false humility, to a heavy burden of responsibility, then resentment at their interference in my life, and finally, back to not caring. Many years went by before I could look at it as simply useful, well-intended information.

There were about sixteen visits altogether and in each one they transmitted huge amounts of information. The information was obviously telepathic, but this term is a very limited description of what was sometimes a complete immersion of myself in that future and the actual experience of events going on there.

Some of these experiences were similar in nature to a lucid dream in which you know you are dreaming, yet can interact consciously with everything in the environment. Other experiences were extraordinarily real, so real in fact, that I would forget about the ordinary reality of everyday life and become completely involved in what the little men were showing me. Still other experiences were characterized by the sort of observation and conversation you might have if you were watching a stage play or television program with a few friends.

It has been challenging to translate telepathic information and experience into written language. So much cannot be translated for reasons that have to do with the broad, inclusive nature of telepathic experience. Large amounts of detail are grasped instantly during telepathy, and the organization of telepathic information is very different from the organization of information meant to be communicated verbally or in written form.

For instance, the little men would present one particular scene or series of events and use it to transmit many kinds of information. Returning to that scene or series of events again and again, they approached it from a dozen changing angles, presenting different details and multiple perspectives, each going deeper than the one before.

Therefore, it was impossible to take that exact scene and write a clear set of paragraphs that followed one another in simple, linear fashion. I could not cover all the *kinds* of information communicated in it, nor could I bring out details in a coherent way while doing justice to the totality of the experience. The result has been that I have just tried to do the best I could.

Some information I saw has not been included for reasons having to do with the privacy of myself and others. Some has been left out because it was a specific experiential lesson just for me, created by the little men to make it easier to grasp certain concepts they wanted to get across, especially around the subject of wave frequencies.

In other instances, such as the healing of catastrophic illness, things were omitted because I wanted to play down some of the healing techniques I witnessed using frequencies and light. Seeing the uses of special frequencies to re-tune molecular and cellular operation in the body, reversing a whole cascade of disease and ill effects, was nothing short of miraculous, yet I wanted to underscore the little men's premise that we must first recognize the importance of our relationship to Earth and not run off chasing another form of technology that we think will save us, ignoring our foundations in the world of soil and green plants. And as the little men made clear, only *after* we have aligned ourselves with the life principle and learned to maintain supreme health at all levels will we be given the secrets to regenerating life and health through the use of frequencies, whether light, sound, or otherwise.

As they once said, "If you're not willing to go after something with your own time and energy, why should it be handed to you? We will show you the possibilities, but you must begin to take a hand in creating your future."

Initially I tried to set out as clearly as possible the events and changes I saw without discussing the strikingly different set of ideas, assumptions about life, work, ethics, values, expectations, daily routines, and beliefs that formed the foundation of the changes they showed me. I also wanted to keep their information at arm's length, taking no responsibility for the words that appeared on these pages. However, those friends and colleagues who read the early versions of the manuscript insisted that I discuss the relevance of what I had written, or at least their relevance to me. As I wrote, I recalled many of the powerful reactions I'd had either during or after the visits. Thus the writing process itself caused one confrontation with myself after another, finally resulting in the realization that I could no more keep the information at arm's length than I could set aside my skin.

More than anything, I have tried to communicate the information with the same level of cheer, insight, practical attitude, and quality of loving common sense that the little men in brown robes maintained. Their emphasis on looking ahead to see what we could create and how we could learn from the situation at hand was inspiring.

If there is any personal wish I could make for all of us here on Earth today, it would be for the continued evolution of the human being toward the opening of consciousness and the practical, everyday use of our full creative potential. And if there is any message I would want to get across beyond the information itself, it is the little men's intense hope that we would wake up and see clearly the reality we have been creating for the past few hundred years or so, take note of where it is leading us, and make the necessary corrections without having everything collapse, losing the truly valuable gains we have made in several areas of life.

As they pointed out so often, if we don't have a vision of what we're moving toward, of what we *could* create, we won't see anything but destruction, won't feel anything but fear as the changes begin to escalate. If this happens we'll be caught up in something painful and ugly at the exact moment we most need to be creative and to be maintaining a vision of beauty, truth, and freedom. 📖

1 📖

FIRST MEETING...

THE afternoon was growing dark, getting colder. Snow was threatening and I kept thinking I should go out to get a few things for supper before the weather got really messy. I didn't have much energy and hated the thought of having to go out in the cold. It meant boots, gloves, a hat and coat, and the mundane decisions grocery shopping required. Worse, the truck would only begin to warm up by the time I reached the store. Still, it was that or cornflakes for supper. Reluctantly, I made the trip, trying to ignore the feelings of irritation that accompanied me.

Shortly before 5:00 p.m. I returned with several bags of groceries and was putting them away when an unsettling feeling that I was not alone in the house began to creep over me. For a few seconds I wondered if Ben had come home from his job on the afternoon shift. There had been no sound of a car in the driveway, however, and my daughters were visiting their father. Turning to look around, I froze. There were at least a half dozen little men wearing some brown robes standing quite attentively next to the table across the room!

For the briefest of moments I wasn't even surprised. It had been almost a year now, since February of 1979, that many strange things had been happening to me. There were lights that glowed and shimmered around everything, I frequently drifted out of the body and thought I was elsewhere, or had little visions in which I saw things happen before they actually did happen. My sleep had been disturbed for months. Some nights I spent the entire night in dreams so real I was sure I was awake, and when I finally did waken, I was exhausted. Other nights I spent hours in a sort of suspended animation, unable to sink into the familiar blankness sleep once offered. I lived in a state of constant consciousness where, at times, the world would begin to buzz and pulse and heat up until I thought I would explode, burst into flame, or both. Other times I existed in a frozen, icy landscape where nothing moved. And my perception, something that I'd never given a thought to before, seemed out of control. Often I was no longer sure what was real and what was imaginary. Wrestling daily with the fear that I was slowly going insane, I had no idea that what I was really experiencing was known as "the awakening of kundalini." Although I'd never heard of it before, it was an ancient eastern term that meant the "full opening of consciousness." [1]

Over the previous twelve months, the stress of these experiences and the fear of insanity had mounted steadily. Life had become an endless string of "psychic" and other unnamable experiences, and now I struggled to decide whether I was just imagining a group of brown-robed, monkish-looking men in my kitchen, or if they were really there.

One of them spoke up and cheerfully said they would like to talk to me about some work I had agreed to do while I was here. I covered my eyes, then my ears in an attempt to block them out, hoping my perception would return to normal quickly.

It didn't, and when I opened my eyes, the little men were still there and still trying to explain what they were doing in my kitchen. I squeezed my eyes tightly shut and covered my ears again, but even with eyes closed and ears covered, their voices kept coming to me in the form of soft, rhythmic words spoken in perfect unison. The words were so clear it was as though they were coming from inside me… either that or every cell of my body had suddenly developed ears. The words created images that filled my mind's eye and for a moment, I was utterly still, watching in shocked silence. Then something in me revolted.

With eyes squeezed shut in a childish denial of their existence, I waved my arms crazily as if trying to erase their presence and cried out to

---

[1] See *The Evolving Human* for a full account of my struggles with kundalini and the aftermath of dealing with a fully awakened consciousness.

them to stop, to go away and leave me alone. When they persisted, I ran out of the kitchen to my bedroom where I crawled under the covers crying, "No, no, no, no, no…" I knew it was irrational behavior but at that instant I simply could not deal with one more perceptual anomaly.

After a few moments it was quiet. I wondered if they were gone. Then I heard them just inside the bedroom door. Surprisingly, in spite of my hysterics, their attitude seemed to be one of patience and understanding and they said they were quite sorry to have upset me. This was followed by something about wanting to show me pictures and answer some of my questions, but that they were leaving for the time being.

"We will return when you are perhaps more open to a little conversation," they announced. Silence followed.

When I finally looked up they had disappeared. Relieved yet still deeply unnerved, I buried my head again and cried. I did not understand what was happening to me and had been hoping every day that my perception would return to normal. Finally, alone for the evening, I drifted into a fitful sleep, forgetting supper altogether.

📖

That was my first encounter with the little men in brown robes. It was neither smooth nor graceful on my part, and I was so sure that it was just another freak show in the theater of my perception that I hardly gave it a thought once they were gone.

Looking back, I don't know why I didn't ask myself the ordinary, sensible questions like, "Who were they?" or "What in the world was that all about?" At that time in my life, I was so afraid of seeing, hearing, or touching the truth that I avoided asking questions or probing too deeply into anything at all.

In the months that followed their first visit, life seemed to be coming apart in every way and most of my energy went into trying to keep it and myself together. In addition, the continuous and uncontrollable psychic experiences left me stressed, strained, and deeply tired.

📖

In September of that same year, the little men startled me with their second visit. The circumstances were almost the same as the first visit back in January. They appeared in the kitchen as I was preparing supper, but this time I did not react hysterically. I was in no mood to be dealing with the far reaches of perceptual reality and when they greeted me in a cheerful, businesslike manner, I slowly turned my back to them, refusing to respond or to acknowledge their presence in any way. I simply pretended they weren't there.

They were persistent for a bit. They pointed out that I wanted things to get better, which was true. They said that at just that moment I had been asking myself what was going to come of my life, and although this was true, I certainly wasn't looking for answers from strangers dressed like monks who appeared in—or disappeared from—my kitchen.

With simple insistence they repeated what they had said the first time, that they had "good news, pictures of the things to come, pictures that would help me understand what would become of me and my life," but I ignored them.

Several times they asked politely if I would be willing to view these pictures, insisting that I would better understand what was happening, yet still I pretended they weren't there. Finally they said they were leaving and would return when I was feeling better.

When they were gone I felt twinges of guilt at my rudeness. I had been raised to be a polite girl. The fact that at the age of thirty-two I still thought of myself as a girl rather than a woman was testament to the level of my maturity, and like a child, for a while I felt guilty. The thought kept recurring that maybe I should have at least explained to them that I was having great difficulty holding my life and relationships together and just wasn't up to dealing with them or their pictures at the moment. "Perhaps I should apologize if they show up again," I thought, but for a second time, I ended up dismissing them as unreal, not knowing how intensely and powerfully they would eventually affect my life. 📖

2 📖

"Earth Is a Living Being..."

AN icy wind lifted the water of the canal into hundreds of dark crystal wavelets while I sat on the living room floor, staring through the sliding glass doorwall. Thanksgiving was only a few days away and I was reflecting on the fact that I had no plans for this important family holiday. I had just decided to get up and call some friends, hoping they would welcome an extra guest for dinner if I promised to bring a dish to pass, when the little men in brown robes appeared for the third time that year.

As if their appearance was expected, I turned and gazed at them with cool detachment, noticing a few details of their presence. By count, there were seven of them, and with stretching they might have been five feet tall. I was five feet three inches, and even from my position on the floor, it was obvious that not a one of them was as tall as I was. Two were completely bald, the rest were bald only on top with a small fringe of silvery-gray-to-light-brown hair that encircled the sides and back of their heads. They wore dark brown, floor-length robes with long sleeves and a white or gold-colored rope around the waist. There were no beards or mustaches, and the faces all seemed to be quite round and ruddy, almost shining, as if they had recently been scrubbed and polished. The whole group had a warm glow about them as if exuding an inner light.

Not wanting to be as rude or ridiculous as I had in the first couple of visits I sat quite still, my mind vacillating between curiosity and pique at another fluctuation of consciousness.

"Why is this happening?" I mumbled half to myself, not sure whether I meant the appearance of the little men, or my generally unstable perception.

Considering my reaction to their first two visits, they seemed to take my quiet mumbling as both greeting and invitation.

"Because the life you keep trying to create has nothing to do with what you came here to do. We are here to help and have some information that may bring understanding. Would you like to see it?" they asked with calm equanimity.

I nodded uncertainly, nimbly dismissing their comment about my life, and continued to sit and stare at them. After a few seconds, they told me to get comfortable, to relax and close my eyes so I could see better. The idea of closing my eyes so I could see better struck me as incongruous but I did as directed, and immediately pictures and sounds filled me, rolling across my mind's eye with all the power and clarity of movie footage in a theater.

I knew that my body was sitting on the floor in the living room of my house, but my entire perceptual and sensory system was standing with this group of little strangers out in space at the edge of the atmosphere looking at a most beautiful planet, the Earth. It appeared like a volleyball that was somehow caught or suspended in a large, 3-dimensional volleyball net. The volleyball net was electrically charged and shimmered with a faint, pulsing glow.

For a moment I was flooded with a deep uneasiness that brought my fears of insanity to the surface. This was a form of telepathy so vivid and real that it would have been difficult to tell the difference between their pictures and the world of everyday events were it not for the content of those pictures.

Then the clear, matter-of-fact voices of the little men distracted me from my uneasiness.

"The first thing you should understand is that the Earth is a living being and is quite capable of healing herself. When she does, there can be a shift of many degrees, even a complete rolling over."

Their words were accompanied by a slight tremor in the earth as we viewed it.

"The net you are looking at is like a network of electromagnetic and other wave forces that move through space and intersect as well as interact with the waves—electromagnetic and otherwise—given off by the Earth.

"As these waves move through space, they strike the Earth from all directions, some holding the planet in place, some moving through or around her, causing a steady rotation. The axis Earth rotates around is the path energy takes as it moves through the body of the planet, and of course this creates your magnetic north and south poles.

"The important thing to be aware of is that as humans create and experiment with technologies using electromagnetic wave energy or other forms of wave power, they can cause serious fluctuations in the waves given off by the Earth, and in the network of waves moving through space around the Earth. Certainly you are familiar with the waves on a beach and the variations in their size and strength. The same kinds of variation occur in the waves that move through space and if you happen to be playing with wave technology at the wrong moment, serious consequences could result. Too great a fluctuation can make the earth roll or wobble seriously enough to create a lot of destruction for humans, thus we would recommend caution."

I did not know what to say at this point. I was still stuck on the very first thing they said, which was that the Earth was a "living being." This seemed preposterous to me. And the idea that the Earth could shift its position in space seemed an impossible fiction. When added to my already serious doubts about whether it was a good idea to watch their pictures, listen to their words, and give the little men the courtesy of acting as if they were real, the information proved to be almost too much. My initial willingness to hear them out or to look at their pictures began shriveling.

I was about to protest or try to withdraw from the experience when the Earth and the volleyball net sort of shrugged. Bulging awkwardly like a pregnant woman in the last trimester, the Earth rolled forward, rolled back, bobbled around a bit, then resettled itself in an entirely new position. The oceans rolled and splashed like water in a bathtub, and even from my distant vantage point I could see considerable destruction as whole sections of land rose up and folded over on themselves, burying everyone and everything, leaving the surface as bare and new as the moon.

For a moment I forgot my disbelief. The blank, empty surface areas in some places looked as though no one, human or animal, had ever even lived there. Then curiously detached, I found myself wondering what happened to Michigan. Immediately the little men responded.

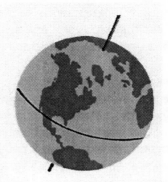

"It is approximately at the latitude that Arizona once sat. The total amount of this particular shift was only about 17 degrees. Once everything has settled it would look something like this."

The whole planet was resting at what appeared to be a slightly unusual tilt. As it rotated slowly in its new position I could see what was left of Japan was just outside the Arctic Circle, and a couple of islands at the northern edge of Russia were the center of the new North Pole. The tip of South America appeared to be inside the Antarctic Circle and formed a continuous bridge onto the ice of the new South Pole.

The equator was running at a slightly different angle as well. It crossed just north of Australia and headed in what used to be a northeasterly direction across the Pacific, cutting through Guatemala in Central America, crossing the Caribbean Sea and skipping past the top edge of South America. From there it moved out across the Atlantic, heading in what had been a southeasterly direction, and entered West Africa south of the Sea of Guinea. Moving along the southern edge of Zaire, it exited East Africa to run through the northern half of Madagascar, then across the Indian Ocean and back to the northern coast of Australia. The Nile River had changed course, in fact, many rivers had changed position, or course, or both, and some were not there at all anymore.

The northern edge of Alaska was just outside the Arctic Circle and was plagued by an increase in volcanic activity, while Greenland's southern tip rested just inside the Temperate Zone. Europe had moved northward and almost all of Norway and Sweden were inside the Arctic Circle, while India, China and most of Southeast Asia were all in a much cooler, more temperate zone.

I was silent, not knowing what to say or even to think.

"You know," the little men interrupted my silence, "ongoing change on the part of Earth is to be expected, and the activities of humans will certainly either aggravate or ameliorate these changes. At the very least, you should be aware that these things have happened in the past and will continue to happen in the future. At best, your lifestyle could be much more fluid, more prepared to deal with such changes."

"Are you saying this could happen in my lifetime?" I asked them, thinking that if it was going to happen far into the future, I needn't get upset or feel I had to do something different.

"If the Earth changes come in your lifetime and you are in the habit of expecting others to feed you, to provide the electricity that makes your homes livable and your appliances useful, to provide fresh water and fuel, and the knowledge of healing, then you are lost. Even very small changes in the Earth would require you to know how to provide these things for yourselves.

"If the changes come in the lives of your children, then *they* are lost, for you would not have taught them what they needed to know to survive in the face of changes that might require fending for one's self.

"If the changes come in the lives of your grandchildren and great-grandchildren, then *you* are lost again, for by that time you will have returned to a new life on Earth, for another round of lessons in soul-development, and will suffer your own consequences anyway.

"Humankind needn't suffer at all if there could be a little more development of the human body/mind. In fact, we have much more we'd like to show you, but first we'd like to ask you to read something."

When I didn't object, they continued.

"If you would read a book called *The Third Wave* by a man named Toffler, it would help you to expand your perspective, making it easier for us to explain some things about the future. When you have finished, we will return."

Then the little men bid me a congenial "good afternoon" and faded away as the gloom and chill of approaching twilight returned me to the present. 📖

3 📖
PERCEPTUAL SHIFTS...

FROM the time of my birth until I left home at age eighteen, the whole of my life rotated around the extensive family into which I had been born, along with the seasons of planting, growing, and harvesting. We did not live in town, nor were we well-to-do. Until I was twelve, we had a tiny 2-bedroom house, our one radio was rarely on, and although someone gave us a television set when I was about eight, it didn't work most of the time. So when I wasn't in school, I played freely along the creek, ran through the fields, or explored the woods. For me, the rest of the world barely existed.

Now in my early thirties, and in spite of several years of college courses, I was still snugly wrapped in the cocoon of my own ignorance surrounding political, economic and socio-cultural matters when I began to read Toffler's *Third Wave,* never suspecting that it would catapult me out of that snug indifference.

I had grown up in a huge family whose maternal roots were in farming and cattle dealing. My mother was one of fourteen children and my father was one of nine. Most of my aunts and uncles had grown up to have big families of their own. I was one of six children, and in eyes of our extended family, that was on the small side.

My mother started out as a milkmaid, delivering milk in her hometown. From there she went to work in a small local factory making mirrors for automobiles, and later she was both secretary and bookkeeper in the office of the local lumberyard. My father, a radio operator in the Pacific battles of World War II, had returned home to marry my mother and go to work for Consumers' Power Company. After baby number four came along, my mother left her job at the lumberyard, stayed home, and took care of her children.

Always close to the roots of tradition on my mother's side, we grew the majority of what we ate in a huge annual garden. Spring planting was a family ritual and as the garden grew, we worked in it daily. By the middle of each June, we had already begun the steady and sometimes exhausting processes of picking and preparing fruits and vegetables for the various kinds of preserving.

We also spent a great deal of time with my maternal grandparents who were still on the farm. One by one, each of Grandma's fourteen children had left to find work outside the farm, but various family members returned regularly, sometimes weekly in the summer, to help with farm work. This included feeding cows, pigs, and chickens, collecting eggs, milking, churning butter, planting gardens and field crops, threshing wheat, harvesting corn, butchering, canning and freezing, making wine, and occasionally even helping Grandma deliver eggs, butter, milk, cream, and freshly cut chickens to her customers in town.

When we weren't at Grandma's farm, we were working on our house. My father built our house with a hammer and a hand saw, and this ongoing project, which started when I was three, was—along with the garden—the topic of most conversations in our immediate family for all of my childhood and into my teen years.

If my parents ever discussed questions of money, politics, race, or even gossip, I never heard it. What I did hear in detail, however, was the inner workings of family. My mother was intensely involved with her eight sisters, a handful of sisters-in-law, several already-grown cousins, a few neighbors, various women friends and acquaintances, and our home was a constant gathering place for an ever-changing assortment of women. At least two or three times a week it was common for me to arrive home after school and find my mother and two, three, even four of my aunts or adult cousins gathered there.

They sat around the kitchen table, drank coffee, often played cards, and always discussed in depth the inner and outer lives of the members of the family and how to view—or help them through—the various life crises that came and went.

Sometimes there was trouble in a marriage, the serious shortage of money in a family, or someone who needed surgery and help with suppers for a few weeks. Other times they discussed someone who drank too much, another who worked too little, or someone who was cheating on a spouse. They wept when a child was dying or in trouble, and grew somewhat indignant when dealing with family members who exaggerated things for drama's sake, were lazy, or continuously bungled facts and details. They disagreed only minimally on how much bluntness was required to handle those who talked too much, thought they knew too much, thought they were better than others, or didn't take the hints to shut their mouth or change their attitude.

When someone was having difficulty coping, was depressed, or even having a nervous breakdown, they decided among themselves what needed changing, who would care for the affected children and for how long. When someone was angry with another family member, they were absolute masters at discerning the real reasons why, and what were the "other" sides of the argument.

Sex was a favorite topic, there was an endless debate about birth control, and they knew who was a good lover, or the reverse, a jealous despot. They cried with each other over the never-ending trials of raising good, decent children, they were forever dieting and discussing which diets worked and didn't work, they kept track of who needed help building a house or a garage, who was gay, who was getting married, who was pregnant and not getting married, who was divorcing, going off to prison, going away to school, dying, being born, or being buried…along with the thousands of subtle, individual motives and matters that drove people to do what they did. No subject was taboo and since the family was populated with a large and amazing assortment of saints and black sheep, I grew up steeped in what people did and why.

With this intense background of family and kitchen-table analysis, opening the covers of *The Third Wave* was like walking through the doorway of Toffler's house and taking a seat at his kitchen table. Except that his family was the entire human race and instead of the waves of changing seasons, there were "waves of economy" based on agriculture, then industry, and now communication. He looked at nations, their relations, their people, money, dreams, and difficulties in the same way my mother and aunts had discussed families, their individuals, and the motives and matters that drove, dogged, or inspired them.

Reading Toffler's book revealed how meager my high school and college courses had been. They had merely assembled boring descriptions of our colonial roots, compiled a few names and dates to be memorized, or skimmed disjointedly through shallow, biased versions of U.S. government and world history.

In comparison, Toffler took me inside the belly of humankind, painting clear and complete visions of a history that lived, breathed, and moved with a passion, all of which shook my mind powerfully. In place of the few scattered pieces of human history that I had accumulated in school, my awareness of mankind slowly began converging into greater coherency, taking on the contours of a common reality shaped by everyday people.

With startling clarity, I saw for the first time the larger human family of which I had always been part. Thus began a slow and steady turning in which I began to forget my distaste for all things historical, political, social, and economic. Bit by bit my attention began to wander beyond the tiny circle of family-based tradition that had bound me for years. Although it was to be a decades-long process, my view of life began its trek toward a global perspective as it was polished first by the little men, later by my own growing ability to see both the ethos and the pathos of Earth and her populations.

While reading *The Third Wave*, the effects of kundalini with its gifts of clairvoyance and the ability to be in more than one place at one time worked in my favor. Entering other times and places, I found myself actually re-living some events in the creation of industrialism. Toffler's approach to history became not just a course of study, but an invitation to go behind the scenes and experience the forces and fates that moved the human family, and if there was anything I was familiar with, it was family.

Fourteen years earlier, anxious to get away from small towns and the cycle of the seasons, I had left home and family, moving to Detroit for its money and educational possibilities.

Leaving my huge extended family had thrown me into culture shock and created a gaping hole in my life, which I diligently ignored in my race to get ahead. Now, half way through Toffler's book, I found myself unconsciously filling that gap with a new family—the human family—with all of its foibles and frailties, its reasons and seasons, its joys and sorrows. This family had a history, I was part of it, and it was weaving my life with every moment. When I finished the book a month or so later,

I felt like a new sweater that had been washed for the first time, then dried all out of its accustomed shape.

📖

Accentuating my budding global perspective was the fact that never in my life, until the little men in brown robes first brought it up, had I ever read, heard, or contemplated the idea that the Earth might be alive. Ditto for the idea that the planet could roll around in space. Gingerly I placed the pictures they had shown me and the comments the little men had made into a temporary mental suspension cabinet at the back of my mind.

Newly concerned about the family of humans, I would, at odd moments, reach into this fragile place of suspension, choose something they had said, and examine it under the microscope of my mind. Other times I reviewed the pictures of the Earth rolling over or wobbling seriously enough to mess up the shorelines, buildings, and energy systems we humans had created.

The little men hadn't said it *would* shift, they had only said it was *capable* of shifting. Their statement that it had happened in the past and could happen again was deeply disturbing—but had it? Where was the evidence? Why had I never heard of this possibility before?

The fact that they had referred to the Earth as a living being, and had put the possible rollover in the context of "healing herself" opened a door that presented me with an entirely new view of this place I had been born onto.

Who or what was the Earth? I couldn't actually say that I had ever given this planet I lived on even a first, let alone a second or third thought. And why had they referred to it as "herself," as if it were a female? If someone had asked me what the Earth was before my meetings with the little men, I might have said it was a glob of rocks, sand, and mud that we lived on, or simply that it was a planet.

I had seen one or two pictures of Earth taken by the astronauts during one of the moon landings, but it did not have the same impact as standing at the edge of the atmosphere with the little men and seeing it floating, spinning there in empty space. The experience had served up a powerful shock to my perception of place. I tried to imagine going outside, gathering up a handful of stones, sand, and dirt, wetting them down with enough water to make them stick together, and then trying to get them to float together in space and spin steadily while traveling in a circle. The more I thought about the problem of how to accomplish this, the more awesome the fact of Earth's existence and her travels through space and around the solar system became. What held the rocks, mud, and water together? If it was gravity, what was causing the gravity? How was it that this huge glob of matter just happened to float in an ocean of apparent nothingness? And how was it she moved so smoothly and effortlessly, like a ballerina in pirouette, in spite of weighing billions of tons and having a waistline measuring more than 24,000 miles?

For a while, I was awestruck. When I walked out the door of my house and stepped onto the surface of the Earth I was flooded with unusual feelings. Was there a living being buried deep in the soil somewhere? Was it a "she?" How could I have walked around on her face for almost thirty-three years and never once noticed her?

For the first time Earth was more than just a patch of ground that I walked across unconsciously. Sometimes I was startled by what I was sure was her breathing. Other times I was sure I could feel her move. There would be just the slightest sense of rumbling movement followed by a shiver that ran up my legs to my belly, causing me to stop and notice, asking anyone who was around, "Did you feel that? Did you just feel something like a little shake or movement in the Earth?" However, no one ever seemed to have noticed it.

Other times I asked myself, "Why would the Earth need to heal herself? What was wrong with her? Was she aware of all of us humans living here, spreading crazily across her skin like so many bacteria in a Petri dish? *How* was she aware of us? Did she see us? Did she know us individually? Could she feel us scratching and digging around on her face like so many chickens? If she was aware of us, what did she feel about us?"

From time to time I would find myself thinking about the Earth and aware of a deep ache in my gut. Was this her ache or mine? Did she have a bellyache and was this what made her think she needed to heal herself? How bad could the ache get before she decided to start a healing program? What did she need?

Turning my mind in a new direction, I would discard all possibilities of the Earth as a living being and decide that what I had seen was merely symbolic of my self.

"The little men in brown robes must have shown me these pictures to make me think about my own life," I would tell myself. "Maybe they're trying to get me to turn over a new leaf. Maybe there is an unknown woman buried deep inside of me and I've been walking around behind this face for all these years and never noticed her. Maybe I'm the one who needs to be aware that I'm capable of healing myself..."

Frightened by this line of thinking and incapable at the time of assessing what the little men were trying to do, I would put them and their information back into mental suspension and try to go about the business of my life. 📖

4 📖

BREAK-UP OF NATIONS...

IT was January of 1981 and an entire year had passed since my first encounter with the little men in brown robes. I had just returned from a ten-day trip to Arizona where I explored the state in search of a new home. Ben and I were having great difficulties with our relationship and I kept thinking that if we parted, I would go to the southwest and settle down. However, something in my gut knew it would be the wrong move. I returned to Michigan feeling tired and low-spirited.

Alone in the house with a cup of morning tea, I sat in my favorite spot staring out the window across the frozen canal and wishing it were spring, when the little men returned.

"Good morning!" they announced brightly.

"Yes, good morning," I answered quietly. My dejected voice was a sharp contrast to their bright energy.

"We have information about the future... Would you be willing to look at some pictures of coming events?"

I nodded absently, struck by their odd combination of patience, peacefulness, and a sort of cheery, businesslike approach. How did they manage to maintain such an attitude, I wondered as I sat back and closed my eyes for what was to be a very long visit.

Their pictures swept around me, and within minutes I was watching crowds of unruly people quite intent on chipping away at a great stone wall. I wondered momentarily if they were chipping at the Great Wall of China but when I got a good look at the people they didn't look Oriental. They sang and shouted as they worked with great energy until holes and serious breaches appeared in the wall. When they finally broke through to people on the other side of the wall, there was wild celebration.

"First the Berlin Wall will come down," said one of the little men, "and this will be one of the earlier, more unmistakable signs of the changes to come. You, yourself, will be there just before it happens!"

This was an incredible statement and I was distracted somewhat. The Berlin Wall was an institution, almost an immutable fact, and I could not believe it might come down.

Neither could I think of a single reason that would induce me to go to Europe. Without knowing why, for most of my life I had felt a vague mix of sorrow, anger, and shame when I thought of Europe. Or perhaps it was a sense of irritation, not quite antipathy, more like anxiety, and thus I had never been particularly interested in traveling there. I had neither the money for nor the interest in going to Europe.

For equally unknown reasons, I had always been drawn to Hawaii, Tahiti, and the South Pacific. If I had the kind of money it would take to travel across an ocean, I would be heading in that direction, not across the Atlantic to the European countries.

Just then a huge map of the world appeared before me, bringing my attention back to the little men and the pictures they were showing me. They directed my attention to the U.S.S.R., which began breaking up into pieces. The first pieces then broke into smaller pieces, and then those pieces broke into even smaller pieces. Long before this process was over in Russia, the same process started elsewhere. Canada broke first into two, and then into progressively smaller and smaller sections. The breakup of Canada was hardly even begun when the same thing began in Africa, Mexico, India, the United States, and the European nations. Even giant China began to split into independent regions.

"What you are seeing represents the break up of the nations and, in most cases, the passing of democracy as well as the end of the huge national governments," came the voices of the little monks.

Their words did not register at first and I continued to watch the disappearance of old national borders and the appearance of dozens of new, much smaller... smaller what? What were these new areas? Were they baby nations, countries, revolting factions, something else?

"The most important thing for you to remember as you look at these events," said the little men, "is that things could be so much easier for you and your fellow humans if you understood why these things are happening, and if you worked with them instead of against them. For you to work with them, however, you must have some idea of where you are going.

"When things change and people see only destruction, only the loss of what used to be, and not the good things they are moving toward or what they have the chance to create, then they feel heartache and pain. They resist what is normal and natural in the cycles of life. There is panic, and much more suffering than necessary.

"As you watch the coming changes increase in number and deepen in effect, keep in mind that part of the reason they are occurring is because human beings have grown past the structures that presently exist. Your new ways of life will express the levels of awareness, function, and organization into which you are evolving. *The evolution of the human is built-in*. It is an essential part of your being that cannot be undone... and why would you want to undo it for it moves you ever closer to the joy and love that is your source."

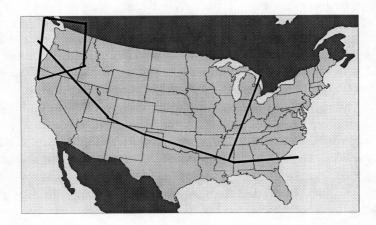

Then the map that was before us changed again and, as in the first visit, we seemed to have an aerial view of the entire planet. Facing us were

North America and the United States. As we looked on, what was once a single entity began to fracture and the U.S. broke initially into roughly three main regions.

The area laying west and south of a line that began in Oregon, extended in a southeasterly direction, passing through the northern areas of Texas, then the southern parts of Georgia and Alabama, was one region.

The middle piece of the U.S. was composed of an area that stretched from Washington state and Idaho, east to Ohio, and from the border with Canada to Oklahoma and northern Texas.

The third piece included most of the eastern seaboard from north to south, along with the northern parts of Louisiana, Mississippi, Alabama, and Georgia.

I was gathering my thoughts about this breakup when a series of earthquakes occurred, mostly minor ones, but with a few major shake-ups. Because of these, east and west coastlines gradually changed, then the mid-west changed. For years I had heard that Los Angeles was about to be reclaimed by the sea, but to my surprise, New York City also met her final days. Even more surprising was that the area in and around Kentucky and Tennessee seemed to sink, filling with water from the Gulf of Mexico, which then exposed a bit more of Florida.

Because of the difficulties caused by the earthquakes, the initial divisions within the U.S. did not last long and soon areas within each region began to define their own new boundaries and autonomy. Some areas appeared to experience serious civil disturbances, and not long after the most serious of the earthquakes, Hawaii broke away from the union. Then the northwest corner of the U.S., including Washington state and part of Oregon, broke away to become an independent region. Eventually the entire U.S. began breaking up into smaller and smaller units. As the break-up continued the little men provided an accompanying narration.

"This will give you some idea of the changes in your political and governmental arrangements as well as the physical changes in your land, since they will begin about the same time and are meant to complicate and complement one another so that you cannot ignore the need for change."

"But why? Why is this going to happen? It doesn't seem possible," I half asked, half stated, acutely aware of the doubt and disbelief in my mind. I did not want to be argumentative, but it all seemed too dramatic.

"Nothing *has* to happen," the little men replied, "but in the physical realm, everything cycles. Cycles are the means by which all basic power is regenerated. As it happens, the cycle of human development is about to move into its next phase at a time when several astronomical and planetary cycles will also be shifting. These are not just imaginary shifts. They involve cyclic changes in the energy fields of your sun and the galaxy, which affect the waves of force that surround, hold, and rotate your Earth."

Directing my attention back to the map, they continued. "It is difficult to predict with exactness the impact of astronomical phenomena or any shifting of the plates, and thus your land may not physically change in exactly this way, although there will be some re-shaping overall, especially along the coastlines and in the deep center, due to factors both natural and man-made,

"As we have pointed out, you and all of the humans here are moving beyond your present structures. In your lifetime you will see the passing of democracy and the folding of nations. If you do not destroy yourselves in the transition, you will enter into a new kind of world with new perceptions of yourselves and new forms of organization at every level. Most importantly, you will help to shape the direction and chart the path for the next few stages of human development, and there are several, each stage being a foundation for the next."

By now, some of what they were saying began to sink in and I was struggling to deal with their statements that the U.S. would break up. I was also having trouble with the idea that there was something, anything, beyond democracy. I vaguely recalled that Toffler had said our current form of government was becoming obsolete, but I assumed without question that we would clean up the political process and get on with our democracy. Wasn't democracy the epitome of civilized possibility... and didn't the U.S. set the world standard for self-government? This couldn't possibly change, could it?

"Democracy was a big step in human development but it was only a step, and it has its limits," the little men said in answer to my thoughts. "You are now well beyond those limits, and if you do not move on to the next stage, you will disintegrate as a people and a civilization. The number of people now on earth precludes any further working of democracy except as a background tool for teaching the preliminary attitudes that set the stage for local communications and global agreements.

"It is important that you and others see insides what is happening and understand the whole nature of the changes. In fact, this is part of what we hope to teach you.

"As a people, you must also learn to be careful in your thinking. If you think the changes in the United States represent a 'loss of power' on the world stage, that is what it will become. Within the present family of nations, many look upon the U.S. as a model and try to copy you. If you are frightened, angry, and offensively trying to get back your old forms of position and power, you will waste time, energy, and resources, and set a poor example of how to deal with such changes for the rest of the world. And you will alienate many in the process, making things more difficult for all, especially yourselves.

"The change to a different form of organization or structure does not necessarily mean a loss of power. It does mean a change in the way power is understood, maintained, and shared."

Having given no thought to the nature of power over the course of my life, I had no useful understanding of what it was, and only a childish definition of power in general. It was the ability to make others do what you wanted, what you told them to do. The idea that power could be understood differently, or that it needed maintenance was beyond me at the moment, yet the little men moved right on.

"Let us look at the Russian people. For over fifty years, their entire perception of power has been based on fear. Fear of what? Mostly fear of themselves and their own perceptions. They are afraid of their own thoughts! When fear is present, love is absent, and without love it is easy to allow the fear to become personified in one man, which is what they did! In Germany it was the same thing. In China, the same. In many other places, the same.

"Our question to you as a people would be, 'What has gone wrong with your understanding of power that millions of people will focus their fears in one person or one organization, and then let that person or organization manipulate them using their own fear?' *There is nothing to fear!* And how is it that millions of hearts, working together, cannot come up with enough love to convert even one fearful leader and a few misguided followers? The world has truly fallen out of love!

"When groups of people live in constant fear, the result is always the rise of the singular individual who will gladly represent and act out the fears running rampant in the general population. Soon there are weapons, which are the symbols of fear; next there is war, which is the fear projected onto others. In the end, power is severely twisted and misused.

"It is important for people to understand that their leader is their own creation, created with their own power, brought before them to demonstrate what they are capable of. This leader embodies the reality of their situation in all of its aspects, whether that situation is love, or fear, or something else altogether, and works to bring the people to greater awareness.

"The really great kings, the excellent presidents, and truly wise leaders of men are able to make their people see themselves more clearly. They are able to express through their own use of power what the individuals in the population are capable of and what they should be striving for. The entire dynamic is an exercise that transfers the gifts and abilities that live in the hearts of the people into the king or president, and then, in turn, back into the people in an enhanced way.

The real responsibility of the good king or leader is always to study his people well, learn their strengths and weaknesses, then empower them to become the best and the most they can become.

"Somewhere along the way your kings began to hoard and abuse the influence they had. They began keeping this power for themselves and not bothering to teach the hearts or nurture the gifts of their people. Instead they began to *demand* gifts.

"Today your heads of state are exactly that, heads only, with very little heart, and therefore no wisdom or ability to bring the people to a wise and wonderful way of living."

Drifting backward through time I recalled running along the edge of the woods with one or two other children from down the road. We were about ten years old and angrily shouting names at two or three boys who had discovered our fort and wrecked it. "You stupid Communists!" I screamed furiously, having no concept of a Communist other than as something bad. Why had I been so obviously biased against something I knew nothing about? Who had taught me to judge others so ignorantly, so viciously, so mercilessly? For the first time, I turned the idea of cultural conditioning around in my mind.

Now thoroughly distracted, I thought about the world as it existed outside the walls of my home. It never mattered to me what town I lived in or what sorts of activities went on in the mayor's office or the town hall. I knew little about what went on at the state capital, cared nothing for national politics, did not vote at all, and knew even less about international affairs. Although my interest had been kindled by reading *The Third Wave*, I saw that I really had not grown much beyond the understanding of that ten-year-old girl shouting epithets. Suddenly I felt peasant-minded and shallow, but the little men did not seem to take notice of how I felt. Either that, or they already knew how I was and wanted to educate me with their pictures. I returned my attention to what they were saying.

"As your population continues to grow beyond the limits of your political system, the most common reaction among the people of your nations will be to ignore the voted decision. Many will begin to live in an existential lawlessness. From there, it is only a short distance to total disregard for your political structures, and from there an even shorter distance to total—and perhaps angry—disregard for the social and cultural structures you have built.

"Not everyone will travel this short distance to apathy and anger, nor will those who do arrive there arrive all at once. Not everyone will move to the chaos of lawlessness, but you will see more and more people making the transition into an apolitical limbo. This will be followed by a stubborn indifference to many man-made laws, and all but the most basic, time-honored laws such as 'do not kill or steal' may be ignored.

"From this will develop a sense of national confusion, accompanied by rejection of the limitations that citizenship imposes on basic human rights. These rights are 'the right to be who you are, and the right to decide things for yourself.'

"Among those who are insecure and underdeveloped there will be great confusion over *who* has the right to decide *what*. This group will be so steeped in the concept of outer authority that the idea of deciding for themselves will seem absolutely unnatural. As their fears grow, they will feed the growing anger that leads toward chaos.

"Passage into chaos will be aggravated by other forces. One will be a tendency for those with time and money to buy the laws they want, much like the wealthy nobles of the Middle Ages bought blessings and indulgences from the clergy, blessings they believed they needed in order to get into heaven.

"What do you mean?" I asked, wondering how anyone could have been foolish enough to spend real money on something as vague and intangible as a blessing.

"In the Middle Ages priests, bishops, and corrupt monasteries began selling blessings and indulgences," they replied. The practice was similar to your idea of collecting green stamps and redeeming them for a new lamp or a pretty dish.

"Sales were based on the Church's teaching that you needed to earn a certain number of indulgences to atone for sins. They could be used to obtain release from the guilt of pursuing earthly desires, or to gain entrance to heaven. When people couldn't earn blessings or indulgences fast enough, they began to buy them.

"This money encouraged priests to overlook the wealthy landowner's unjust practices. It convinced bishops to make favorable rulings in various causes and issues that involved land squabbles, marriage, divorce, annulments, and other mayhem. In short, such practices enriched the priests and bishops, who then assured the nobles that they now had a direct line to the power in Rome, and an assured seat in heaven.

"In your immediate future, those buying various rights, laws, and rulings will be doing the same thing. They will be trying to get something they think they need, something they believe they can only get from someone outside the self. And when they get it, they will think that they are making a reasonable exchange, that they are quite sophisticated and successful. They will make great efforts to keep up this facade and to promote the perception that the government is truly a 'government of the people' and is still working reasonably well. Few will notice or care that millions of people have fallen outside the circle of government. They will fail to see the signs of crisis approaching."

"What kind of crisis... or signs?" I inquired.

"The most obvious signs will be the inability of your government to satisfy anyone. Delays will become more and more prolonged as committees and meetings are scheduled endlessly. However, it will be backdoor dealings that determine the decisions; decisions that contradict all common sense.

"Other decisions will end up being made in a default mode through which few get what they want and no one takes responsibility for the decision or its results. These decisions will lead to rules and regulations poor in substance and effect. They will drive many people further into the existential lawlessness we mentioned earlier, and finally to take matters into their own hands.

"Other forces arising to pressure your nations will be the rise of a global network which will facilitate the passing back and forth of ideas, decisions, and trade outside the circle of government. This network will eventually be joined over the entire planet and will be used in an ever-growing manner to manage many aspects of life and daily routine, including de-structuring of the nations and restructuring of people into smaller, self-governing groups. It will coordinate the actions of your people, and be used to send huge numbers of messages to those in Washington D.C.and elsewhere, announcing the intentions of the populace. It will also facilitate a great deal of trade between all peoples of the world, bypassing governments and giant corporations.

"Key forces working against nations everywhere will be the growing imbalance between the poor and the wealthy, as well as those who have developed themselves and those who have not. The sheer numbers of people, the need to feed them, and their increasing dependency on being fed instead of feeding themselves—all are forces that will work against your current structures of power.

"Among the signs of the end times will be the fairly rapid influx of women into government. At the same time, a number of long-time politicians will begin leaving their positions like critters fleeing a sinking ship. Of course, this will not be what they tell the public, and each will have a reason based on an intuitive sense that the job requires too much energy, is no longer a source of satisfaction, or does not create a feeling of power or of doing good in the world.

"Women, long remanded to the home yet wanting to get into the power structure, will suddenly find themselves in the mayor's chair, the governor's office, the Parliament, the House of Representatives, and the courts. They will think they are finally changing things at a core level. Some women will believe that time, maturity, or luck has made the difference for them. Others will be convinced it was their persistence that finally paid off. They will not see that they are rushing in where more experienced politicians are saying "No thanks!" They will not see that they are being left with the hollow remains of a system that no longer works and is about to come undone. In many ways, those that care the most and are the bravest in creating the changes they think will help the ailing democracy will reap much of the blame for its unraveling.

"Yet the touch of women in the structure will be good for the most part. Women have a tendency to foster common sense, nurturing, and doing what must be done regardless of comfort levels. Their leaning is toward preserving and healing without need for fanfare. They will preserve what is useful in its time, and lead many toward healing. Women, both in and outside of formal government, will end up working mightily to soften the slow collapse of the ship of state."

By this time I was working hard to maintain a sense of calm in the face of the idea that the government I had always known might not be there one day. For some reason, I clearly recalled a brief but intense exchange between my father and I some years earlier.

We were having Thanksgiving Dinner; everyone was at the table eating when I mentioned that I had received a distressing letter from a former childhood friend in Vietnam. He had lost an eye in battle, and I went on to say how stupid it was that we should be in a war. My father, who had fought in the Pacific during World War II and was one of two men who returned alive out of a company of sixty-two, took immediate exception to my comment. This was unusual because he had never talked about the war before. Now he looked over at me and said quietly, "Sometimes you have to fight."

I was still for a minute and then said, "*I* wouldn't. And I think anyone who goes off to kill other people just because their government tells them to is a fool."

At this he became visibly upset and stopped eating. He looked at me and we locked eyes. "Do you know that I went across an ocean and killed other young men that I didn't know and didn't want to hurt just to save this country's peace, and now you're telling me that you wouldn't fight to keep what I risked my life to make sure you had?"

"N-n-no-o," I said slowly, "I wouldn't kill anyone for any reason."

Without hesitation he pursued me. "Do you mean to tell me that if you were in your home and soldiers were coming over the back fence to kill your children and take your property that you wouldn't fight to keep them away?" he demanded to know with an air of incredulity.

With eyes still locked and the dinner at a standstill, I opened my mouth to say 'no, I wouldn't' but as I pictured the imaginary soldiers grabbing and hurting my children, my voice died away and in the silence I simply stared at him, unable to deal with the magnitude of a confrontation that might force me to kill or be killed.

After a brief eternity, still obviously upset, my father looked away and muttered a few words to the effect that there was something wrong with me. The dinner conversation resumed and within minutes all was apparently back to normal, but I never forgot this exchange and his question remained unanswered. Now the pictures shared by the little men in brown robes had triggered the same anxiety my father had triggered. Did the collapse of the U.S. involve being invaded? Would I have to answer that question put to me by my father?

"Will the coming apart of the U.S. be the result of any kind of attack by other countries?" I interrupted the little men.

"Not necessarily, and not in the way you're thinking," they said, "but we'll come back to that in another visit."

I was left with fears fluttering and a sense of dissatisfaction with their answer, but they continued in their cheerful, matter-of-fact way.

"The collapse will occur in fits and starts and stops and restarts, during which time little is accomplished by the political structure, other than trying to hold itself together.

"Those dependent on the political structure—schools and libraries, hospitals and clinics, banks and research labs, armies and embassies, to name only a few—will make a determined effort to carry on as if nothing unusual or threatening is happening. Many people will be caught in that self-deception and thus, for a while, it will appear that nothing *is* changing.

"Yet one of the most significant signs of the passing of nations will be the slow rise of business to power, for during the transition into the next stage of human development, the structures of big business will temporarily arise to replace nations as the structures that hold and manage world power.

"When business begins openly trying to run the government, the closing of the nation's doors is not far away. In an effort to deny the looming demise, your government will continue its struggle to be of use. However, more and more power will fall onto the shoulders of business; power placed there by governments themselves.

"Over the past few decades there has been an ever-growing tendency for governments to make laws that will empower businesses, all in the belief that a healthy business climate will keep many people employed and an employed man is a man who is too busy to bemoan his lot in life. This also means he is too busy to interfere in the affairs of government or to pay attention to what is really happening in Washington D.C., London, or Hong Kong.

"But governments will not realize until too late that they have played directly into the hand of big business. After years of making decisions that favored or were owed to various corporations, your governments will discover that most of these decisions had no common sense.

"To their dismay they will discover that they have bankrupted the land and its resources, and that they—the major power structures of the nations—are little more than puppet arms pulled by the strings of the large, multinational corporations who operate and thrive without loyalty to people, land, governments, or boundaries of any kind.

"At just about this point in time, people will begin to ignore government in more organized and calculated ways, further helping to bring about its demise. This will make way for big business to take up the yoke of power. However, the reign of business will last only a short time, perhaps as little as five years, more likely between ten and thirty years, perhaps as long as fifty. Then gradually the reign of multinational corporations will come to an end. Disruptions with the earth which interfere with their people, interruptions in their supply of resources, trade taking place via the global network, whole new ways of viewing and organizing life—these will be only some of the factors that they cannot adapt to. In the end, the nations and the multinationals will be replaced by the emergence of a world council."

"But what about people... how... will we be safe?" I asked still trying to ease my burgeoning anxiety over what looked like a lot of chaos.

"As the nations break up or are stalled by dysfunction, people will return naturally to the tribes and regions of their ancestors, finding a sense of belonging and safety there. In fact, people's insistence on returning to the tribes and regions of their ancestors will begin even before your nation restructures itself, and this will exert additional pressures that tend to speed the break-up of the nations.

"This re-grouping of people into their original tribes and regions will be an important step in your human development and necessary for your physical survival.

"At first there will be great resistance to this re-grouping. Those in power, as well as people whose entire life has been steeped in the idea that nations are the best or only way to organize life, will consider this re-grouping process to be utter rebelliousness. These patriots will be those who fought in the two world wars. As they begin to die and pass to the other side in great numbers, they will take their patriotism with them.

"Among the generations born after them will be an increasing movement of people in the direction of their origins and the homes of their ancestors. Even those who remain where they are will continue to group and regroup themselves, and the nuclear family will be swallowed up in a new arrangement of people that comes to resemble a cross between the old feudal estate, the commune, and the corporation.

"Slowly, these extended forms of family will evolve into a socio-economic structure known as 'family business' and your concept of democracy will evolve into a system of individual self-development with a code of self-governance known as 'personal responsibility.'"

I was well into overload and having difficulty absorbing the amount of information they were giving me. My ostrich side wanted to dismiss most of what they were saying, while the practical side of me, with its broad streak of curiosity wanted ten thousand explanations. The curiosity won out, but with all the questions they had triggered, I was still unable to get beyond the idea that things could change to the point that the United States might not be there.

Still worried that we might collapse into chaos and be invaded, I stammered unevenly, "Um… but why?… does this mean the United States will be taken over or destroyed?"

The little men responded brightly. "As to *why*, we have already pointed out that you are evolving as individuals, *must* evolve as a people, and the structures you currently have in place will no longer serve you as your development continues.

"Our hope is to help you through this transition with a sense of peaceful change, practical creativity, and relief from the difficulties of systems that no longer work well or even make sense. There is nothing to fear in making these changes. They will take some work, some time, and energy, but we think you will truly like the new structures, customs, and ways of your future, for you do not realize how much true freedom and inner authority you have lost, or how much your development as humans has stalled.

"In the course of the past two millennia you have moved from the power structures of the church to the power structures of nations. Although there will always be a need among humans for a basic form of organization that helps to structure daily life, in the two power structures mentioned above—government and business—there are limited possibilities for self-development.

"The people who share life on your planet at this time have only a cloudy perception of Self, most of which is based on how well you are complying with the rules and expectations of the church, the school, or the state. These institutions were originally meant to exist for your convenience; now the reverse is true and you exist for their convenience."

"But I thought you said that national governments as the structure of power were going to be replaced by big business as the ruling power structure, so how would anything really be different?" I asked

"Although big business will have its heyday and its impact, these forms will be very transitory and will not last long. The main value of the large corporations is to model the concept of how to organize large numbers of people in transnational ways. Once a number of you have realized this, you will go beyond the forms of the big corporations. The church held power for 1500 years, the nations for roughly 500 years, and if they are extremely lucky, the big corporations may hold it for fifty years, probably less.

"Human development is moving at an ever faster rate. If you and your people manage to transform yourselves and your way of life without destroying the huge global network and the ability to communicate, you will move ahead toward greater realization of human potential. If not, your world will collapse and you will return to extremely primitive forms. Being primitive is not bad, it is just that most of you have forgotten how to survive in this way, so you would either die quickly or suffer greatly.

"All of what you are seeing today is simply an overview. We will address the subject of business, as well as other issues and perspectives, in more detail during later visits, but for now we would like to stay focused on the coming apart of the nations.

"Since you have asked specifically about the U.S. we will give a bit more information that would be of help here, although much of this information will also apply to other nations around the globe, including and especially China.

"It is unlikely that the U.S. will be taken over by strange and foreign powers. It would be far more accurate to say that it will be taken over by its own people who have decided they need to make some changes.

"In the final days, although there may be some violence and anarchy, it will not be these troubles so much as it will be health that becomes the last straw for your ailing government. We will deal with the issue of health in more detail later on, but for now we will say that all over the world, many will die of starvation or malnutrition, there will be plagues both old and new that arise, and many will die outright from these.

"There will come a time when your children will be so ill and your old people so sick and degenerated that those in the middle years will have great difficulty carrying on. Stretched to the limit, they will be unable to find the time and energy to work for a living because they are bravely trying to nurse the fevered children, care for and comfort the old ones, bury the dead, and keep themselves well enough to keep going.

"The government will try to pass laws that provide care for everyone. But this will be one of those 'cursed if you do and cursed if you don't' situations. If the law is passed, it will bankrupt the remains of the governmental bank account much faster and bring about a quicker end, for they will not have anticipated the seriousness of the decline in overall health among their people. Later they will complicate things even more by trying to pass laws demanding optimum levels of health, how to achieve this, and the need to prove you have good health before you can enter public and even some private places. But health is not something that can be decreed from outside the self. Health is a way of life, and the hurried attempt to legislate health will be useless.

"If these laws *are* passed, they will seriously restrict freedom of choice and movement. Both business and government will be adversely affected. If they are *not* passed, things will carry on with an aura of normality for a bit longer, but eventually your people will become so unwell, so pressed for a sense of calm energy and secure well-being that they will no longer pay attention to the rituals of government.

"There will come a time when the people, acting in unison, will pass over the April ritual of the taxes mostly because they are too tired, too ill, too overworked, and too stressed to deal with this rite of spring. The collective action will go from an irritable 'don't-bother-me-with-paper-work-right-now' attitude, to an out-and-out protest of the whole concept of taxing, to a demand for a complete reforming of your ways of self-governing.

"At present, when miscellaneous people do not file their taxes, some get away with it and some are persecuted. But when the entire nation, acting as one mind, refuses to follow this annual directive, the message conveyed to the government will be that its ways are unacceptable and it must change.

"Although in the beginning there will be attempts to make examples of isolated taxpayers with a flurry of new rules and some confiscation of property, this will not last and all properties will eventually be returned to the owners. In the end, your whole approach to land and ownership will change.

"The truth is that your government began acting like a corporation some years ago and people do not realize that it is not a political system any more. It is, like most nations, an economic structure and cannot operate without money. When you realize that it is really a business masquerading as a national government, you will also realize that no other business in the world demands its customers pay a certain amount of their income whether they want to buy the goods and services or not.

"Thus, after operating in deep debt for a number of years, when the shakedown among the giant corporations begins, your government, actually a bankrupt corporation, will shut down slowly and painfully.

"Eventually, it will go the way of the Catholic Church, becoming a hollow shell of power that once was. Some will nostalgically send donations to the few public schools, cancer charities, and bridge-repair projects that it continues to try and support, but in the main, people will ignore the old institutions that arose during the time of national governments. Their relationship to it will be similar to the sort of curiosity reserved for other relics of the past."

By this time, I was numb. I didn't think I could watch anything else that the little men had to show me, or listen to any more of the future. Just as I was about to say something to that effect, the pictures began to fade. I was back in my own home looking at the little men wordlessly.

"I'm not sure what to say," I told them, when what was really going through my mind was something more like "I'm not sure what to believe."

"No need to say anything," they replied, "and no need to hurry or worry. Take your time, think about what you've seen, and begin in simple ways to prepare for change." Then, with courteous nods and the comment that they would return with more, the little men disappeared. 📖

5 📖

FREE-FALLING THROUGH AN EMPTY WORLD…

AFTER the little men were gone, I continued to sit quietly. I stared at the cold cup of tea beside me and tried to organize the things I had just seen and heard. From a logical or scientific standpoint, there was no proof that such events would come to pass, and the new information seemed outrageously impossible. It could even be seen as oppressive. Yet the little men had conveyed a sense of practical excitement and promise in the tone of voice and point of view with which they presented the various pieces of information. It did not feel oppressive either. Nevertheless, I could not seem to get my mind around the bulk of the information. Like a simpleton I sat there while the words, "Things might be changing here…" ran through my head in endless loops, punctuated by the scenes that had moved across my mind's eye during the long visit and narration by the little men.

Finally I got up, dumped out the cold tea, and went to get dressed. I began moving through the day as best I could, but my mind was not where my body was. It was wrestling with the possibility that the little men in brown robes were real, that the information and pictures they showed me were real and might actually happen, and with the assortment of issues these possible changes brought up in me.

I tried to assess the situation calmly. It had been over a year since I'd first laid eyes on the little men and until now I had not seriously considered the possibility that they were anything other than a fluke in a mind that was suddenly prone to all sorts of unusual perceptual events. Yet I had just had the fourth in a string of visits that most people would consider impossible, unreal, or both. The little men had indicated that they would return for at least a fifth. But were they real? And if they were, why were they showing me their pictures and telling me about the future?

I couldn't answer these questions; part of me didn't even want answers, and the result was that I skipped over the questions, which was my usual approach to things I couldn't deal with.

That afternoon, on the way to do a few errands, I could barely pay attention to my driving. I stared out at the land, the streets, the streetlamps and stoplights, the signs, the hardware stores, and shopping centers, asking of each, "Are you the United States? Would you still be there for me if the U. S. government were not there? Maybe the land would be, but I wasn't sure about the streets and the rest of it. Who gave somebody permission to make a street or hang a light? With all the force of divine revelation, I was suddenly aware that I had no idea how things of that sort were done in the common world. In the same way that the little men had appeared in my life one ordinary day, things like stoplights and signs appeared in the land-scape as if placed there by some mysterious hand.

On the heels of this revelation came a second. It was a feeling more than anything, combined with curiosity, that I was groping for an authority figure, aware that in huge areas of my life I had always assumed someone else would take care of things because I had no authority to do so. It was not that I had given away this authority, it had never been mine enough to decide that I had it or had the right to give it away. It was simply an aware-ness of how much authority I had assumed was "out there," somewhere, anywhere but in me, and with the power to decide everything about my life and its setting.

For the first time in my life, I was viscerally aware of the sense of security and comfort I felt under that huge invisible umbrella called the "United States." I tried to imagine it not there and couldn't; it was so much a part of my conscious and unconscious reality. Still, as I drove toward the supermarket, the thought kept coming back to me, "What if the U.S. was not there?"

As long as I couldn't imagine such a thing, I was able to push the question aside. But then, just as I was turning into the grocery store parking lot, unexpectedly there came a clear and lucid moment when I experienced the complete absence of that umbrella labeled "United States" and suddenly, without warning, I was free-falling through empty space, tumbling blindly, end over end, with nothing to hang onto, no one there to help me or protect me. Who was I?… Where was I?… I was frightened… unnerved… the world I had always known was gone… it had dropped out from under me… or maybe it had actually rolled over like the little men had said… I couldn't seem to get my breath… what if there were strange soldiers coming over the back fence like my father had threatened and there was no one there to help me… I was alone here on this huge planet… just me and nature… wild nature, dangerous nature, uncontrollable nature… and gasping like someone who had been held underwater for too long, I struggled to right myself, to find solid ground, to calm the fluttery, helpless feeling in my stomach.

Until that moment I did not realize how much my identity and security was tied up with the concepts of a nation, a country, or even a sense of place. I had never considered myself to be particularly patriotic and thus the power of my identification with this nation in this place rocked me to the core. Sitting in my truck in the middle of downtown Mt. Clemens, Michigan, I was so shocked I could not even open the door and step out of it to begin my errands.

Instead I looked around at the physical structures of shopping center and grocery carts, bank building, and parking lot, wanting them to be as familiar and as serenely transparent to the structures of my thought as they had been only a few moments before.

Somehow, the highway and the houses, the office buildings and the local café, the schools and the stoplights, even the river, and the bridge that allowed me to drive over that river without being conscious that water was flowing there, all formed a backdrop against which my perception followed its usual, rutted routines. These structures stood for the U.S. and our way of life. They symbolized us, they were us, and again I thought, "Are these things the United States or are they just buildings and land and streets and stoplights to which we apply our attitudes and perceptions?"

As I stared helplessly out at the once familiar urban landscape I suddenly understood at levels I had never touched before that the United States was not a building, a place, or a people, it was simply an idea. It was an agreement between all of us living on the land of our particular continent. We were all living under an umbrella of illusion, albeit a handy one. The U.S. was an idea in the mind, a projection of mankind that, once in place and accepted, allowed us to make all sorts of assumptions about reality, secure routines, and the course of The Everyday.

The alternative seemed to be a life of isolation and fear. What if there was something dangerous or life threatening out there, waiting to get me?

In that moment I understood something of why primitive man had lived in groups, had insisted on the existence of his gods, and why he maintained such elaborate rituals and relationships with them. Through the idea of "the gods" he assumed a deep sense of security, and through this security, he developed a stable identity, a sense of who and where he was, along with his place in the order of things. His group and his gods were *his* umbrella, and living under its shelter he felt safe enough to go about his Everyday, performing the dozens of chores, simple and complex, that needed to be done regularly in order to survive on the planet.

By subscribing to the idea of a nation, and organizing that nation to take care of wild neighbors, unpredictable nature, and other unknown aspects of life, I could be free to follow the routine of my own work and daily chores. The illusion was that I was free... free to do or become what I wanted or needed to do or be. But was I free? Did I know what real freedom was? The little men had mentioned something about loss of true freedom. What had they meant?

Now my mind took another tack. What was true freedom? Was it the freedom to do whatever I wanted whenever I felt like it? If I could do what I really wanted in life, what would I do from day to day? Certainly I would not be going off to work each day. Yet if I did what my heart really wanted, how would I get the money I needed to survive? Who would feed me? How would I get a house, or afford a car so I could get around from place to place, picking up the food that would feed me, the furniture that would make me comfortable in my house, or the tools to repair or remodel that house?

Anxiety flooded me. I'd have to spend all my time growing food, or perhaps building and re-building my house. Where would I get supplies? Without the idea of a nation and an economic system, I might be totally free to do what I wanted, but if I had to spend all my time looking for food or trying to maintain a warm shelter, was I any more free than in the present system?

Now I felt trapped. It was a conundrum, a riddle with no solution. Finally, I prodded myself to get moving, to go through the motions of The Everyday and finish the errands I had driven to town to do.

Slowly I did them, yet all the while my awareness was still free-falling through the space that was empty of the U.S., underscoring some innate need for a connection to both people and place.

Once back home, re-runs of the scenes I had watched with the little men ran through my mind relentlessly. I saw myself in a strange house in Germany that was made of an unusual brick—and resolved to go to Hawaii if I ever had the chance to go anywhere outside the U.S.

I tried to think about business as a new form of government, but simply could not imagine any corporation that would be able to take over the functions of government.

Letting go of the confusions of business-as-government, I turned their comments about the limits to democracy over and over in my mind. Were there too many people for our form of government to work? If that was the case, we needed to cut back on the number of people. This provoked as much anxiety as the absence of my national umbrella had. We couldn't tell people that they couldn't have children... we couldn't just get rid of people either. We were civilized, and civilization was about people, and creating a safe home, a healthy life... but... they had said that health would be the factor that drove us to the breakpoint with starvation and plagues... Surely our medical system and its technology were a match for anything that might come along, weren't they? And if they weren't, if we could not learn to heal the illnesses and diseases they had predicted, was that the answer to too many people as a limit to the workings of democracy? This did not feel like a comfortable solution and I felt guilty about having had such a thought at all.

Thinking I could sort through some of the problems the little men had so smoothly covered if I wrote them out, I sat down with paper and pen to outline the issues. Instantly I was confronted with the difficulties of having to translate non-linear, telepathic information into linear sentences.

It took forever to decide where to begin, and once I did, the written words were so drab and frightening that I stopped. How could I communicate, even for myself, the feeling of practicality, the common sense, or the peculiar attitude that combined the good cheer and positive approach that the little men brought to the information? Clearly, it was important not just to write down what they had said, but to keep the mood and the perspective with which they had said it. Then there was the tremendous amount of information to deal with. What's more, their telepathy included powerful, colorful pictures, a soft, chant-like rhythm that they used for words, and an immense range of feeling, insight, and sensation that made me feel I was right in the thick of whatever they were showing me.

I was at a loss as to how to convey the power of their "pictures" with a mere paper and pen. After staring at the paper for three-quarters of an hour I gave up and went off to do something else, hoping to distract myself.

As I bent over, sorting clothes, getting ready to do some laundry, my mind continued to sort through the information I had seen early that morning. Once more I was struck by the little men's comment that the government would go the way of the Catholic Church. This triggered the memory of their discussion of the sale of blessings, which brought back their comments on the passover of the spring rite of taxes, which reminded me of their statement that it would be health more than anything else that would bring down the structures and institutions of the U.S. and once again I was back in the grip of a mind that cycled furiously and without relief from one topic to another. Little in the way of The Everyday was accomplished that day. 📖

6 📖

LEADERS, WELFARE, AND LAND...

A few days later, before I'd even begun digesting their information about dissolving nations and disappearing democracies, the little men in brown robes returned.

Shuffling around in the darkened kitchen of early morn and not quite awake yet, I jumped when I realized they were there. They apologized for startling me, but there was no need to apologize.

"No, it's okay," I said, "I just didn't expect you back so soon or at this hour."

"You seemed confused at the end of our last visit and we thought perhaps a bit more information about the changes that will occur might help to clarify things," they remarked. After a slight pause they asked politely, "Would you like to see some additional pictures?"

"Sure," was all I said, then went into the living room and sat down, putting an afghan over my knees for I knew it would be chilly just sitting there. Once settled I closed my eyes and a few scenes of the disintegrating nations I had watched in the previous visit promptly unfolded as the little men began to speak.

"When the break-up of the nations begins, there will be the appearance of a new breed of clear-sighted, practical leaders in your country and elsewhere around the planet. They will see the need for a whole new level of wisdom and practical operation in the laws that now guide human actions and assumptions.

"With one finger on the pulse of the human mind, one eye on the disintegrating governments, and a personal penchant for following the natural evolution of human beings, these leaders will be among the first to champion a new approach to the basic issues of land, an important step in moving you forward toward the inner and outer harmony required for human evolution.

"Let us look back to the beginnings of the Industrial Revolution for a few moments. The invention of engines to replace human energy and the development of complex machinery was driven by a deep need for self-expression, a basic need that exists in all beings. It was also driven by the desire to make physical labor easier for all, and the hope of making life better for your fellows by providing basic material goods for as many people as possible.

"As the first factories took shape, it soon became evident that those who put these new inventions to work could gather power over others and become quite wealthy as well. Gradually the drive for self-expression, making work easier, or life better, twisted into a whole new set of goals designed to gather power and money. To reach these new goals, it was necessary to get as many people as possible off their land and into the factories where their lives could be more easily controlled.

"Soon the measuring stick of a man's value was not how healthy and able to survive he was, it was how much money he possessed, or how many people's lives he controlled.

"The result over time of removing people from the land has been the growing regimentation of daily life according to the clock which undermines basic health, brings about the loss of self-sufficiency, causes deep disconnections from Nature, and loss of much of the knowledge necessary to feed, clothe, and shelter oneself directly from the land.

"When money is the only means of getting basic survival needs met, the foundations for crime are laid in place because only a small percentage of people have unlimited access to money. People need free access to food, water, land, clothing, shelter, medicine, and a means of transporting themselves when necessary, and they will do whatever they have to do to get these. This includes not only spending entire lifetimes doing work that is hated and stalls personal growth, but going outside your system of laws, regulations, and expectations when necessary. Much of the crime you see and hear all around you is a direct result of this drive to survive in a situation where there is unequal access to the basic means of survival.

"In the decades to come you will see your prisons fill up with people who are not intrinsically bad. They are simply people who never developed to full maturity—which means to reach full adult power—and who were unable to cope with their inability to get what they needed within the existing system.

"Your streets will fill up with people who do not have enough money to buy a piece of land to sit, stand, or sleep on. You will watch as they are driven from place to place, and will feel bad that they do not have a home.

"Instead of examining your basic assumption that everyone should buy a piece of land and build a home on it, you will continue to push your assumptions about land onto the homeless by putting them in government housing where small bits of money are doled out to them and they languish day after day. Their valuable time and energy will be wasted, and there will be no opportunity for self-reliance or self-sufficiency. Worse, you will make others responsible for feeding, clothing, sheltering, healing, educating, and burying them—all things they should be doing for themselves if they are to learn and grow as humans.

"You will hear those in government or the general population complain about the huge numbers of poor on welfare, and asking, 'Why are they allowed to do nothing while we must work every day?' Yet the more realistic questions would be, 'What do you expect them to contribute? Can you really expect people to take responsibility for themselves when everything they need in order to do so has been taken away from them?'

"As these issues begin to escalate, your new breed of leaders will come to recognize that many present systems of money and government have become unworkable. They will see that the more things collapse, the more people will turn to the government to 'do something.'

"You cannot add burgeoning numbers of unemployed people to a system of welfare run by a government that is itself collapsing. Thus it will be clear that if something practical is not proposed, millions will be left with nothing to fall back on; chaos, revolution, and suffering will result.

"These leaders will point out that refusing people a piece of land, or forcing people off of their land because they do not have money for taxes, is somewhat shortsighted and has led down some very unproductive paths for both sides, the government as well as the greater population.

"Looking into the future, the new leaders will see not only disintegrating governments and nations, but a rising tide of unmet needs in every area of life. They will recognize that the government simply cannot meet so many divergent needs and attempting to do so will lead to confrontation, anger, and disservice in too many sectors of the population.

"These divergent needs will represent individual and group survival issues of a wholly different nature, and a government, like a religion, is charged only with examining and setting guidelines that help define the ethical aspects of human behavior. It sets the rules of fairness humans agree to follow in their treatment of one another, but is not meant to play nursemaid, savior, papa, or rich uncle.

"Although many nations will be taking more and more responsibility away from their people, the new leaders will see that this only infantilizes people, blocking maturity and extending subservience. It is not wise for government to provide the basic human needs; humans must do this for themselves. As with parents who have spoiled their children, the children refuse to grow up and move out into the world on their own. After making ever more selfish demands for food, clothing, safety, shelter, schooling, jobs, transportation, health, entertainment, a variety of services, and even pocket money, they indulge in deceit and temper tantrums when they cannot get something they believe their parents should have provided.

"As the spoiled members of the population continue to demand care and convenience from an aging government that is less and less able to provide even the basics, frustrations will grow. Like parents who have become unable to work or to carry on, yet somehow feel responsible for the entire situation, government will try to pacify at least some of the demands. The tragedy will be that if the children continue to lay around the house, refusing to work, stagnant, and incapable of doing anything for themselves, when the parent-government falls ill and finally dies, the entire family will collapse and disintegrate because none of the children ever learned how to take care of themselves.

"It is this looming prospect of unnecessary suffering and collapse that will cause these new leaders to speak out more boldly. Some of them will begin efforts to cut back the structure of government in order to wean the people from their dependence on it. Some will teach new ideas and encourage people to take responsibility for themselves. Some will focus on building a base for the new structures that will evolve as the old ones become dysfunctional, and some will try to illuminate the nature of true relationships between leaders and their people.

"In spite of the work of brave new leaders, as governments slowly come apart, it is likely that people will become more and more angry about the ineffectiveness of the care, the loss of the conveniences they were receiving, the disruptions within the financial system, and the sudden return of self-responsibility or self-sufficiency without the land or the freedom to exercise that self-responsibility. Many of these people will fruitlessly fight or waste their energy on angry protests and complex legal strategies.

"Some people who are very angry will refuse to give the government any more respect or compliance. They will want to withdraw from the government and tear apart what exists with a sense of vengeance.

"Some people will not be able to imagine a life without governments and huge institutions. They will have the attitude that perhaps government is only guilty of trying to help too much and all that is necessary is to strip away governmental fat and provide only the most basic assistance.

"Some people will insist on change but have no clear picture of the changes that are needed, thus they will support every change that is proposed, even those that are contradictory.

"And some people will slowly begin detaching themselves from dependence on governments, as well as corporations. They will begin developing a real sense of personal power, a sense of responsibility that is based *inside* the Self, and that results in an expanding awareness of their right to govern or manage their lives in ways that seem fit and fair to them.

"Here and there among groups of these people the realization will dawn anew that the government belongs to them. They will remember that it was meant to be a government of the people, by the people, and for the people.

"From this point, there will emerge the wish for a government that is more accessible, more responsive to individuals, something closer to the idea of a 'personal government.' This idea of having a more personally responsive government will evolve through a series of temporary, sometimes ill-defined stages, similar, in some ways, to the evolution of your concepts around a personal god.

"Like the idea of a personal god, a personal government can be talked to directly, can be bargained with, can be petitioned to for every form of wish and desire. A personal government can become a scapegoat, and can also be ignored if it fails to produce the desired results. Decisions can be pushed onto it when convenient, and if these decisions turn out to be poor or inappropriate, it can then be held responsible for the poor outcomes. Later it can also be blamed for usurping the decisions that really belong to the human being. Like a personal god, a personal government can be held accountable for every kind of disaster or complaint, be it natural, manmade, or otherwise, *and* be expected to avert or make amends for these and every other situation that goes awry.

"As the growing sense of personal responsibility in individual humans creates the concept of a more personally responsible government, *and* since this is not what current nations or their governments were set up to be, there will be increasing dissatisfaction with governments in general.

"Finally, your ideas will evolve into the concept of personal self-government we have referred to as 'personal responsibility' and it is this as much as anything that will aid in the gradual undoing of the concept of national government. A great deal of the actual undoing will be the result of simply too many people making too many demands on a system that is not organized for continuous personal communication and ends up first overloaded, then paralyzed.

"In truth, this insistence that the government respond to each of you as a valuable individual will be a good sign of renewed human development. For too many of you, too much power and responsibility is imagined to be outside the self, which is why many of the new leaders will initially be teachers and guides who will not appear within the structures of government, but who will lead you toward your own maturity."

Abruptly, a stray thought struck me, "Maybe now people will understand why I don't vote..." as I drifted backwards into my childhood. I was young, maybe eleven or twelve, and we had just finished eating supper one night when my Dad put on his coat, got his keys, and told my mother he'd be back shortly. It was my night to do dishes and when he left, I asked my mother where he was going.

"Up to vote," she said.

"To what?" I asked, surprised.

"To vote. It's time to vote for a new president," she explained and then went off to the utility room to finish some laundry.

I continued to clear the table, outwardly silent but inwardly in turmoil. How could he waste his time with that, I asked myself over and over. Didn't he understand that it would all come to nothing? Couldn't he see how this idea of voting was childish, silly?

For a young girl who was not given to considering the outside world at all and who knew little or nothing about politics and elections, the waves of sorrow and incredulity over my father's involvement with voting were unprecedented. Where such thoughts and feelings came from was a mystery. All I knew was that they were deep and intense.

The next day I had forgotten the whole business. It remained forgotten for years, until after my first marriage. I was about twenty and it was an election year. Although voting was legal for those over eighteen, I had not voted for anything and had never even considered it.

As Election Day approached and my husband kept asking me who I was going to vote for, I kept having the same intense, inexplicable reaction toward his interest in voting that I'd had toward my father's at the age of twelve. Even at the age of twenty, I could not explain what I felt, and knew that he wouldn't understand even if I could have explained. There was no logical reason for my feelings, and I had barely enough self-awareness to realize that other people didn't seem to feel what I was feeling, so I remained generally silent on the subject.

One day, when he had asked me for the hundredth time who I was going to vote for, I shouted out, "I'm not going to vote for anyone, not now, not ever… I'm not part of that system."

He reacted angrily to my tone and attitude, stomping off in a huff and asking 'who the hell did I think I was?' But I reacted in shock to my own words.

"Where did my attitude come from? What did I mean by that? What system am I not part of?" I asked myself.

Embarrassed and without answers, I dropped these questions in a flurry of confusion, and as Election Day arrived, my husband continued to press me to vote until I finally capitulated and went over to the school where the voting was taking place.

Once in the voting booth, I panicked. I did not read newspapers, watch television, or listen to the radio and now I stared at all the names as if they were some indecipherable language. Neither could I remember the instructions for making the machine work, and after trying to push several different buttons, I pulled a lever. Somehow, when I pulled the lever, I voted for the whole Republican Party. When I tried to undo my sweeping choice, I couldn't. With deepening panic I abandoned the machine, turned around, and fumbled frantically with the curtain that separated me from the next person in line. When I couldn't figure out how to open it, I picked up the bottom edge of the curtain and half-crawled, half-ducked under it.

I left the booth sick to my stomach, feeling I had done something dishonorable, something untrue, as if I were a liar, a fool, or both. In the end, I decided never to vote again. I didn't have any reasonable reason. I just knew that I couldn't. Whenever politics came up, I tuned out. If someone happened to ask which candidate I was thinking of voting for, I stated simply, "I don't vote." If they pressed me to explain and I asked them why they were concerned, I found that some people assumed I was going to be out of town and wouldn't know how to get an absentee ballot, which they were always happy to tell me how to get. Others assumed it was because I didn't like the candidates, or that I was too lazy to go out, or too apathetic and needed some political cheerleading.

When I continued to state quietly, "I don't vote," and they continued to ask why, I often ended up saying, "I'm not part of that system." Usually that was enough. I didn't know what I meant, and they didn't either. Most backed off in confusion and the subject was quickly changed.

Now, the issue was staring me in the face. The little men had touched something so deep I could hardly breathe when I allowed myself to contemplate it. Backing away from my own thoughts and feelings, not wanting to know any more about myself, I again focused with some effort on what the little men were saying.

"… the new breed of rising leaders will realize what every mature human eventually realizes, that power does not come without full responsibility. They will see that many political systems have become powerless and ineffective. This will be so partly because of their unwillingness to take responsibility for fear of the political consequences, and partly because the people have outgrown them.

"The new leaders will be unwilling to play the expensive political games that would bring them into the world of traditional politics and although they will not be speaking as senators or parliamentarians, they will have the strength, the voice, and the vision to propose a series of changes.

"Firmly believing that the Earth can and will supply almost everything that is really necessary for a good life, and that it is essential to get as many people as possible moving toward self-sufficiency as quickly as possible, these leaders will make an effort to move people off of governmental support. In time, they will propose that interested people be given small plots of land that they can consider theirs for life and on which they can be self-sufficient.

"Others will point out that the government has been myopic in taking land, property, and houses away from the common people who do not have money yet are perfectly capable of staying on that land, supplying their own food, clothing, and shelter, and making their way peacefully through life. In addition, they will go on to teach a new view of managing life based on human evolution and self-sufficiency.

"As they do so, others will begin to see that it is foolish for governments to take away the land and homes of the poor, forcing them into government housing supported by taxpayer money just because they have no money and severely limited opportunities to make the required amounts. There will be an effort to make clear how it is a disservice to induce people to take food stamps when they could more reasonably learn to grow and eat much healthier food themselves, food which is free from the earth for relatively little work.

"The new leaders will see that collapse is already beginning and irrevocable change is in progress. They will see that people will suffer if they are not prepared to take care of themselves, and thus they will work to create as much change toward self-sufficiency as possible, knowing that this will create islands of stability in case chaos should follow.

"They will point out that in view of rapid changes in corporations and the loss of many jobs, it is misleading to encourage people to sign up for educational programs that will prepare them for meaningless work in nonexistent jobs. They will also point out that it is unethical to force other taxpayers to pay for the meaningless education meant to draft the new workers into an army of taxpayers and an American way of life that used-to-be and is destined for even deeper change."

Now I was looking at a desert-like area where a shantytown had sprung up. It was somewhere in the southwest U.S. and was populated by a large group of brown-skinned people who moved about several luxurious gardens in a relaxed manner, nearly all of them carrying something in their pocket with a short antenna-like wire on it.

The scene changed and I was looking at a nearly empty city, a shell of what it had once been. Pockets of people were tending a series of small machines that did some kind of drawing while other people tended a number of gardens. I wondered who these people were, what they were doing, and why they were living in such ruins, but didn't interrupt to ask as the little men continued briskly.

"In many ways similar to your land rush of the 1800's in which people were given the deed to a plot of land if they lived on it and worked it, those formerly dependent on government money will be encouraged to accept a parcel of land build on it, grow food on it, put their small business on it, raise their children on it—any or all of these.

"Discussion of this proposal will trigger a wave of demand from people everywhere who want to be given the same opportunity to own and work a piece of land that can be considered theirs for life. Gradually, this idea will catch on and, in time, due to the faltering government and deep changes in your attitude toward land, many will begin to ignore things like deeds and ownership payments. Others, like some in present-day Mexico and Africa, will simply set up home and family wherever they will be bothered the least by the disintegrating governments and absent or un-threatening owners.

"The possibilities for helping people to help themselves will range all the way from giving away pieces of national forests with the stipulation that they must be maintained as forest, to offering tracts of polluted or otherwise damaged land in return for restoring it to healthy, natural balance.

"This will be only the beginning point at which your perception of land will change and you will have to be careful as a people that you do not descend into squabbling over land in the way the old gold miners once squabbled over claims.

"As the earth changes, and nations and governments slowly pass away, so too will old attitudes toward the land. Land, once the necessary prize for any nation of means, will take a back seat to food and the power provided in the large global network that grows to encircle the earth. In time, all that the nations will have left to help their suffering people will be the land, which will be gradually parceled out as needed.

"Following the example of those who transformed the desert area now known as Israel into a self-supporting economy, many small groups of people will take a nearly barren piece of land and create a whole new environment that is self-sufficient and self-supporting.

"Of course, people knew more about making a living from the land back in the 1800's and there will be the arguments that the government is abandoning its people to sink or swim. After years of home-based colonialism founded on the dogma that your government was raising your standards of living, this will seem an abrupt about-face. Some will claim that dumping people back into the lap of nature would condemn many to certain death by starvation, freezing, or physical stress.

"The truth is, all of you are already on your own in the lap of nature and do not realize it. Worse, you are destroying nature, the source of your physical existence, and if you do not take steps to re-connect yourselves to Earth, you will perish.

"To help you make it through the coming transitions you must realize several things. First, there must be the awareness that the changes *are* upon you. Second, the changes will be extensive. No area of life will remain untouched. Third, if you prepare properly, you *can* transform yourselves and all of the ways you organize your lives and your time without undue suffering. We consider undue suffering to include being hungry, cold, sick, or under attack. Those who resist the changes and refuse to let go of their present ways of life will likely suffer, and will be choosing to suffer unnecessarily.

"If you have at least a rough idea of what the future looks like and how the human is meant to evolve, you will not be afraid. Leaders will arise to help you through the transitions. If you are paying attention, you will recognize them and the wisdom of their solutions.

"In the end, if you are wise, and if all goes well, there will be changes in your entire way of life and even in your reasons for being. Your people need to grow in terms of perceptual development. Some of this development will bring an expanded perception of the self, combined with an instinctive recognition that the individual can re-create that self end-lessly.

"You have a saying that says the only things you cannot avoid are death and taxes. The truth is that your idea of death is a mistake in thinking, and taxes are an illusion. *The only thing you cannot avoid is your own human development.*

"In the old societies it was the job of shamans, yogis, and griots to help members of the group continuously recreate themselves, and to help the group as a whole transform their visions of life into meaningful action in the everyday routines. In your society, and in many places around the Earth, the new leaders will be teachers who will arise when and where needed to help you transform yourselves and access new visions.

"The rise of the large global network will also help you learn to enhance your sense of self and re-create your way of life, for technology tends to reorganize thinking. Every thought, every communication, every perceptual experience has an effect on the inner you, as well as on the outer world around you. It is time for you to not only recognize this, but begin using the body/mind system to practice the expanded creating and communications you are capable of."

The pictures now came in closer and with more detail. Fighting had broken out in areas of Georgia and South Carolina, across Florida and Texas, in the upper Midwest and the Southwest. Gangs of young people were everywhere, attacking, scrambling for power, taking what they needed, and causing much grief. They seemed to be the children of no one. I watched them sadly, anxiously, and wondered where or to whom they belonged.

"You will eventually come to think of these children as the lost generation," the little monks remarked. "They have agreed to come here to teach you that what you sow is exactly what you reap. Once you understand human development a little better, you will understand what went wrong for these children, but we will go into this more deeply at another time.

"In closing we would like to emphasize that as we go deeper into the coming changes, we hope you will understand why learning to see backward and forward in time is one of the most basic of skills in human evolution and why it is so sorely needed by the people of your planet."

With that enigmatic statement, they faded away.

📖

I found myself back in the present, and for a while I continued to sit. The future did not look either simple or smooth, and although I wanted to ignore the little men and their pictures as easily as I had their first few visits, somehow I could not.

Instead, a new view of money, land, housing, and other necessities began blossoming. It wasn't very coherent, but it was taking shape. For the first time I was aware that everyone needed food, yet in the current system there were few ways of getting it other than going to the grocery store. Education was supposed to be the key to more money, yet you had to have thousands of dollars to get that education in the first place and given the current economic system, it was beyond my humble means. I was willing to be responsible for filling my own needs for shelter, clothing, healing, transportation, and many other things, but in the current system there were narrowly-prescribed ways for doing this as well. Either you were in the system submitting to its dictates, contributing to the illusion of a certain and necessary standard of living for all, or you were out of it, poor, disadvantaged, needy, and trying to get into it.

"How did we get such limited options? Who is running this system?" I demanded to no one in particular. Where were the people who could open more options, make it make sense? Where were the leaders the little men had described? Was it a new, wiser president? Or the governor? If it wasn't either of them, who was it? And where would they get their authority? From the Senate? Or the House of Representatives? How would they go about changing the system? Wouldn't that be considered revolutionary? Where did one go to get permission to be a revolutionary? What sorts of papers would you have to file to get an okay to set up a new system?

This train of thought ran on for a minute, leaving me feeling naïve, then helpless, finally cynical. "This is crap. Nobody's going to change the system. It isn't possible, any of it, and those guys are nuts," I said, referring to the little men in brown robes.

I got up off the sofa to begin my day but wandered over to the window and stood staring out the window at the frozen January landscape. In my mind it was the summer of 1967 and I was seeing a jeep with a machine gun mounted on the back. The gun was casually pointing toward the upper flat I lived in on Manistique Street in Detroit. The Detroit Riots had erupted a day or two earlier and was in full motion.

The night before, shortly after dark, Effie, the only other person on our street that I knew, had come over and asked me to go with her to pick up a friend. The friend, Carol somebody, was stranded in a trailer park over by the Cadillac plant on Conner near Gratiot Avenue. Bullets were flying near the trailer park, Carol was six months pregnant, and she was frightened.

Driving through the littered streets had been like an excursion through a war movie. The sky was red-orange from the fires that burned out of control everywhere. The sound of sirens, guns, and shouts came from various directions, broken glass lay splashed across sidewalks, and dark figures hurried furtively in and out of gaping storefronts.

In the trailer park, most of the lights were out as we made our way to Carol's trailer and beeped the horn once, lightly. After a minute the door opened and Carol came crawling out. Moving as quickly as her swollen belly would allow, she scurried on all fours to the open car door, crawled inside, and shut the door quietly. We backed out the way we had come in, turned, and headed home.

It was a tense, quiet trip, and in retrospect, it was clear we could have easily become a target for the snipers that seemed to be everywhere. Yet we made it without incident, and in my memory the whole night remained surrounded with a thick aura of safe, almost romantic adventure.

The next day when the soldiers and machine guns showed up on our corner, it had not seemed so romantic. Indignantly I stared out the window at the gun and thought, "They wouldn't dare use that thing here!" Even more shocking was the soldier who manned the gun. He was only a kid, young, white, maybe nineteen or twenty, like me. I gazed at him from my window thinking, "Do you know what you're playing with, boy? Do you honestly think you can kill? What's wrong with you, thinking like that?"

Looking back it seemed that everything about that summer had ended in disillusionment. On the one hand, the script of life seemed to have been taken from a comic strip that poked jeering holes in the hope that people could just up and change things. On the other, the pall of tragedy lay over everything. The hopes of black people, the dreams of the hippies, the expectations of the young men going to Vietnam, the demands of the adults who wanted an end to the war, the fears of those in power... no one was getting what they wanted.

Gradually my vision returned to the present and the frozen canal outside my window. "Get going!" I told myself, "There's no point in worrying about whether the system will change... that's just a myth... I need to get out of the mindset those guys always get me into." 📖

7 📖

WORLD WAR III?...

WHEN the little men returned for a third visit in less than two weeks, they found me in a disagreeable mood, trying to pay the January bills without enough money to cover everything that was due.

True to form, they addressed my mood with a new version of their usual greeting. "You seem to be feeling poorly about your life. Would you like to see some pictures of the things to come so you will have a better idea of why things are unfolding as they are?"

Somewhat exasperated, I didn't answer right away. Instead I contemplated their presence, wondering why they were back again and what more they could possibly have to show me. I didn't have time for this sort of thing today! And I didn't need more information, especially when I had no idea what to do with the information they had already shown me. Were they going to continue taking up all my free time without regard as to what I needed to do each day?

They stood, watching me quietly, saying nothing, and it was clear they intended to stay. It didn't occur to me to say "go away" like I had the first couple of times, or even to suggest they come back when I had more time. Finally, I agreed to look at their pictures, and with a sigh, sat back and closed my eyes.

Swept quickly into a river of awareness, I watched scenes of fighting with growing alarm. There was violence in Eastern Europe, terrorism in France as well as North Africa, and just plain terror in a number of South American countries, especially Columbia, Argentina, Chile, Peru, and Brazil.

Quiet tremors of raw anger ran through the streets of China while waves of revolution covered Mexico. Huge demonstrations of protest erupted in the U.S. and Canada, while the Middle East remained an active volcano of discontent.

Groups with machine guns were running around in Russia, the Caribbean, and Africa. In scattered places over the rest of the world, trains, boats, and planes exploded or were taken hostage. Here and there, angry, screaming people threw rocks and sticks at office buildings. Elsewhere, people streamed out of factories and offices, unable to get out fast enough as bombs exploded from within.

I continued to watch and although things did not get better, they did not become catastrophic either. Nevertheless, by degrees, I noticed that people seemed afraid to drive anywhere or go out of their neighborhood, sometimes even their houses. Fewer and fewer were going to the markets or malls, sending their children to school, visiting shops and restaurants, or any of the other places where large numbers of people had gathered to relax or do their daily business only a few years earlier. It appeared to be unsafe everywhere. Schools, hospitals, malls, and other public places had become favorite targets of destruction.

At last the little men began their narration.

"As the old ways come to a close and the new ways open, you will see the unfolding of struggle, fighting, and destruction, in nearly every corner of your world.

"In the beginning there will be no nuclear weapons used in these battles, and there will be no major, international military conflagrations of a protracted sort that characterized World Wars I and II. But many kinds of serious conflict will spread across every land, bringing quick invasions based on greed and the desire to control others.

"As the nations begin breaking apart, this fighting will escalate and spread to many new places. Along with the 'official' international conflicts, there will be regional conflicts everywhere. This will include conflicts between cities and states, within cities and towns, and between tribes and old groupings as neighbor suddenly turns against neighbor.

"Some of the battles between nations will be fairly big, using air power, missiles, and heavy equipment. Others will be characterized by a series of small yet destructive, strong-arm hostilities designed to intimidate. Some fighting will employ stealth in the night and guerrilla tactics in retaliation for imagined insults, while others will consist of offensive maneuvers planned by those who hope to ward off attacks based on fear of shortages.

"There will be acts of sheer terrorism designed to frighten one another or get revenge for imagined faults. Some fights will be bloody man-to-man, hand-to-hand battles between groups of people who refuse to move any further into what are considered frightening changes with uncertain outcomes. And some will be bloodless, yet vicious battles between powerful individuals, using the lives of other men as pawns.

"These battles will be fought for all kinds of reasons—over food, water, land, air, animal rights, mineral rights, trade rights, and human rights. There will be arguments and bloodshed over boundaries, the right to govern, the right to speak the truth, the right to live where one wishes, and to die when and how one chooses.

"You are familiar with these kinds of wars, and therefore what we hope to illuminate here are the wars you may overlook, and the powerfully destructive effects they will have on your reality. These overlooked wars will be fought using your legal systems, yet you will be so hypnotized by the more obvious war dramas being played out in many areas of the world that you will not see that your courts have become a battleground and your legal system has become an insidious weapon of attack. Because it is bloodless, you will not see that it has become distorted and manipulative, or that it is being used by the government to maintain whatever shreds of power it can, as well as by the large corporations to gather increasing amounts of power.

"Although the common man will be welcome to use this weapon of attack to fight whomever he chooses—including the government and the corporations—he will quickly discover that it takes extraordinary amounts of money to do so. Since the amount of money he has access to is likely to be controlled by the corporate system he works in, and a portion of what he earns is taxed by the government, it becomes an easy matter to keep his money, and therefore his power to fight, severely limited.

"In the meantime, more and more laws, regulations, and rules that erode inner authority will be enacted, all of which the common man is subject to and cannot fight simply because he cannot afford the cost of the legal weapons. Gradually, the basic rights of self-government and self-determination will be sneaked away.

"Soon, many words, thoughts, practical actions, and ideas will be out of reach. To use them will be illegal. They will be off limits to the common man who trudges through his daily routine, not thinking, not speaking, and having barely enough energy to perform those specific tasks that will get him the little bit of money he needs to buy his survival.

"Some of the more serious disagreements will be fought among governments, businesses, or ordinary men and women, each of whom wants the exclusive right to use certain words and ideas. Each will want the final say in these battles, for each believes that whoever has the final say will have the most power and control.

"No one will have the sense to say, 'Why don't I create my idea, and you create yours, and perhaps we will find valuable elements that will teach us both, carrying us beyond the original ideas to something even better or more useful?'

"Instead, the war over words and ideas will accelerate the loss of your inner authority because you will not recognize what is really happening—the strangling of creative self expression."

Then the little men presented a scene involving a courtroom. As I watched the interaction between the lawyers and their clients, it became clear that there was a serious disagreement over an advertisement. The thing being advertised was a toy, and it appeared that someone had created something similar to compete with the original design. The first company was not only objecting to the similarity of the product, they were arguing that the words their competitor used to describe the toy were words that belonged to the first company.

I recognized that this kind of argument had to do with copyrights, or perhaps trademarks. I had zero experience with these kinds of issues and was shocked at the cool, ultra-logical fight for power, the bribery involved, and the mechanical application of rules and regulations. I was also surprised by the intensity of the fight for a mere toy.

The case came to an end with a financial settlement, but others followed. Some centered on disagreements over how to interpret a particular phrase in the law. Others fought fiercely over whether an individual had the right to use certain words when describing another individual, a business, a government, or a product.

Although the people involved in these arguments were struggling to settle what they believed were some very serious issues, the whole question of who owned words and ideas reminded me of the little men's comments about selling blessings and indulgences. It was all just another scheme for power and money.

"To underscore the tragic side of these battles," continued the little men, "it is important to understand that words are a form of expressed energy. To speak a word is to take an intermediate step in creating something, the first step being the thought or concept itself.

"All words are characterized by sound frequencies and when you give voice to a sound, you are shaping and manipulating energy into the basis for form. Let's say the form is an automobile. Once the automobile has been created, it continues to emit the entire symphony of subtle sound frequencies that were used to create it because these sounds are emitted by the pattern of wave frequencies that hold the automobile's atoms and molecules together.

"Once created, the automobile and its sounds continue to have an effect on you and your physical reality. As a result of this feedback effect from the automobile, you may be inspired with new ideas for creating other sounds and forms, since there are endless possibilities for these. Thus you can say that creation is a highly interactive process. You grasp an idea, the idea emits a sound or matrix of sounds in the form of tones and words, these sounds help to both create the form, and to inspire new ideas!

"Words are a form of energy, and energy is—by definition—a moving force directed into either form or further action. When people try to own words or prevent others from using them, they interfere with the movement of energy, with the transformation of energy into form, with the interactive potentials of that form, and thus with the creative nature of life itself. And the truth is, you must create if you wish to survive. It is not a luxury for artists and those who are wealthy.

"When people are fighting, they surround themselves with destructive forms of energy which arise from the angry, hurtful words that are expressed during the argument. This destructive energy acts on everyone involved, extending even to those who maintain relationships with those engaged in the fight. This anger also acts on the original objects, words, or ideas being fought over, tainting them with destructive energies. The result is that those who win often find that the objects or words they were fighting over have lost much of their magic as well as the power to do creative work for the owner.

"Many humans have lost their inner authority and have tried to fill the gap with money. This is the real problem behind the argument, not the ownership, but we will get to this a bit later. First we would like to look at another war that will also be overlooked.

"This will be the war involving what is 'true because science says so' versus what is true 'because you know it in your heart or have experienced it in your own mind.' As this issue comes to the foreground, you will begin to realize that there has been a degradation of your beloved scientific method. This degradation of science is based on the widespread but erroneous assumption that there is only one way to observe a set of events, one correct conclusion to be drawn, and one truth associated with this conclusion.

"When you subscribe to the belief that there is only one way to define a given word, action, or idea, and only one correct—therefore allowable—conclusion, you again have a stifling of the life force as well as the drive for creative self-expression. Disturb these two forces and you disturb your ability to survive and thrive.

"Once upon a time, science and the empirical method were exciting, useful approaches for observing and studying a reality. Over time, they have deteriorated into a means of control. Now only select processes of observing, studying, and testing are recognized. Other observations and personal experiences are dismissed as 'unscientific.' Again, this dismissal has slowly, imperceptibly, robbed ordinary individuals of a sense of inner authority, undermining their ability to perceive for themselves, to make decisions, to exercise common sense, to nurture wisdom, and to tap their potential as humans.

"Once the inner authority of a people has been usurped, the unbridled growth of religious institutions, national governments, and corporate entities is an inevitable outcome for people must have something to believe in.

"Once these institutions, with their tendency to decide and manage everyone's affairs, are in place, the main avenue to power is through them rather than through the Self.

"At this time in your development, if you want any semblance of power, you must join one of these institutions. Yet there is serious disillusionment among those who structure their lives according to the dictates of institutions. Once inside, you find that above and below you are dozens, perhaps thousands, of people who have lost the path to their own true power. All are caught in a delicate but pointless balancing act in which each tries to garner power by building small kingdoms through which those below them can be controlled or otherwise forced to do as they are told.

"Refusing to follow the religious dogma, the corporate propaganda, or the governmental party line leaves you threatened with cutoff of the money you need to fill the basic needs for survival. Quickly you find that you are just another cog in the gears. You, the self-governing, have somehow slipped into a position of being dictated to.

"Although some may make an effort to regain their own authority, most attempts to do so end unsuccessfully because they still insist on trying to get others to do their bidding.

"Those who try to gather power by sitting down and refusing to move until someone listens to them are simply picked up and carted away like Monday morning's trash. Those who use direct opposition to get their message across by engaging in public temper tantrums such as riots and marches, seldom get anywhere and usually run out of energy. The more deadly among you turn to sabotage through assassinations, bombing, and arson, yet these people frighten everyone and end up becoming direct targets of the power they are confronting. Quite a few are satisfied with the small moments of power they feel when shopping, complying with rules, or joining the rituals and services that institutions offer, yet this perpetuates the existing system and their dependencies within it.

"Frustrated, most people look for some indirect way to manipulate other people and events, while trying to make the world conform to their own wishes. Yet while running other people's lives, very few feel they are free to run their own life the way they truly wish to. The truth is that all efforts to regain inner authority must begin by focusing on the Self, not on others.

"As people of the democracies continue to grow in maturity and awareness, they will come to feel that the institutions of national governments, business, and religion are no longer serving them well, a fact that those in power will worry about. This worry will lead those in places of power to keep a sharp eye out for any form of challenge. As some of the newer structures of the future begin taking shape, there will be strenuous efforts by government, business, and religion to take control of these new structures, or at least make laws to control them.

"This will foster resentment and resistance toward government's interference in an area of life that has nothing to do with why government really exists. If there is not the acknowledgment and recognition of this resentment, it will fester and grow, creating an explosive climate. Unless it is dealt with constructively, only a short time into the new millennium people will begin to be caught up in fighting which will eventually spread around the entire globe.

"In every nation and group heart there is a desire to avoid another confrontation on the scale and horror of World War II. But while you are all trying so hard to avoid doing anything that could be labeled as the start of the third world war, you will fail to pay attention to the fact that there is fighting in every corner of the planet. If you are not careful, only a decade into your new century there will be few places left to run to that are not engaged in fighting, or where human beings are not suffering small wars, persecution, death, environmental disaster, or serious deprivation in large numbers. Those that *are* hanging on to some semblance of peace will not let anyone else in.

"At this point you will realize that, for all intents and purposes, the world is engulfed in what will eventually be termed World War III. It will not *look* like the first two world wars with a common battlefield, trenches, and two sides lined up to confront one another, but it will *be* a world war due to the fact that almost everyone is fighting over everything. As you have seen, some of the fighting will be over land and food, words and ideas, or money and power. But the real reason for the fighting will be that everyone is feeling the effects of the loss of inner authority, and too late it will become clear that you are trying to follow too many conflicting rules served up by too many masters chasing after some kind of temporary power.

"In order to survive you will have to regain a sense of purpose and direction in life, and to gain a sense of direction you will have to do things very differently. Therefore, a great number of the battles will be between those attempting to hold on to old ways of doing things and those who want to move ahead to new ways.

"Over the long run it will be important for all of you to know that the dissolution that begins angrily in Russia *can* be accomplished sensibly in Canada, the U.S., Mexico, and other places around the world as newly expanding waves of regionalism and allegiance to ancient tribal boundaries force national governments to reverse their earlier colonialism.

"If you are wise, you will work to find peaceful and creative ways to help one another. Once there are precedents, and people can see fairly peaceful means to taking back their own authority, or their land, or the means for survival, these can be copied and used as models in many places. They can serve as a point from which to develop even more satisfactory ways of organizing groups of people that live, love, and work together. In your current situation, you can only disintegrate at all levels, physically, mentally, emotionally, and spiritually.

"For now it is quite important to underline several ideas. The first is that if you can see in advance how and why the world could become caught up in a new version of a world war, you might be able to avert, or at least reduce the problems and heartache involved.

"The healing process could begin early, giving you time to create new paths to peace. This would be quite helpful since most of the old channels used to create peace were designed to work in an environment that will no longer exist, or is crumbling into dysfunction.

"Entirely new approaches will be required, approaches that must first address how to change the perception of those who must live the new ways of peace. The changes will necessitate a global consciousness of true priorities for *humans*, not for Americans, Arabs, French, Chinese or all of the other groups with artificial boundaries between them and impractical limitations around them.

"These new approaches to peace will require a tremendous amount of activity in both the letting go of some traditional structures, the set-up of transitional structures, the development of the ability to imagine whole new ways of living, and the acceptance of a few basic truths—one of which is that anything unnatural, anything which does not create and extend life, will not self-sustain.

"Ideas, words, objects, actions, and life-styles are either aligned with the life-force or they are not! If they are not, they will soon become uneconomical and require ever-increasing amounts of time, energy, and resources to keep them going. Since you are running out of these on every continent, it is time to begin a new way of life. The stage is being set for the human to move to a new level of functioning and in order to accomplish this you must not only survive, you must evolve."

With that, the pictures and the little men faded away and my attention returned slowly to the room around me.

📖

The pile of unpaid bills stared at me expectantly, but I had lost interest in them. I was thinking about the little men's comment that when people were fighting over something, they were surrounding themselves with angry energy that tainted their lives and their project. At that moment in my Everyday, I was involved in a legal fight with the City of Pontiac.

Ben and I wanted permission to open a small bar and restaurant there. All the city council had to do was give us a permit to occupy the location we had rented. Yet month after month they stalled, using one excuse after the next.

The facts of the matter were that General Motors had built an entire complex of executive offices down the street from our location and we stood a better than average chance of being able to attract a good lunch crowd from these offices. Just up the street was a older man who also owned a small bar and restaurant. He didn't want us opening a new place just a few doors from him.

Unfortunately for us, the mayor pro tem of the city council was the nephew of our would-be business neighbor and the two of them had been blocking the approval of the location for almost two years.

The fight had become a public matter with bad press, back room promises, and all kinds of plots and distractions. It was costing us a fortune and we were already in serious debt with no sign that the occupancy permit would soon be ours.

With unexpected clarity I deliberated as to whether or not I was caught up in the very situation the little men had just described. Was I going to lose because I did not have the money to continue buying the lawyers that would allow me to keep on fighting for what I wanted? And if I got it, would it be tainted with negative energy that prevented the bar and restaurant from working creatively, specifically to create the money I needed to buy my survival?

The specter of this was so overwhelming that I instantly got up from the chair I was sitting in and went to make a cup of tea while my mind worked furiously to assess the possible outcomes to our fight with Pontiac.

At this point I couldn't afford to give up the fight for the bar and restaurant, and I couldn't see any other means of forcing the city to give us the permit. I also couldn't afford any doubt and it was this thought that prompted me to begin criticizing the little men and their pictures.

"What are they talking about with this business of negative energy?" I thought with disdain as I slipped into a more comfortable frame of mind, one that did not admit little men in brown robes, telepathic communications, inner authority, or the possibility of failure.

    "I need to get these bills paid!" I told myself, clucking my tongue at the clock and how late in the day it was. In no time at all I was caught up in the task of writing checks, putting them in envelopes, stamping and sealing them with approximately the same kind of vigor my mind was sealing off the accumulating evidence that I might be on the wrong track with my life. The hints that people were not going out much in the future to places like bars and restaurants, the scenes of civil disturbance, the possible disintegration of our government, not to mention earth changes— all were neatly set aside, refused admission beyond the shallowest of acknowledgments because I stubbornly did not want to see or to know anything other than what I wanted to see and know. 📖

8 📖

WEATHER EXTREMES ...

AT the very end of January the little men quietly returned. I did not think I was dealing very well with the information they kept giving me, yet because of my good mood at the moment I felt a small start of pleasure at their appearance. They smiled, nodded, and in the same way as always, asked if I would be willing to look at their pictures.

After wondering briefly what more they could have to show me and why they thought I should see it, I agreed and closed my eyes in order to enter their world of telepathic movies.

As the pictures opened, I found myself in what appeared to be central or eastern Europe. Judging by the old-fashioned clothing and carriages it was sometime in the 1500's, perhaps 1600's. There were small villages dotting the hills and some of the houses had a touch of what struck me as "gingerbread" architecture, but all of them were very solid and well-built with huge beams, thick plank paneling and hardwood floors. In the houses, the exquisite furniture was large and heavy, with intricate carvings, and was nothing like the cheap papery paneling and dressers that were so common in the present time.

A group of men was walking through the woods and I became deeply engrossed in watching them. There were five of them and they seemed to be from a family of woodcutters and carvers, who were out selecting trees for something they were building or planning to build. They moved among the trees, stopping to gaze at this fir or that oak, visually seeing the finished piece in their minds and superimposing that finished piece on various trees, noting how the grain would likely move in a table, or how the shape of a branch changed direction in a way that could be utilized for the back of a curved chair or a bed.

With small, broad knives they lifted pieces of bark to look at the color of the wood, noting which were champagne pale, which were rosy colored, or a dark gold. With careful attention to soil and slope, they assessed how wet the tree's lumber would be and how long it might take them to dry it, whether it would shrink out of shape too much, and how the placement of various branches would accentuate the shrinking and distortion of the wood. Fascinated, I lost track of time and place, moving about with them until the scene began to change, then again, and again, each time more quickly.

With each change there were a few more people, all still dressed in old-fashioned clothing, and still cutting down trees to build houses, furniture, and other items. Slowly the clothing became more modern but the people were still busy cutting down trees for ships, for factories, for more houses in the growing cities. Little by little, people began to appear everywhere over the surface of the earth, always moving, ever restless, seldom secure or rooted. And slowly, the sparkling cool greenness of the planet began to dull.

Hordes of people moved back and forth, into and out of Africa, others moved westward to North America, and still others to Central and South America. Following the hordes of people came fleets of bulldozers moving mountains out of their way, or piling up the earth to contain rivers, create lakes, or build houses, factories, and business centers. Teams of workers were flattening the land to prepare it for railroads and highways designed to make all the moving back and forth even easier.

I had not noticed the air at first, but now it became heavier, less sweet. Then it turned dark, smoky, and acrid smelling. Particles in it stung my nose and made the landscape look dirty, dusty. Thick, smoky air hung over the cities, factories, forests, and even the water. I recognized some of these locations by their architecture or the ethnic faces of the people.

The scenes reminded me of news reports that talked of acid rain and other ecological disasters, and suddenly I pulled back, highly resistant to what the little men were showing me. I didn't want to see or hear any more. I was so tired of what I thought were over-exaggerated reports of ecological damage and environmental pollution. I considered such reports to be over-dramatic, fearful propaganda pushed by people who wanted some of that same power and freedom held by factories and corporations. The little men should have known that I was not an ecology activist by any stretch of the imagination and nothing raised such feelings of irritated helplessness in me as the constant bad press regarding the environment.

"Who cares?" I thought with a disgusted sigh, suddenly feeling that the little men were guilty of trying to brainwash me.

A portion of me was still back in that magnificent forest with the family of woodcutters and carvers, however. I had truly been interested in how they went about their work.

"It's too bad we can't make furniture like that any more..." I thought, "...no one takes that kind of time anymore... and where would we find those kinds of trees these days... too bad..."

My train of thought was interrupted by a series of violent storms that moved across the landscapes I was viewing. The storms were accompanied by the commentary of the little men.

"The weather will begin to be more extreme everywhere," they stated as I watched torrential rains and widespread floods wash over the same area of central Europe where I had just been wandering through the forest with the woodcutters.

"There have always been the rainy seasons, the dry seasons, sudden and dangerous storms, as well as the unexpected, like earthquakes, volcanoes, and sudden glacier activity. But this new extremism in your weather will be an undoing force, exactly equal to your undoing of the matrix of nature.

"The weather will become seriously unpredictable and violent, constantly interfering with your regions, your crops, homes, roads, routines, and the economics of all these.

"Your rigid economics based on predictability and control, will shatter again and again, leaving many people thirsty, hungry, sick, cold, and financially broken. You will waste time and money repeatedly rebuilding what nature has ripped up. This constant rebuilding in inappropriate places will waste your dwindling resources of wood, water, oil, and minerals until there is nothing left to build with, and many places are no longer habitable. Gradually you will come to see that a much more natural and flexible way of life is necessary if you want to survive on the planet."

The scenes I was watching now included water and mudslides in California, Central China, India, and Venezuela. There was flooding in northern and central Europe, on several islands of Japan, along the entire southeastern coastline of India, in central and east Africa, in multiple regions of the U.S. In some of the places bodies were floating in the water.

The little men went on. "To stay alive on this planet you must have air, water, food, and shelter—not necessarily a good job, lot's of machinery, or a nice bank account. Let us say you are a modern farmer growing food for the global population. If a serious local flood destroys your home, your car, your agricultural machines, and your roads, you have some difficult choices to make. Should you grow another crop first, put up another house first, borrow money to repair your car and tractor, or fix your roads so your wife can continue to go to work to make dollars? Which is truly more important... a place to live, something to eat, fertile land, well-maintained equipment, or a possible source of immediate income?

"What if an earthquake destroys both your cropland and your irrigation system or water sources... then what? Can you even think about planting again? Suppose it is an unusually severe and prolonged freeze in winter or late spring? What about a drought that lasts a decade? These extremes of weather can cause losses that are long term, that cannot be restored the following week, and that your multiplying population can not withstand."

The little men continued their lecture as I watched strings of tornadoes move across the interior of China and the U.S. Hurricanes pounded India, the southeastern coast of the United States, the north and south coasts of Australia, Japan and southeast Asia, both sides of Mexico and the Caribbean, as well as Hawaii and the islands of the South Pacific.

Freak winds and unending rains plagued a succession of regions in England, Europe, North Africa and the northern portions of the U.S. At the same time, droughts and a burning sun fried everything to a crisp in the Russian, North American, Central American, and South American grain belts.

"Your air is composed of various electromagnetic pockets. Some of these pockets are large and some are small, some are dense and some are thin, some are positively charged, while others are negatively charged.

"The earth's land surface also carries and transmits electro-magnetic energy, and as with the pockets of air, some land areas are positively charged while others are negatively charged.

"The wind that you see moving the trees, or feel blowing across your skin, is mainly the result of the interplay of these positively- and negatively-charged areas in the air and on the land. Simply stated, some pockets of air and land are attracted to one another, while others are repulsed, and this attraction or repulsion is one of the driving forces behind what you experience as a spring breeze or a powerful hurricane.

"Trees and vegetation are other critical elements in moderating and controlling electromagnetic fields, and therefore the wind. Trees are themselves producers of magnetic fields, and their fields interact with the magnetically charged pockets of air and land in two main ways.

"One is that they keep air moving through sheer intelligence. Trees are intelligent beings capable of shifting the electromagnetic signature of the E-M fields they produce. Thus they are capable of attracting air pockets containing moisture when they are dry and want something to drink.

"The other is that through their magnetic fields they can hold air in a given area, even pull back at and redirect air moving across them, thus helping to reduce erratic and viciously high winds that would otherwise race across the land at 100 miles per hour, even 150 miles per hour.

"The absence of trees and vegetation is why winds at the arctic ends of the earth are as constant and dangerous as they are. It is why hurricanes over bare water easily reach 100 mph or more. And the clearing of your trees in huge numbers over the past 250 years will begin to show its effects in extremes of wind and changing temperature patterns since these are very dependent on the vegetation in any local region.

"As trees and a certain density level of vegetation are lost, their work as physical obstructions and deflectors of wind are also lost. In addition, not only does the electromagnetic signature of the earth's surface change as a result of a tree's presence or absence, the interaction between the earth, the remaining vegetation, and the air changes.

"Of course, the presence or absence of sun and shade, the raising and lowering of temperatures, the number and type of particles in air, and the amount of moisture in both air and soil all play a part in air movement as well, but more basic to these is the interplay of electromagnetic fields.

"The wind performs a number of important services and you will see problems in many areas as trees are cut and wind patterns change.

Among the tasks of wind are the balancing of the ozone layer; the mixing of various particles to achieve an even, breathable air; pollination of trees and plants; the bringer of cool breezes in summer and warming winds in winter; and an important moderating effect during a freeze or a heat wave.

"Wind is the force that trims dead branches from trees, and the carrier of many ionic particles needed by the soil. The wind helps in small ways to generate many small electrical and electromagnetic currents in the soil itself, and these currents provide some of the energy used by plants to take up nutrients and minerals from the soil.

"Without wind moving over your earth, soil would end up either disabled or statically neutral. If soil becomes static, plants do not grow and people do not thrive.

"As we have already mentioned a moment ago, the wind is also the holder and carrier of rain. For example, when the vegetation in an area begins to disappear and dry out, its electromagnetic signature changes. This change sets up a polarity in which the electromagnetic signature of *no rain* among the trees and vegetation begins to attract the electromagnetic signature of air holding *lots of rain*. In effect, the trees and vegetation in an area are the beings that call for rain. Without a cover of trees, there is a great weakening in the strength of the electromagnetic signature, thus a weakened call for rain. This is the beginning, or extending of a desert area.

"When a region stops calling for rain, the result is that extra rain is dumped in other areas. Flash floods as well as unusual, long-term, or repetitive flooding is the result, with heavy amounts of rain that simply cannot be absorbed.

"In addition, if vegetation is cut around the belly of earth, more rain and snow can be pushed into the upper and more northerly regions where a heavy and uneven build-up of snow and ice at the polar caps can help set the stage for a shifting of the entire planet. *If* the build-up of ice becomes heavy enough, and *if* the magnetic pole wanders too far from its accustomed orientation or in an unfortunate direction, or *if* human activities and experimentation with electromagnetic war technology cause uneven pulsations in the electromagnetic framework that holds the earth in place, the combination of excess weight and magnetic bobbling can cause the earth to roll or shift a bit.

"Of course, this would create much havoc and could even result in the earth settling in an entirely new position. A new position would create new Polar Regions in the places that end up occupying the traditional pole areas at the top and bottom of the planet. It would also cause the melting of a lot of ice that has been displaced. There would also be dramatic alterations in the relationship between land and water, changes in the delicate balances that keep volcanic action at a reasonable level, shifts in the climate of every region, and disruption of life at every level, plant, animal, and human.

"We do not want you to feel fear, but from the universal point of view, your entire way of life and its estrangement from the natural world is somewhere between artificial and senseless. You have organized life with an eye on the short term, and set yourselves up for a maximum of pain, difficulty, and disruption over the long term. The way your civilizations are arranged at present, if anything were to change, you could all be lost, and this is something we would like you to avoid."

They paused briefly and looked at me pointedly. I was so caught up in what they were saying that I had no response and wondered if I was expected to say something.

Stammering just a bit I said, "Um, what would you suggest we do to begin moving toward...?" I stopped, feeling slightly defensive. Were they suggesting that my own life was included among those that were inflexible and badly organized? Was I living for the short term in an unnatural, artificial way that was headed toward disaster? What were they suggesting I do? Or was the message broader and more general?

The little men waited for a moment and when they realized I was groping in the dark, they continued in a most helpful, partially probing tone. "At the very least you have to be aware that the building of large dams and nuclear power plants are two things that would seriously aggravate and complicate your attempts to cope with any changes or shifting of the earth... are you not?" they inquired gently.

I considered this for a moment, and my first thought was a defensive block, "I didn't build any dams or nuclear plants!" Then, unable to comprehend life without electricity, aloud I said, "But those dams and power plants bring water and electricity to many people."

"Yes, they do," they acknowledged. "But are you sure these are absolutely necessary, or just necessary to this particular way of life? And if you feel electricity is absolutely necessary, is the nuclear plant or the high dam the best way to get it?"

With that they nodded a brief good-by and disappeared.

I sat at the table for a long time. I did not know of many other practical ways to get electricity and simply could not imagine a way of life that did not have electricity. In fact, I could not imagine any other way of life at all. 📖

9 📖

RISE OF BUSINESS...

ON a damp, cold night in mid-February I was hovering over the stove, soaking up the heat rising from under the teapot, waiting for the water to boil, when I heard the light clearing of throats behind me. It was the little men.

"Good evening," they greeted me.

"Yes, good evening," I replied, although it did not feel like a good evening. The occupancy permit for the bar and restaurant had just been denied again, and I was facing the fact that I needed to find an interim way of making a living until we could get that permit and open for business. Should I go back to engineering... look for a management position somewhere... try to find something that would refine the skills needed for a bar and restaurant business? Go in a whole new direction? I was out of time to make decisions about which direction I would go during this temporary period, but over the evening, all I had accomplished was a frazzled mind, and a churning stomach.

Brightly the little men offered their usual invitation saying, "We have some information that will surely help to clarify things so you can make good decisions. Would you like to see some previews of coming events?"

In the same way that they did not vary their greeting or invitation, I did not alter my usual response much either. I just did not have the energy. I turned off the stove, sat down at the kitchen table without the tea, and closed my eyes.

They began by picking up the threads of disintegrating governments as if the two intervening weeks since I'd seen them had been only a moment.

"As each national government begins to slide into dysfunction, the population within that nation will begin to slide into confusion. We have already looked at several of the reasons for this, including government's interference in every detail of daily life, the need for new attitudes toward land ownership, and other issues. In this visit we would like you to look a bit deeper at the interactions of people, government and business, as well as the rise of business to power.

"By the end of this century it will be obvious to everyone that the government has inserted its influence into every corner of daily life with an ongoing flood of laws and regulations. Although many of the old laws will not be enforced, a continuous stream of new ones will be hastily added to cover some area of life or economics that seems out of the reach and control of the government.

"Existing laws will also be modified continuously to suit the thinking and attitudes of whoever is in power, and this constant re-writing of laws will accentuate competition rather than cooperation at a time when the need for cooperation is becoming essential. It will also create the percep-tion that your laws are arbitrary, merely man-made, and no longer imbued with honesty, justice, good will, or common sense. This will be a dangerous perception, not only because it sets a poor standard of morality, but be-cause people will be inclined to ignore such laws. Worse, it will strengthen the destructive idea that power is merely the ability to force others to do things your way.

"Adding to the realization that a large number of your laws no longer concern themselves with fairness and the correction of wrong-doing or injustice will be the recognition that far too many laws are designed to set financial traps. Those who are caught in these traps will discover that the punishments are designed to extract money from them, money which is then funneled into the collapsing institutions in hopes of keeping them afloat. Those who unwittingly break the rules, as well as those who knowingly resist going along with such laws, will find their own supply of money seriously interfered with, and thus their ability to meet their own needs will be compromised, along with their access to the games of power

"In the minds of the people, this confusion between a government designed to set standards of ethical justice, and one designed to create laws that serve as traps providing an excuse to collect money and stay afloat, will not be clear or even suspected for quite some time. Instead, people will have a vague feeling that they have been betrayed by their laws, yet be unable to pinpoint just how or where.

"In time, this feeling of betrayal will come to be focused in the attitude that if the name of the game is money, then governments and corporations will have to move over. Everyone will want in on the financial handouts flowing from government offices, corporations, and courtrooms, and government will find itself in a web of its own making as people discover they, too, can play financial games.

"The battles will be joined in a financial melee of suing over words, ideas, rights, ownership, insults, belief systems, and injuries—both real and imagined—all because of the instinctive attempt to regain some sense of power and inner authority. This will increase the pressure upon governments to write more rules concerning individual legal rights and money. From special interests to interest rates, from false papers to trumped up injuries, from nuisance lawsuits to outright grants, these financial games will multiply.

"This will increase pressures on the huge multi-national corporations who have gotten used to being the only ones able to manipulate the government for legal and financial favors. These corporations, like dinosaurs in a jousting match, will be suffering from sluggishness caused by swollen payrolls, a shrinking bottom line, severe competition for resources and global markets, and the growing use of expensive technology required to stay competitive.

"In response to increased financial pressures coming from every direction, they will begin shedding people by the thousands. Many people will be without jobs, and because they do not understand what is happening, they will suffer because of it."

Now I was looking at people working in offices, processing plants, and factories. I thought back on my work as a tool and process engineer for Chrysler, and for a moment I recalled the anger and the agony I had witnessed there.

I could still feel the smoldering resentment of the men and women called "factory rats," human beings treated as if they had no more feeling or common sense than the machines they ran all day. Outside the factory these people were ordinary mothers and fathers who raised children, paid steep house payments so they could live in the suburbs, and made expensive car payments so they could drive into the city to work each day. After work they went home, cooked, cleaned, shopped, and sometimes took care of aging parents. Yet inside the factory they were treated as stupid or ignorant, childish adults incapable of thinking for themselves.

I was caught in these reveries of my own past experience when the scenes before me began to change. The offices and factories began shrinking in both number and size. People were streaming out of buildings with unhappy looks and a general sense of depression. Some offices and factories began to look forlorn and unkempt; some closed.

At that moment, the little men picked up their narration.

"Those of you who are first to be let go will, in some ways, be the most fortunate. You will have the greatest amount of time to restructure your lives and reorient your time and energy to what really matters.

"Of course, there will be those who cannot see what is happening, nor will they ask themselves, 'Why did this happen to me and what is the gift hidden within this difficulty?' Foolishly, they will run frantically to another corporate position and struggle to get back into the same trap from which they were just released.

"Those who are the first to be released from their illusions of corporate security and power will have the hardest time because there will be so few clues evident in the general culture that give any idea of what is happening or of how extensive the changes will become.

"Some of these individuals will be angry and feel like they have been unfairly chosen to be shut out of the good life because they did not conform to some meaningless rule in the chains of command that once bound them. They will not understand that the unwillingness to conform to that small detail was the reason they were chosen to be given the gift of freedom in the first place.

"Those of us working at the unseen levels have looked diligently for humans who still show signs of thinking for themselves and would perhaps have a better than average chance of surviving the coming changes if they had a good start. This small sign of independence was what resulted in their selection to be given the first opportunity to restructure their lives.

"Those who are released further along in the changes may have less time to adapt; however, there will be many more signs and supports in the culture as to which direction to head in. Those who are able to look at twenty or thirty years and tens of thousands of other casualties from shrinking corporations will be able to recognize that something significant is happening.

"If you and your people are wise, you will read the signs of your time and begin to think of security as a small business of your own, run from your home. A 'cottage business' as Mr. Toffler calls it. You will learn to grow your own food, and to invest in and use the large communications network that will be spreading over the entire planet. You will begin to re-educate yourselves in terms of true necessities and the wisdom of a more self-sufficient life-style, which will teach you not only about true caring for the self, but also about the necessity of maintaining a relationship with the Earth. For if Earth decides to heal herself and to repair the scars and scabs upon her face, it is those who are self-sufficient who will survive!

"Now, returning to business, as the boards of the big corporations try to decentralize and shed people, there will be a corresponding effort in your national government to cut back as well. But while corporations cut through thick layers of over-organization with ease, politicians will be far less free. At the very least, they will fear the loss of the next election. The politicians' efforts to look like an impartial government yet act with the freedom of a corporation will greatly handicap the government in what will still be, at that time, their very hidden struggle for supremacy with the big corporations.

"Then the corporate mood will shift very slightly. With allegiance to nothing except power and the dollar, they will continue to cut people, but this will now be a deliberate attempt to create problems for government, distracting it, leaving it less able to pay attention to corporate maneuvers and goals. The corporate attitude will be that people out of work are a governmental problem. They create a drain on the financial resources of the government and perhaps a problem for those who work in social services, but they are not of concern to business.

"Since those in government will be unable to raise taxes like a business raises its prices, nations will have great difficulty with the huge sums of welfare and unemployment dollars suddenly needed, and with the amount of time, human energy, and paperwork required to track all these.

"Hamstrung in their efforts to deal with the changing situation, and under attack for their confusion of rules, paper trails, and people who fall through the cracks, government will attempt to cut expenses and simplify processes. This, they believe, will not only help them out of their difficulty, it will help their people. Thus the cutting will begin, and so will the arguments, sometimes about who or what to cut and how much, and always about what to do with the few dollars they imagine they have freed up.

"Once the government is thoroughly at cross-purposes with itself, and its attention—like Narcissus—is wrapped up in what image to maintain and how to sell this image to people, the corporations will begin their moves to consolidate power. Huge mergers will take place as more and more multi-nationals recognize that national governments are ineffective and beginning to crumble.

"Implicit in the corporate recognition 'that now is the time to make a move' will be a central paradox. On the one hand, corporations will understand that when the largest of the first world governments are gone, something will have to take the place of these structures... and only the most timid of corporations will refrain from fantasizing about their role in such a new and open power arrangement.

"On the other hand, they will see that if the national governments collapse, the corporations themselves may have more difficulty implementing and enforcing their own legal contracts without access to the legal, law-making puppetry called "national government" whose strings they have been pulling for quite some time.

"These huge companies will still want to protect their power to decide the terms of any agreement, to set the prices, payments, and interest rates they want, charge punitive fees, and have a number of legal avenues to pursue if the consumer does not comply or changes his or her mind about the terms of the payment or the product.

"Excited at the prospect of global power, yet wary of losing governments that can make laws in their favor, they will back off a bit, temporarily supporting governments by supporting the candidates of their choice, and conversely, making efforts to publicly crucify those they want to get rid of. Publicly, they will defer to government rulings, but in many cases they will do as they please in areas where they are fairly certain they can get away with it. In many ways, their power over the government will remain unnoticed for a long time.

"Meanwhile other dramas will escalate. The ordinary people in your hometowns and on city streets will slowly become aware of a myriad of factors that are deleterious to their life, their health, and their babies. Connecting their problems to both big government and big business, they will respond to this distressing awareness by increasing the already considerable pressure of the financial games another notch or two, suing for every kind of problem and difficulty, regardless of who is responsible.

"Hoping to put an end to this, and head off any future ability of the common man to define what he wants in life, to set the terms of his own agreements, have a say in his own payments and fees, or sue for damages suffered on ever-expanding grounds, corporations will push for new laws and legal protections for themselves. And all the while they will be increasing the rate of mergers.

"No longer able to ignore the possibility of global power, yet still unwilling to openly acknowledge it, many corporations will recognize that the company holding the most assets in the key markets of the future will be able to exercise the most control in what they will see as a global restructuring of power completely in their favor.

"With control over huge amounts of wealth, their own spies, teams of lawyers and legal analysts, communication networks and expanded customer service centers, armed security and even assassins, they will hope to step seamlessly into the position vacated by governments, dropping any corporate structures that belong to the old ways or do not make money, and picking up as much power as they can.

"As mergers get bigger and pink slips proliferate, corporations will go to great effort to disguise this plan and keep it far from public consciousness. They will make careful attempts to bridge the growing gap between national governments and the multinationals by keeping the markets operating as smoothly as possible from Wall Street to the local strip mall.

"These goals will be helped both by manipulation of Wall Street so that serious difficulties can be short-circuited, and in the discovery by many common people that they can make money even while they are out of work simply by having a little bit of money work for them in the stock markets. Thus, as the markets balloon, few will be thinking about what is going on under the surface.

"To help bridge their reach for power, some corporations will begin offering services formerly offered only by government. Some will create entire social and cultural communities among their workers, offering everything from banking and loans, healthcare and ongoing education, childcare and temporary welfare, to bowling leagues, counseling, book clubs, and travel.

"Some will try to develop the family concept, others will develop the team concept, and still others will rely on the old favorites—various versions of competition and conquest, from friendly to cutthroat. Regardless of how it looks on the outside, all will be looking for powerful partners who have not only the size but the boldness to see the world on their own terms.

"For those who are paying attention, it will be obvious that businesses are indeed, slowly and quietly placing themselves in carefully selected roles, especially where they believe there is long-term power to be gained as well as a profit to be made. In short, the large multinational corporations will begin to look and operate more and more like small national governments.

"As the big nations stop, start, and continue to crumble, people will begin communicating with one another in unprecedented ways via the large global network. Big corporations will watch these developments and be divided as to whether or not they should support, oppose, or ignore these newly evolving forms of communication and organization. In the end, most will opt to follow the dollar and in doing so, will help create the structures of communication that will eventually become the seeds of their own retirement from power.

"As for the general population, after a time they will begin to split into many antagonistic groups. This will be a time of many refugees and homeless, immigrants and ethnic tribes. The inherent weaknesses of widespread poor health in first world countries will also begin to make itself felt. Complicating this will be the extremes of weather that we mentioned in an earlier visit, and growing shortages of real food.

"The fraying and degeneration of that formerly solid core referred to as the middle class, will begin to be evident. Many people who are too embittered to carry on emotionally, too fatigued to carry on physically, too cynical to carry on mentally, and having long ago lost much of their spirit of national pride, will simply pull away from government and corporations, putting their time and energy where they believe it will help them to survive. When they do, they will move in a surprisingly measured way toward an entirely new way of life that will bring them into conflict with both the remaining institutional structures and the giant corporations."

I interrupted the little men here to ask, "What new way of life? Could you show me more about the cottage industries that Toffler talked about where everyone… or maybe not *everyone*, but lots of people work at home?"

"Well, yes, we will discuss new ways of living in another visit, but for now we would like to finish dealing with the demise of national governments and the fact that as the mask of government falls to the side you will come face-to-face with big business and some very difficult decisions."

"Okay," I said, somewhat reluctantly, and the little men continued.

"Even after people begin to see the power struggle that is really going on between governments and big corporations, there will still be many people who continue working for these corporations. These employees will have watched much of the uproar, the takeovers, the cut backs, and the shrinking payrolls, and many of them will be grateful for having been spared the disruption and discomfort of being let go from their jobs.

"They, along with those who were put out of one corporation only to wiggle back into another, will feel quite fortunate and will unconsciously resolve to support whatever their corporation supports, simply because they will be grateful for having been saved from the difficulties of joblessness and the challenges of change. Thus, employees working for corporations that still find the legal powers of a national government to be useful, will support both their corporation and their government. They will think they are being loyal and patriotic.

"In a second group of corporate employees there will be the opposite orientation. This group will find themselves working for corporations that want national governments out of the way. Unconsciously they will adopt the attitude that they could do their job so much better and easier if they did not have to waste so much time dealing with governmental obstacles and paperwork.

"Meanwhile, a third group will also be forming which will consist mostly of those outside of the large corporations altogether. This group will have little or no use for either corporations or national governments, and thus you will find your populations polarized into several very different camps with the potential for serious strife.

"The real issue, however, is not whether governments should rise or fall, it is whether the individual has created the necessary supports for staying alive in the face of governmental collapse *and* extremes of weather *and* shortages of food *and* faltering health *and* a roll or shift of the Earth.

"Many will ignore the fact that they are resisting the changes in perception, decision-making, and self-direction that are required in a mature and evolving human. Later, their avoidance of their own development may well backfire when they discover they cannot always buy what they need, or that they have lost the skills necessary to survive in a changing world. Yet the biggest difficulty for some individuals may well be in their disappointment with themselves when they recognize their part in a corporation that may have been slowly destroying the earth, her resources, and her people.

"And this very issue—the deepening destruction of Earth, her people, and her resources—may well end up becoming the flaw in the corporate soup. As governments flounder and corporate markets are awash in waves of change, there may be little interest in reviving them in their past forms. People will recognize what they need to know and do to survive well, to have joy and health, and they will begin asking with some seriousness how to end the damage that is and has been occurring in themselves and in the natural world.

"Reinforcing this attitude of the people, the global network will release a great deal of information about pollution, poisoning, poor food, and destructive research or development projects, facts that were formerly ignored, denied, or suppressed.

"Paradoxically, as governmental problems escalate, and a variety of crises follow—especially those of an ecological nature—one group of citizens after another will demand justice, hoping to get as much of their money back from the government as possible. When they cannot get either the justice or the money from the faltering court system, they will demand retribution directly from the companies either supporting or producing the harmful goods. When they cannot get it from these companies, they will create havoc with their anger.

"After a long period of co-existing uncomfortably yet with little visible friction, the three major groups—those still inside corporations that do support government, those still inside corporations that do not support government, and those outside corporations who have no use for either government or corporations—will break into openly antagonistic camps.

"Those who are outside corporations will begin to look at those who are still working inside them as a form of enemy. They will see a whole new power structure taking shape with the same bad habits and destructive values as the struggling governments. They will see huge numbers of have-nots, with a handful of elite at the very peak who have everything and believe they can control others.

"They will also see that, just like former governments, the big multinational corporations are still using the resources of earth recklessly, creating useless things because they think it will remind people of the good old days of mass consuming when there was a mass belief that Uncle was taking care of them and all their problems.

"At first a few individuals, then increasing numbers of ordinary people will grow to bitterly resent the creation of tremendous wastes and poisons that cannot be easily undone, poisons created because of a greed for profit, control, and power. They will see a perpetuation of uncaring destruction in spite of corporate efforts to create extensive facades meant to assure otherwise.

"Over time, those who are still part of a functioning corporation will become divided in their loyalties. Some will see what the corporation is doing as good, as a needed service, and won't believe the product they produce can be produced any other way. They will fight to keep things operating and keep the product moving.

"Some will see the product itself as trivial and unnecessary, and they will fight to stop the production of such useless items and take up production of something more meaningful.

"Some will see what the corporation is producing as useful, but will see the corporate structure as bad. They will fight to keep the product but change the structure.

"Some will begin to see the corporation *and* its product as bad, and as something unnecessary in the new world. They will become inside saboteurs and fight to eradicate both product and company.

"Some will see the corporation's production processes as destructive and feel guilty about what they must do to produce their product. They will fight with themselves in order to hang on to a sense of security.

"Others will feel that what the corporation is doing *is* polluting, but production could be improved and made to conform to the laws of nature and the general population's support of these laws. They will fight for inner change and for an investment in new research or technology.

"Others will feel that all corporations are breeding grounds for the development of miniature kingdoms based on power and control of others. They will fight for dispersion of ownership and yet still cling to their own source of power—their paychecks.

"Still others will live in fear of the corporate power structure and do what they are told in the same way that they did what the political governments told them to do. They will fight those who are fighting for change because they are afraid to be without the illusion of authority above themselves.

"Others will feel that the corporation has a successful business going and this is reason enough to allow it to continue, after all, it keeps a large number of people busy and occupied and thus out of trouble. They will fight because they believe in an ethic of loyalty to success and for recognition of whatever good they feel the corporation is doing whether intentional or unintentional.

"Others will believe that no structures of the old order should be allowed to continue. They will fight to bring down the old and to erase the damage and pain of the immediate past while creating something new.

"Some will see that the past is quickly disappearing and feel a deep sense of nostalgia at its passing. They will fight change out of a sense of romanticism.

"And some will see that change is inevitable. They will fight to accomplish the change as quickly as possible and get it over with so some new kind of normal can be established.

"On one side of the struggle, people will say that business as a power structure for the new times is an attractive, reasonable idea because it gives people a structural base around which to organize daily thinking, and has none of the dictatorial sheen of politics or the potential dogma of religion. They will say it makes sense because life makes it necessary to buy or barter for certain things and there are too many things you simply cannot make for yourself because you lack time, energy, money, resources, or the specialized knowledge.

"On the other side will be those with a new vision, who will see that the multinational corporate system has every potential of becoming even more destructive and power-hungry than the national governments were. These people will insist that all businesses destroying either soil, water, or air be halted immediately, and they will make it clear that they are in no mood to tolerate being dictated to or controlled by any of the old structures, no matter how reformed they may try to look.

"Thus, fighting will break out. During this period of fighting, both employees and products from targeted industries will suffer the gamut from outright attack, to active sabotage, to being absolutely ignored in the marketplace. In this way, people with a new vision will force the large corporations to deal with them in the same way they once forced national governments to respond to them.

"Corporations, who are used to buying men's minds and time in order to get their way, and who still believe the old saying that 'everyone has their price,' will resort to buying influence and power from thugs and anyone else riding the opportunity bandwagon. There will be serious attempts to frighten and attack those who will not accept corporate power.

"It is at this point that you must be most cautious or you will degenerate into the World War III conditions we showed you earlier in which there is tremendous fighting, man against neighbor, at every level of life—physical, mental, emotional, and spiritual.

"For those who have been waiting, this is the long predicted 'War Between Good and Evil.' On one side will be those businesses and people who are working in harmony with the earth and nature. They will consider themselves and their ways to be Good. On the other side will be those corporations and people who are still destroying earth and nature with their technology and chemicals. They will be considered Evil. The struggle against the big corporations and their destruction of earth has the potential to trigger your 'battle of Armageddon,' and may be the last chance to return to a healthy, balanced life for yourselves and the planet.

"If you do not remain aware, you will find yourselves caught in the clutches of fighting that is passionate but has no focus, and that displays such vicious yet generalized conflict that you will not be able to see what is happening to you. To complicate matters, the unfocused, generalized nature of this war will exactly reflect the unfocused, degenerated nature of the human being who has no inner vision or strength to sustain him through difficult times, and has lost all sense of meaning, therefore has no spirit.

"For the term 'spiritual' has little to do with your ideas of religions, Gods, or churches, and much to do with the processes of individual human development. The term "spiritual" refers to the meaning you give to your life. An individual without a vision of how his life could be has no goal, no spirit, and therefore no meaning in his life. No amount of church-going and prayer can bring a true sense of spirituality and meaning into the life of someone who has forgotten why they were born or what they originally intended to create with their life.

"At present, people all over your world have created such a tangle of artificial rules and routines that life has little meaning any more. A man or woman who carries out his or her work with a spirit of cooperation, creativity, and peacefulness has powerful, positive effects on surrounding family, friends, co-workers, and community. An individual whose life is filled with a spirit of anger or martyrdom or languor has an entirely different effect.

"Spirituality is simply 'meaning.' It is having a vision of your purpose and your life's work, and a population without it will disintegrate. Meaning and vision bring great strength and focus, and a sense of direction in creating, which brings us to the reason we are showing you these pictures of what is to come.

"If you know that the world must change as human beings develop, and you can see the kind of world you are moving toward, then you need not destroy one another in the process. You need only for each to confront the self, privately, wrapped in the security of knowing that you have some time to make the changes.

"This self-confrontation will pose challenges of a far broader and deeper nature than you have faced so far, for while you once thought you owed allegiance to a flag, you will now discover you believe you owe your life to the money that comes in on a regular basis. You will discover that you are in the habit of believing that any joy you experience is the result of the things you own or the amusements you can buy.

"Nearly everyone on the planet believes they must have money in order to stay alive. But money cannot be eaten, burned for warmth, or worn on the feet for comfort and protection. Thus, when money is not available, more than a few will think that life is over. Others who have no idea how to grow food or build the things they need, will think the only way to get what they need is to take it away from someone else.

"And this is where a most dangerous moment will be reached. At this point, you will have to face the fact that you must do away with money as you know it. This money is the beast of your ancient pro-phecies. It has long been told that the beast would be identified by the numbers '666'. The account signature of the biggest financial computer in the world is #666 and is located in the north of Europe.

"You, yourselves, have created this beast, step by greedy step, and thus, confronting it will look and feel as if you are tearing apart all that you have put together in the past five hundred years. This is not true, for confronting it will open the doors to a whole new world, however, as long as you believe money will save you, you will be lost. As long as you do not know how to survive on your own, you will continue to be subject to the power of remaining governments and corporations, and in danger of death in the face of natural earth changes.

"Facing the problems created by money, as well as the ongoing poisoning of yourselves and the earth, will bring you to see that the power of the large corporations is based on the economic threat they hold over people. If you believe you must have money to buy the right to live on a piece of land, buy the wood to build a house on that land, buy bottles of water because what is in the river is no longer fit to drink, or buy the food and clothing that you no longer know how to get for yourself, you will be subject to the power of the corporations.

"Once you have remembered how to feed, clothe, and shelter yourself, you will begin to look at corporations with new eyes. You will wonder why you ever thought you needed to have a big corporate job with lots of money in order to have the good life. It will dawn on you that people working together can accomplish the same thing freely.

"You will more easily see that corporate profits are often based on destruction of publicly held resources. These resources were meant to fill the true human needs for water, wood, fertile soil, clean air, and nourishing foods—not artificial needs like trinkets and other items that make you happy for a moment then go to the landfill or local dump. You will realize that corporations have long been in the position of being free to draw up legal documents or, if necessary, extra-legal elements, to back up their self-granted permission to continue destruction of resources.

"A great deal of corporate activity is based on deception and the control of people's Everyday, and you have been willing partners in this endeavor, not only with those corporations who produce bombs and guns, but all who produce destructive effects to your earth, water, and air, your relationships, or the human body/mind system itself.

"Slowly you will begin to see that money, as you have created it in modern times, is no longer a balancing force in daily life. Instead it is an unbalancing force, a weapon of division, attack, and control.

"The illusion is that you must have money so you can buy a piece of ground to sit or stand on. The truth is that the land is yours for free. You, yourselves, have set up and agreed to the mistaken idea that you must pay for something that is really a universal gift to all of you. You think you must have money to buy water and food when water comes freely from the sky or out of the earth, and food lives, walks, and grows everywhere that you have not insisted on turning over the earth or putting down concrete.

"As these issues arise, you will find yourselves asking difficult questions about money, power, meaning, about the earth as a home, or life and death and health and what it takes to maintain a body. The corporation as a suitable structure around which to organize life, and the subtle concepts of ownership implied by the corporation will be deeply examined.

"Is it really possible for you to own anything? Why is one of you more suited, more monied, more special, or more entitled to this land, that car, a color television, a swimming pool, or a luxury life than anyone else?

These questions are not meant to imply that ownership is evil or that having luxuries is a sinful waste and those who have them should feel guilty. Rather, these questions are to be taken seriously and answered only after exploring them thoroughly, thoughtfully, and with one eye on the number of people living on your planet.

"If common sense is applied and the problems of survival are approached with wisdom, money as you currently know and use it will disappear. This will occur partly because the money you now crave has become the basis of a particularly destructive form of judgment. The constant judgment and re-judgment that must occur as each new material thrill calls you to pursue it causes you to abandon your deepest values, often shifting them into confusion, and generating very poor results in terms of personal satisfaction.

"The truly deep and difficult questions that you must learn to ask and answer could be stated as 'Do you need money to buy what you already own? Is it best for power to be concentrated in the hands of a few who try to make decisions that run the lives of all? Can you develop yourselves to the point that each individual becomes personally self-responsible? How can a woman or a man learn to access the full potential of the creative powers within the self unless he or she enjoys responsibility for the course of his or her life? In what ways has the freedom, power, and decision-making of each individual been corralled into narrow ruts and then eroded? And exactly what are the potentials of the fully evolved human?'

"Once you begin attempting thoughtful answers for these questions you can begin to develop an entirely new foundation of values and ethics which can be used to make wise decisions and steer a prudent course of action. If you can nurture these questions within yourselves and among one another, there will be a move toward true personal freedom, common sense, and global cooperation. Many corporations and institutions that currently operate only for the money will slowly collapse and disappear in the crucible of change. Some businesses will survive in new forms, especially those in communications, education, and media. Others will be revived later and run by various families who found the original work useful or a good means of personal self-expression, and who will have put time and energy into eliminating or counteracting all destructive side effects to nature.

"Even though some of the large corporations may have disintegrated, the work or goals of that corporation may be picked up later and carried forward on a smaller, cleaner scale by former employees who form a family business and are able to attract the right mix of skills. Attracting these skills will come down to the ability of the family business to feed, secure, educate, and nurture the personal growth of all of its members.

"As you begin to move away from money, many companies, especially those who are providing basic services such as electricity and communications, will be run in an entirely different manner. For example, utility workers at a local plant may temporarily take turns keeping things repaired and running—partly because they want the electricity for their own home, partly because this is the thing they know how to do, partly because they enjoy using their skills, and partly because it is a service that helps others in their region. This attitude of just doing what makes sense or is necessary, regardless of money, will continue to develop throughout the transitions ahead. As you slowly evolve into a whole new way of living, you will discover the incredible sense of satisfaction that is meant to come from a useful, creative daily life.

"Even more importantly, you will begin to implement whole new ways of providing yourselves with energy and the big plants will be disassembled for other uses or will fall into ruin. This will also be true of other industries that operate with messy side effects.

"Gradually, you will all discover that you can have many of the things that you consider essential for comfortable living in a much more relaxed, reasonable way, without destroying your environment, needing money to get it, or expecting money in return for your work.

"We do not wish to over-simplify the challenges that will come with this transition, but we believe you will discover that in order to carry on with basics, it all comes down first to communication, second to the sharing of creativity, and third to coordination, and you are already doing these things in your Everyday. This is what corporations are really teaching you to do.

"You will discover that you know what must be done, that you can arrange it, coordinate smoothly with others, and accomplish results simply because you decided to, not because you were told to or because you thought you had to do it for money. Once the limitations imposed by finances are removed, you will find many more things are possible simply because money is no longer a barrier. You will be on your way to re-discovering true freedom.

"In the end, after a brief period of ascendancy during which the large corporations will fill in as the umbrella of authority, all will be transformed into the newer forms of human organization that come to be known as family business. These forms of organization will be based on personal responsibility as the foundation of self-governance. These families will be groups of people who live and play on, work from, feed themselves from, and manage the care of, a common piece of land.

"Just as the stories of the Round Table once painted a new and seemingly impossible picture of life based on consensus and agreement rather than settling things through brute force, the remaining people of earth's population will be struggling to get their minds around the seemingly impossible picture of life lived freely, without national governments, without what you refer to as your rat race, the need for money, the need to buy land, and all the other needs that lead to poverty of both the spirit and the illusion you call the pocketbook.

"In fact, of all the concepts that have bankrupted your spirit of creativity and a balanced life, the most destructive has been the idea that you can, or must, buy pieces of the earth. This makes as much sense as charging one another for the right to physical existence and basing the amount due on the total number of square inches of flesh.

"Before closing we would like to emphasize that we are not suggesting you go backwards to something you might call primitive living. Quite the contrary! We are pushing you to go *forward* to a life that neatly integrates the best of the old with the best of the new. We hope to encourage you to use common sense about land, about water and air, about food, plants, and animals. These things can be nicely integrated with the information technologies you are evolving toward.

"With real freedom, and time to re-create your lives, there need be no limits to your developmental potential. Mind you, we are referring here to *personal* development as creative beings, not to the development of machines or an artificial standard of living. For machines, although necessary to teach you what you are capable of, can be only *very* temporary supports. All of your machines are crude representations of your own human capabilities. The machine is just an externalized example. This is true whether the machines are designed for transportation, transformation, assembly and processing, communication, remote viewing or hearing, healing, creating, or some other purpose."

With that, the pictures and the little men faded away. 📖

10 📖
PERSONAL SHIFTS...

WHEN the little men had gone I sat at the table quietly and thought about the things I'd just seen. In the past I had been able to maintain a fair amount of naivete. In spite of being thirty-three years old and three-fourths of the way through college, in spite of four children and having been through a divorce, I was still seriously immature.

Trying to assimilate the events I had just seen left me feeling the way I'd felt at age twelve upon being informed that there was such a thing as menstruation. My reaction to the details of what to expect, the fact that all girls menstruated sooner or later, and the advice that I should prepare myself was, "What!? How could this be taking place all around me and I never knew it? Maybe it won't happen to me."

Now picking aimlessly through the future events I had just seen, I tried to assemble a coherent picture. Among the things I'd seen with the little men, jobs had disappeared... but that was good for those who'd been let go... offices and factories had bullets and bombs in them... governments were competing with businesses... no, government had *become* a business... and they were selling blessings... no, not blessings... they were selling rights... or was it regulations... everything else other than regulations was in short supply... people were tired and really hungry... and it was the government's fault... no, wait, it was the corporations who were at fault... something about wrecking the earth... people within corporations were fighting each other as well as people on the outside... money was a bitch... no, it was a beast... *the* Beast... and nothing had any meaning any more...

Confused and tired, I gave up trying to sort it out. With just about the same amount of rationality and reason I'd had when I was twelve, I once again told myself, "Maybe it won't happen."

While I was with them, the information presented by the little men in brown robes was as clear, sensible, and predictable as my next breath. I could see exactly how each situation materialized, the lessons implicit in the situation, the gifts and benefits of dealing well with each challenge, the places we were most likely to trip up, and the shortcomings of ourselves in so doing.

Viewing their pictures, it was clear that the world was coming face to face with what it/we had created. Th e need to see where we were at and not assume the nature of the future was obviously important. While I was with 'the Robes,' as I often thought of them, deliberately creating a whole new world seemed like a practical, feasible task and I could feel confident about our ability as a people to get ourselves together and take on such a task.

However, once the pictures faded and the little men were gone, I always slid unwillingly into uncertainty and doubt. Why were these little men visiting me? What purpose could there be in showing me the future? Why had they picked someone who had never been interested in national or international affairs anyway? What was I supposed to do with the information?

I wanted to believe that both the little men and their pictures were real, and what they were showing me was not a waste of time and mind, but somehow, a clear and logical assessment of them and their information was beyond my grasp. At that time, I could not make the connection between what I was trying to do with my life and what they were saying about the future. In addition, I had never read nor heard anyone mention anything about little monks in brown robes visiting or appearing to them. There were stories of angels and the Virgin Mary here and there, but no accounts of little men arriving to enlighten hapless humans.

The result was that I really did not deal well with the information they were spoonfeeding me. Their pictures hung in the back corners of my mind like a dress received for Christmas that was never worn because it didn't quite fit. I had no mental structures for dealing with such perceptions.

Nevertheless, in subtle ways this new perspective of the world and the knowledge of coming events began to affect me. Without really recognizing it, I had already swallowed the little men's advice that it would be better to have a business of my own. However, it was going to be a long time before I reconciled myself to the kind of business that I was suited to. I went to bed that night avoiding everything, including the denial of the occupancy permit for the bar and restaurant, the need to make a living, and the information from the little men.

📖

Spring was approaching and with it several things became clear. One was that I was never going back to engineering. Another was that the bar and restaurant might never open. I needed to do something to make a living. With a shifting combination of skepticism and hope I placed two small ads in the local newspaper. One announced my skills and availability as a massage therapist. The other was an offer to teach a four-week class in intuition. I hoped something would happen with at least one of these offerings and perhaps I could make a few dollars. To my surprise, several people called to make appointments for massage, and seven students enrolled in the intuition class. Thus I taught for the first time in my life, never suspecting that I had taken the first real steps toward having a business of my own.

After teaching only one class I knew I hadn't done just an okay job, I had been an excellent teacher. I had taken to teaching like a bee takes to making honey. By the time we reached the last night of class, the tiny effort had become a spectacular success and all the students wanted me to teach a second set of classes, something I had neither expected nor really thought through.

As I played with the possibilities of teaching intuition, I was belatedly doubtful about pursuing such a weird path. What would I tell people when they asked what I did for a living? And what would they say if I told them? Maybe I could just ambiguously say I was a teacher. No, they would still want to know whether it was English or math or science, and I couldn't lie. Maybe I should forget this idea of teaching. My heart didn't want to forget it though, and I ended up arguing with myself. I wanted to do at least a little more teaching; no, a lot more teaching. It was fun, I liked it, and in addition to bringing in some much-needed money, it gave me a chance to talk with people who thought intuition and psychic experiences were normal, or at least interesting.

I was also more and more attracted to the idea of working at home so that I could be there with my children, and have time to make decent meals. I did not want to punch a time clock, suffer through rush hour traffic, get up at the same time every morning to the demands of an alarm clock, brush my teeth, flush the toilet, and go to bed at the same time as everyone else every night in a stream of rutted days.

While all this was going on I continued to re-examine the pictures the little men had shown me. The more I thought about what they had shared with me, the more I felt that the information needed to be shared with others.

I set about writing a newsletter that would both pass along their information and offer some hints about growing food, using free-and-available herbs for healing, and coping with change, especially the coming break up of the big nations. Seated at my typewriter, I stared at the paper, unable to think of any way to present the fact of the little men's appearances in a way that was even slightly plausible. For days I wrote and re-wrote, starting over again and again.

In the end I was stuck. There was just no way to present the fact of the little men's visits without sounding like a crackpot. As for hints on food and herbs, I had not grown a garden for over ten years, and my actual experience with herbs amounted to chamomile tea, some peppermint, and parsley. The rest was a bit of book knowledge; nothing that involved hands-on experience. I also realized I had nothing of value to offer when it came to coping with change since I was barely coping with the changes in my own life.

Then there were the problems of newsletter design, production, and mailing. After more than a week of frustration and effort, I had a one-page, poorly typed, partly hand-written, and very badly designed piece of paper that could only be described as pathetic. I looked at it thinking, "Even if I knew where to mail this, who would bother to read such a tacky looking thing? And who would really believe that all this stuff might happen?" That was the end of the newsletter.

The awareness of food shortages that I had glimpsed as the nations fell apart, and the need for self-sufficiency that the little men had repeatedly brought up, were also working their way into my consciousness from the back of the closet into which I had stuffed them. All of the newsletter-oriented thinking I had done to review what I knew about gardens and growing food sparked my next direction.

I decided to grow a small garden as insurance against the future. Carefully I measured the length of the house, which faced west and the afternoon sun. It was around twenty-nine feet without the garage. If I used the entire length of the house, and then came out eight feet from the foundation, I could have a garden that was over two hundred square feet. If things were trained to grow *up* rather than *out*, I could get a lot more food out of a very small space.

Still without a reliable income, I calculated the cost of seeds, trellis, and string like a miser. With a shovel I began turning the sod, a backbreaking job that seemed to take forever. Letting the ground sit for a few days so the sod would dry out, I planned the layout, moving imaginary plants again and again, trying to find room for everything I wanted to grow.

The next weekend a dozen fence posts went in. These would provide supports for overhead crossbars up to which the string trellising would run. A few days later on a warm sunny afternoon I planted the seeds. It was not quite April and really much too early, but I couldn't wait. When the tiny shoots began coming up, I felt a humble pleasure that was beyond words.

On and off I worked in the tiny garden, now and then gave another massage, and in between thought how nice it would be to teach some more. Gradually I admitted that I needed to teach, at least once in a while. My pocketbook needed it, so did my soul, and it would give me something to do while I decided what to do with my life.

For weeks I seesawed back and forth about when and where to set up new classes that I could teach. Finally I called the local adult education office and proposed to teach a class titled "Psychic Development." To my surprise and excitement they accepted, asking for an outline of the topics I would be covering in the class. I began putting the outline together, not realizing that I was learning the ropes of a whole new way of life. 📕

11 📖
FORCES SHAPING 'FAMILY BUSINESS'...

I did not see the little men in brown robes again until May. One balmy morning I came inside after enjoying a cup of tea and toast on the dock, and there stood the whole group of them at the far end of the kitchen.

"Good morning," they replied in a crisp but friendly manner. "We have information that may help you get on with what you came here to do. Would you like to see some of the things to come?"

I wondered briefly what they meant, but didn't ask. Nodding my agreement to look at their pictures, I went into the living room to sit in a comfortable chair and closed my eyes.

Immediately I found myself in a neighborhood of families on the outskirts of a city. It was early in the morning, a man was delivering milk with a horse-drawn wagon, and I guessed it to be the early part of the 20th century. Before my eyes, the neighborhood began changing, moving into the twenties, thirties, the forties, fifties, and beyond. As the scenes moved ahead in time, the entire neighborhood and it's setting changed, as did the nature of the families in the neighborhood.

Even as late as the twenties, it was common for people to have at least one or two extra family members, sometimes more, living with mother, father, and children. By the 1950's, much of this extended family structure was gone and many single people were living alone.

By the second or third decade of the new century, however, the extended family was returning and some families had twenty or thirty people in them. These groupings continued to form and grow, and as the end of the 21st century approached, the average group had over two hundred. Some had more than two thousand people living and working in them! No matter what the size of the group, they referred to themselves as 'families' and after much of the upheaval in the world had passed, they remained as the basic structure of society. Then the little men began to speak.

"As the nations begin to break up and a number of the old tribes begin to re-constitute themselves with great vigor, family groupings will change in response to an assortment of forces which will come to bear on your population.

"We do not even need to take you into the future to show you the collapse of the nuclear family. Even today it is easy to see that this has already begun.

"Although the two-parent family is currently considered to be the ideal for raising a family in modern societies, the most common results of having been raised in a nuclear family setting are fatigue, frustration, and disturbing forms of mental and emotional competition.

"If you look around at your own family and friends, you will see that single-parent and even two-parent families are finding they cannot make their lives work smoothly without the help of grandparents, household help, lawn and garden help, child care help, cooking help, and many other kinds of help from counseling to financial assistance.

"At present you are so pressed for time that you are willing to pay money for the help that was once freely available in the family. The result of this willingness to pay for a number of services will be an increasing tendency to turn everything, even grandparenting, into small businesses. These will become the 'cottage businesses' mentioned in *The Third Wave* and will be one of the forces leading toward re-establishment of the large family groups.

"In the earliest stages of this move toward extended families, you will see that many adults are moving back home to live with parents. Whether they bring children with them or not, they will often feel that they have failed to do what you refer to as 'make it.' Initially many will be anxious to get back out on their own, and in the beginning, some of them will. Later, with the increasing instability of governments, the rise and fall of big corporations, the shortages of real food, and the burgeoning of chaos, they will choose to stay within the family because the arrangement will prove to be more secure.

"Under pressure to remain at home where there is less chance of being caught in random violence, they will begin pooling their energies in hopes of helping each other meet survival needs. Gradually they will combine skills and resources to establish small family businesses that allow for trading, and end up staying together simply because this arrangement works better.

"Slowly you will see that the old version of the extended family shattered because everyone was expected to go after a maximum of money and power. Those who did not were considered unsuccessful misfits. Few appreciated the small contributions of an aging Uncle Joe who cut the lawn, planted flowers, helped do the dishes at night, and served as occasional babysitter. Failure to recognize the pivotal role of these needed small services was like failing to put the chinking among the logs of a log cabin. The cabin would stand, but it did not offer nearly as much support, comfort, and protection from the stresses of weather and nature. In the same way, the absence of all the small services has resulted in an inability to make the basic structure of life function smoothly and allow the human enough time and creative energy for full self-expression, as well as further development of the human body/mind system.

"In the new families based on family business, this trend toward turning every aspect of life into a small service business will help to correct some of the problems that once existed in the old extended families. When you have discovered that you need a particular service because it adds to the quality of life, but you do not have the energy to do it yourself and must pay money for it, you will learn to value the work of all. Each contribution will be appreciated because it relieves the drain on your own energy, and leaves you better able to care for yourselves and your children.

"Some of these family groups will be formed mainly of blood-related members. Some will be formed out of neighborhoods where the lack of a blood relationship is replaced by an unusual cohesiveness in which the level of interaction and caring works just like a blood family. Some groups will come together around common interests, or because they create a good mix of complementary talents, and others will find they live together peaceably.

"Gradually you will learn to combine resources and services that complement one another and allow for fulfillment of needs, unhampered trade, and ongoing personal development of those within the family group.

"As you have already seen, some families will have as few as twenty individuals, some well over two thousand. Many of these family businesses will be connected to one another via the large global network and will keep each other abreast of what is going on in the various families or local regions. By stages, these family groups will grow into greater maturity. Those that do, will experience high levels of nurturing and support for personal growth and human evolution. This will lead to an exploration of identity and purpose in the world, and this will carry you toward the development of the capabilities we mentioned in our last visit.

"Do not expect that everything will work perfectly for all however. Some groups will come together in desperation and continue to struggle with the changes in the world around them. These will be slower in coming to think of themselves as a family. Those who never bothered to learn the basics of self-sufficiency may also have a difficult time until they can reorganize themselves and learn to produce what they need to survive as well as attract new members who can help fill in their gaps.

"Those who have been raised to think that every man is an island, that you must go out in the world to make your fortune, or that competition is the way of success, will have some difficulty coping with these changes for they require new and extensive forms of cooperation.

"Those still operating on the old habits of competition will descend into confusion and depression. Confusion is the result of being unable to access your inner knowing, and depression results from the inability to act on what you know. Those who cannot move forward will waste the rest of their lives fighting for ways they once believed in, unable to cope with the number and depth of the changes. They may refuse to expand their communication and technological skills, or take the steps necessary to band together and protect themselves. Worse, they may deny that change is happening at all, and become caught in either violence or an epidemic launched by a terrorist because they failed to keep abreast of what was really unfolding in the world.

"Some of the children and young people who were produced and conditioned by the generation believing in the 'get-a-good-education-so-you-can-get-a-good-job-because-it's-every-man-for-himself' approach will also be caught in the fires of change and unable to adapt or figure out where they fit in. When the times of disease, hunger and starvation set in, far too many children will be orphaned, or abandoned by adults who are practicing the 'every-man-for-himself' religion. These children will become the lost generation that you have previously seen and felt anxious about.

"Even before these times begin, people will begin keeping children home from school because they do not want to put them in situations where either their bodies or their minds are in danger. Those people who are cast out of their jobs will begin to work from home and teach their own children. This will give a further push to the exodus of children from the schools, especially as the violence and epidemics sweep here and there.

"This trend will continue to grow until the only children to be found in your public school systems will be the children of the poor, the destitute, the hopeless, and those who have lost or been abandoned by their family.

"In time you will come to see how the sad chain of events surrounding children was perpetuated. Once you left the land, your need for money forced you to leave the home each day. In order to leave the home for money, you needed to give up your children. So you sent your babies and children off to nursery centers and elementary schools where one or two harried women took on the job of raising them, also for money.

"In their early years when your children were being formed, when their attitudes were being set, and their intelligence was being programmed, instead of an expansive group of mature, loving family members from which to copy behaviors, learn to survive, and draw their self-image, children had access to only one or two adults, usually a single teacher who was often fatigued, overworked, and irritable.

"Instead of observing and participating in loving adult relationships and mature interactions, the impressionable young minds of your babies had access only to other young minds that were, themselves, still immature, self-centered, and in need of loving models. Since children 'learn how to be' by copying, all that they learned was how to be immature, self-centered, and needy. And since they were not involved in the business of everyday living, they neither contributed in any meaningful way to the family, nor learned the basics of what was involved in making a living.

"Then parents began to suffer severe mental and emotional stress in their attempts to make the necessary amount of money and still have time to shape and nurture, or constantly re-shape and reassure, their child.

Money-getting was the top priority and this was often based on competition, jealousy, and the wish to outdo others.

"Children were slotted much further down in the priorities, somewhere after money, bills, and a car to drive to work. Making matters worse for the children, their adult models of how to live and how to be were now modeling only how to live a life of severe mental and emotional stress with all the wrong goals!

"In mirror fashion, children began to reflect to their parents the same kinds of relationships they had perceived and been immersed in while growing up, one in which money-getting and possession of things was much more important than attending to what other family members needed.

"Through the course of such a childhood, the value of and connection to family was gradually lost, leaving each child searching for something that could not even be described verbally, that could only be felt deeply as something missing, a vague emptiness.

"Whole generations grew up empty, and the emptiness came to be romanticized as the search for love, the search for a 'soul mate.' Myth had it that this love, or perhaps the soul mate, would somehow complete you, bringing the sense of Self and wholeness that should have been created from birth onward in the self-reflection of the family.

"The search for love, for wholeness, then consumed the energy that would normally have been used to sustain creative, healthy lives focused on the development of full human potential.

"Children, no longer connected to the land, were also disconnected from the family and the parents, and thus all three major family groups—children, parents, and grandparents—found themselves isolated and drifting away from one another… children in their schools all day every day, parents away at jobs, and grandparents banished to their nursing homes. The goal of natural growth and ongoing development of the human being had been replaced by the concept of growth and development of an economy.

"The business structures and social institutions that flourished as a result of this separation from the land filled in the gaps of this meaningless way of life so aggressively, so hypnotically, that few questioned it. The stronger and more widespread these institutions became, the more people were drawn into the trap of working for money, consoling themselves with entertainment, and cursing themselves or their children when the children did not turn out to be thoughtful, gentle, or moral creatures.

"Thus you have arrived at your present situation, one in which overwhelming changes are about to happen in a relatively short time because you have thoughtlessly reproduced yourselves and then not nurtured your reproductions.

"Any time a group of people begins to reproduce selfish, inconsiderate, violent, weak, or diseased people, its days are numbered. Any group of people who send their children away, who do not make use of the wisdom of their old ones, and who continue to deny the dissatisfaction and fatigue that they, themselves, are experiencing will soon find their world no longer makes sense.

"When the world stops making sense, you will pass this sense-lessness on to your progeny, and thus the natural intelligence of children becomes dysfunctional. Those without access to natural intelligence will be handicapped in subtle but important ways for the rest of their lives simply because they do not have access to their intuitive functions. [2] These children eventually become adults who find themselves further tangled in efforts to make ends meet, while neither they nor the money are ever enough. *Their* children are even more dysfunctional, and all the while the old ones with their accumulated wisdom, die of uselessness. In the end, unable to function in ways that make sense for survival, the whole culture shatters and disintegrates."

As I watched these scenes of people struggling to get to work while coping with children and high levels of stress, I recalled an incident that had occurred when I was only about three years old. My mother and father, my baby sister, Pam, my Aunt Pat, and I lived in a big, white house on Main Street.

My mother worked afternoons at a small factory just outside the downtown area and this particular summer afternoon she had gotten ready to go to work as usual. I don't know if she said goodbye to me, but I don't recall her doing so. I don't know if she was running late and had to hurry, or if I had been taking a nap and woke up just in time to see her leaving or what. I just remember being overcome by an intense need to have her come back, to turn around and come back at least long enough to hug and kiss me, maybe even to stay with me because I needed her at that moment. I ran down the sidewalk, crying, screaming "Mama... Mama... Mama..."

---

[2] For a more complete discussion of 'natural intelligence' see *The Evolving Human*, pg. 191-196.

but she continued to hurry along. With the short legs of a three-year-old I couldn't catch her, and she didn't turn around once or even hesitate as if she heard me, so I continued running, crying, screaming for her, agonized that she was leaving again and wouldn't stop or even acknowledge hearing me. Perhaps she didn't hear me, I never really knew if she did or not. Finally my Aunt Pat caught up to me, picked me up and carried me back home, while I cried as if my heart was forever broken, asking myself again and again "Why didn't Mama hear me and turn around? Why wouldn't she stop?"

I didn't know what I had decided about myself in that moment but I didn't think it was good. Forever after, something ineffable was different. My spirit felt mute. And what was all the more agonizing was that I had done the same thing to my own daughter in exactly the same way. She, too, had been three years old and ran after me screaming, "Mama, don't leave me, please don't leave me... just one day stay home Mama," in an agonizing way as I walked down the sidewalk one morning, headed for the bus which would take me to work. I left, ignoring her great need and thinking, "One day? What good will it do to stay home one day when I have a whole lifetime of days to go to work yet. If I stay home today, she'll just want me to stay home tomorrow, and the day after that..." and I kept walking.

To this day I regretted that decision. What would I have felt or decided about myself if my mother had just turned around and come back to give me one little hug? Would it have allowed me to believe that what I needed was important, or more basic—that I had needs? And that "one day" that my daughter wanted, it was only one day. She wasn't asking for more days, just one. Who knows what a difference one day could have made for her?

Now I was weeping openly, aching at what had happened to me, at how I had done the same thing to my daughter. Oh God, what the little men were saying was terribly true. They interrupted at that point and suggested I go get something to wipe my eyes and blow my nose. It seemed they had touched something that went to the core of me and for a brief moment the floodgates were opened. I cried with all the agony of the three year old I had once been, and with all the sorrow of a mother who felt she had unwittingly done the same terrible thing to her own child. 📖

12 📖
THE MAIN HOUSE...

WHEN my tears were exhausted, I returned to the living room where the little men in brown robes were still waiting. With some effort I closed my eyes again, expecting them to resume their commentary immediately. Instead they projected something else my way, some kind of energy that was warm and soothing and made me feel greatly loved and appreciated. My eyes flew open when I realized they were doing something to make me feel different. For a minute I was going to ask them what in the world they were doing. But I changed my mind, closed my eyes quietly, and basked in their loving warmth.

When they finally began again, I didn't know if they felt bad that I had cried; perhaps they decided to change their approach, because now we were above the earth's surface and they were saying very little.

Hovering over the planet from the edge of the atmosphere, I could see for quite a distance and the most immediately noticeable feature was the absence of the huge cities with their long, straight city streets and row upon row of identical, closely set houses. Even the suburbs with their carefully curved streets and deliberately mismatched houses were gone. In their place were a combination of remaining ruins, reclaimed buildings, and a few sites with a whole new set of homes and buildings. Populating this amazing variety of sites were the large families, many with over two hundred people who lived and worked together on good-sized, carefully tended acres of land.

Then we were on the ground again, moving from family to family, looking at how they had reconstructed their homes and their lives during the dissolution of governments and the growth of the large global network.

Some families had built a collection of individual homes near one another. Others were in apartment buildings or condominium-style houses grouped together into a small, private neighborhood. Around this group of homes was open acreage, some of which was used to grow trees, some was under grain or bean cultivation, some was used for vegetable and flower gardens, and some was deliberately left wild.

In the majority of these neighborhood groupings there was a large building that seemed to be there for the support of everyone, and when I asked the little men for more information about it, they commented only briefly.

"What you are seeing here are some early examples of the family neighborhoods and the structures that will evolve to support the family business. The neighborhoods usually consist of a large 'main house' surrounded by a variety of smaller, more private houses inhabited by family members. If the family is large there may be a second main house, but either way it is often the place where the major work of the family business is carried on. In some cases, if the nature of the family's work requires it, there will be complex equipment and processes housed in two or three smaller buildings that are nearby.

"These combinations of family-plus-business structures will help to heal and stabilize life in many ways. Within each family the customs, rituals, and routines will vary tremendously depending on the original beliefs of the group members, but many will have similar characteristics."

Now we began going into some of the buildings, looking around. The main house of each family compound varied in size but was unmistakably larger than the private homes or group dwellings around it. On the outside, the main house design almost always included a large porch that wrapped all the way around it, with many of the rooms having direct access to the outside.

Inside there were workspaces used for the family business, several offices, and a common area used for relaxing, for informal get-togethers, or family meetings. There was usually a music room, a large central kitchen with dining area, a food processing area, and an area referred to as the healing center. Frequently connected to the healing center was a large exercise room, and in every single case, an impressive and well-equipped communications center. Every main house had a room used as a schoolroom, and all had a small entertainment theater, or even two. There were usually a few private rooms or apartments for those who ran the main building, and beyond this most had a variety of storage areas, a large laundry and clothing area, a repair shop for metals and plastics, a wood-working area, a maintenance area, and a technology shop.

The most striking feature of these main houses was the amount and kind of technology each was using, especially in the communications center. The equipment in these centers was sophisticated and consistently busy. Some of the technology looked familiar, and some was like nothing I had ever seen. In my own life, I was pleased to have a telephone and a manual typewriter! In the world of the future, every main house seemed to have a whole room, sometime two or three, filled with what appeared to be large and small TV screens, speakers, headphones, microphones, cameras, large machines with an array of blinking lights and buttons, an assortment of telephones and 2-, 3-, or 4-way radios, something that reminded me of a teletype, and quite a bit of other equipment that I did not recognize at the time. It reminded me of pictures I had seen in connection with NASA's space center during the space flights, and according to the little men, most of the equipment was used to communicate over the large global network.

There were always a number of spaces devoted to producing the family product and these spaces were large and well organized, For some this was simply a specialty food or herb and the kitchen was larger than usual or designed to handle this. For others, the family product was a piece of furniture, or technological equipment, sometimes cloth, or dishes, perhaps windows and doors. For some it was music, for others it was news, education, or programming that was broadcast over the large global network.

All of the families worked directly with the large global network, compiling, evaluating, adding to, or disseminating the information found there. Where the family business involved the making of unusual ceramics, plastics, cements, or chemicals, there was a separate building away from the main house. These families were larger than average and I was impressed with their technological expertise, the esthetic designs of their homes and work places, and the completeness of their attention to detail when it came to creating their product then using or transforming all by-products.

I was surprised at the look of most of the offices in various main houses and the casual atmosphere with which they were used. I had worked in numerous offices since graduating from high school and they were always cluttered with books and papers. Worse, they were invisibly stamped with the territorial aggressions of supervisors and managers. In contrast, the offices in the main house looked quite bare and were used by anyone who needed one for the day. Without money there seemed to be no bookkeeping or accounting, but complex inventories of supplies-on-hand were kept and updated regularly, trade records were carefully maintained, directories of other families that were communicated with frequently were kept in printed form, and personal records of education, health, and individual development were common. Other offices were used for settling misunderstandings, counseling sessions, private meditation, special educational tasks, or some aspect of trade required by the family business.

In the large central kitchen there was always food for those family members who did not have the time, the kitchen, or the inclination to prepare their own. Most of the foods were fresh from the gardens and consisted of a tremendous number of salads and vegetables. Breads were baked for everyone, sometimes using grains I did not recognize, and a variety of condiments that looked like jellies, jams, catsup, mustard, pickles, relishes, and sauces were made there.

A sumptuous variety of fruits and many vegetables were continuously harvested from the gardens and frozen or dried for use during both winters and hot seasons. Root crops of all sorts were grown and stored in great quantities. Herbs were also grown, dried, and stored in large quantities, and many families kept a few treasured animals such as cows, goats, sheep, or chickens for the milk, eggs, and meat. I had always been a big meat-eater and was surprised to see very little meat in the average diet. Neither could I find anything that resembled a box of Trix, Cheerios, or Rice-a-Roni. Qite a few foods were ea ten raw, most others were made from scratch and this included breads, butters, yogurts, and cheeses as well as juices, soups, pastas, and casseroles.

Near the central kitchen in each main house was a healing center. This group of rooms included a massage room, an exercise room, a music room, and several single-bed rooms, each with an attached bath containing a whirlpool tub, showers, or sitz tubs. Sometimes there was a sauna or hot tub as well. The exercise room was spacious and contained mats for floor work, a variety of free-weights, and sometimes physical therapy or body-building equipment.

The music room also had multiple uses. Individuals utilized it for music therapy, for giving impromptu concerts, or playing music by private individuals. It often held "old fashioned musical instruments" like pianos, trumpets, guitars, and such. Otherwise most musical instruments looked like a box with a typing keyboard, yet made a variety of sounds from violin and clarinet to harpsichord and xylophone. [3]

At least one of the rooms in the main house of the compound was a schoolroom and children would spend an hour or two in this room several times a week. Accompanied by an adult, I was astonished to see them sit back in a lounge-type chair, wearing what looked like headphones, sometimes a set of goggles over their eyes, or perhaps other headgear that looked like a helmet. It appeared they were watching something inside the goggles!

At other times they watched pictures on the large TV screen. Occasionally they talked on the telephone to someone whose picture appeared on the TV screen, or typed on a keyboard that looked like a cross between a typewriter and a keypuncher's unit.[4]

The rest of their education was experiential and hands-on in nature, and every child was involved in a variety of useful projects mentored by several adults who acted as part-time teachers.

Frequently located next to the schoolroom was the entertainment center which resembled a tiny theater having a dozen or so comfortable chairs that adults relaxed in to watch programs or listen to concerts coming from elsewhere. At times this room was used as an extra education area for adults, and in some smaller families the schoolroom, entertainment center, and music room were combined into one.

Within the main house there were always a few private apartments set aside for those who ran the kitchen, the healing center, and the communications center. Other individual rooms were given to visiting apprentices or guests, although at first there were precious few people traveling or visiting openly.

Elsewhere within the main house could be found a laundry area that resembled today's public Laundromats but with several washers and dryers that were dramatically smaller than the machines I was familiar with.

---

[3] These were obviously some version of the computerized digital sampling equipment now widely available.

[4] This room seems clearly to have been a highly sophisticated communications center with programming selected especially for each child.

There were many natural fibers and fabrics in use and this was quite evident in the sewing area, which was in almost constant use and frequently included small but automated weaving or knitting machines. Although the idea of doing one's own weaving and sewing struck me as old-fashioned in concept, it was clear that these weaving and knitting machines were highly advanced in their design and operation. Some of the families even had a small machine that you stood in front of which somehow took a picture of a body then created a set of basic patterns that were used to make an individual's clothing. The finished piece could be viewed on one of the TV screens and small details changed—a different collar, a higher or lower neckline, a particular kind of button, shorter or longer length—until it was exactly what you wanted. Another automated cutter then cut out the pieces and someone quickly sewed them together.

To keep all of this technology going there was always a maintenance and repair shop, sometimes two, that worked with everything from metal to plastic to wood, and a technology shop where some of the communications equipment was created, while some was repaired.

Besides the main house and the individual homes, there were a variety of storage buildings, and often a small animal building which also housed farm or garden equipment. The farm equipment appeared to be very small in scale and many of the pieces looked like toys compared to the large equipment I had grown up seeing!

Now I began to watch more closely what people did in the course of day-to-day living in one of the family business neighborhoods. Especially noticeable was the fact that everyone was involved in growing food, and within the larger families there were individuals or small groups who took additional responsibility for making special food items like unique sauces, jellies, pastas, or spice mixtures. A few people grew trees, herbs, or flowers for use by everyone, while others focused on gathering and preparation of special plants used in healing. A central kitchen with someone who loved to feed people often produced tasty snacks and meals, and the three-meals-a-day concept seemed completely absent. People ate whenever they were hungry.

I had the impression that disease and illness were rare. However, when some unusual or unknown health condition appeared, a regular procedure was followed. The ill person's finger was pricked and a few drops of blood were placed on a series of slides. These were then taken to the communications center and run under some kind of scanning machine with lights, all of which seemed to be connected to some kind of data source somewhere in the large global communications network. The blood was analyzed minutely for dozens of possible diagnoses, and then recommendations for correction or balancing were given. A variety of healing techniques were used from lights and sounds, to foods, diets, and herbs. If unique formulas or plants were needed, the names, addresses, and communication numbers of where they could be found were sent with the recommendations, along with directions on the best way to use or prepare the substances. Sometimes the directions were given in a brief movie format that appeared on the large TV screen via the same network.

In the midst of watching what people did from day to day I began to notice some of the individual houses that family members lived in when away from the main house. Homes and apartments were similar to today's homes, although all were clearly more energy efficient. Some had unusual domed or rounded shapes, with a tough fabric stretched over them, which was then sprayed with something that looked like stucco. There were no garages, but everyone had an outbuilding or two, a basement, and a small cellar where foods were stored.

The interiors of the individual homes were only slightly reminiscent of today's homes, and space was used in a different manner. Surprisingly, not every home had a kitchen. Those kitchens that did exist were larger and looked quite commercial. Usually they were part of a home that housed two or three families, a family often consisting of one to three people. The unique aspect of these kitchens was that most were oddly designed to be partly indoors and partly outdoors. There was usually a comfortable eating area designed around several tables and chairs, with one in the indoor area and one in the outdoor area. Cupboards were smaller and contained things I did not recognize, probably because of the absence of mass packaging, and it was obvious that diets and foods were much different.

Almost every individual home had a small, relatively soundproof relaxation room where meditation was practiced or music was used as part of the healing routine. Individual homes also had a full communications room that doubled as an office. Like the one in the main house, it was filled with television screens, radios, telephones, and other equipment as well as a desk or two, chairs and a table, and perhaps a storage cabinet for printed records, although there still seemed to be a shortage of paper around.

A number of private homes had exercise rooms similar to the exercise room in the main building. Gone was the large "family room," there was no sign of a living room in most homes, and there was a complete absence of the traditional dining room.

Bedrooms were slightly larger and most of them were more like suites with a small sitting room and spacious bathroom attached. I was quite surprised to see that bathrooms were *much* larger, more complex, and were frequently called "healing baths" or "the healing room."

Another thing that intrigued me was that, like the main house, almost every room in every house opened directly to the outdoors onto a large porch that encircled the house. Around most porches were small salad gardens. Even second floor bedrooms opened onto an outdoor deck, or at least a large landing-with-stairway that descended to the lower porch, allowing everyone to come and go privately, without going through the main part of the house which was usually the kitchen area if they had one, or something resembling a common lobby if there was no kitchen.

In the cold regions, a small section of the porch facing south was often glassed in and people used it to sit in the sunshine even in the winter. There were no roads as we currently knew them, and it appeared that the requirement set out by every urban and suburban building code that houses be built on a public road with a certain amount of frontage was no longer in effect. I intended to ask the little men what happened to the roads, but my curiosity was too intense to allow questions at the moment. I left to walk along one of the wide footpaths that connected dormitories and private homes to the main building, the gardens, and in some cases to the homes of favorite family members, so I made a mental note to inquire about roads later.

The little men had continued to escort me through these rooms of the future and finally they spoke up again, this time zeroing in on an unexpected theme.

"In the coming times you will have many chances to change your perspective, your priorities, your lifestyles, your goals, and your basic system of values, self-governance, and self-development. Although you will *all* change depending on which stage of the transition you are in, do not expect someone to suddenly appear and insist you make these changes. An unalterable law of survival is adaptation. It is best for you to recognize this and make change part of the flow of life rather than wait to be told what to do. Those who refuse to see and acknowledge that life on a daily basis is gradually forcing them to give first priority to good food, sustainable shelter, communication, and health will simply die and disappear.

"Those who see the changes that are required will come to divide their time between growing food, developing their potential and wisdom, and producing a product or service to be shared with others, with the priorities in that order.

"Over time you will all begin to ask several questions. 'If the goal of human experience is to develop each individual's power to express love, communicate, and become aware of their creative potential, and if it is necessary for both men and women to pursue their own development, then who will have time to give birth to children? Who will raise these children and nurture them until they learn how to continue their own self-development?' Slowly you will realize that to give birth to a child is a monumental decision and commitment, and one that might best be made for an entirely different set of reasons than you now tell yourself.

"We will come back to the subject of giving birth in our next visit, but for now we will point out that in the fully developed human there will be no need to regulate or make laws regarding birth, abortion, or the limiting of population, for fully developed human beings have no neurotic drives to reproduce in order to find the love that supplements the missing connection with the Self. Self-governance around this issue will be a matter of personal development.

"To try to pull together some of what we have shown you so far, imagine, if you can, a planet on which there are no giant cities and where daily life has become a combination of old and new life-styles. The huge, powerful institutions you once knew are gone and in their place is a large communications network that links people all over the earth. Most of the information that was once held in the large institutions is now held in this network and many of the functions once performed by these institutions are now planned and completed via this network.

"Through this network a small family producing a product west of what was once Lake Michigan may send their goods to another family in old Virginia, to a second family in the south of what was once Spain, maybe a third family along the east coast of Africa, and another southwest of where St. Louis once thrived.

"Imagine a way of life in which money as you once knew it is gone, there are no taxes, no schools as you once knew them, no factories, shopping centers, or office buildings, and you do not 'go to work' every day. You live in a *family* instead of a town, and your goal is to contribute to the survival, health and well-being of the family.

"The pace of most days is steady and relaxing compared to your present 'rat race' and your time is divided among tasks that take you into the garden where foods are grown all year, into the exercise center as part of your own health maintenance routine, and the communications center or perhaps the school room where you pursue learning and self-development on a continuous, life-long basis.

"If you are directly involved in producing an item in the family business, you might spend time working toward that end. On other occasions you might spend time meditating, or working in the healing center with a private mentor. This mentor will teach you to develop a particular healing skill or therapeutic technique.

"If you were a repair person, you might linger at home, going off to get tools and repair something only if someone called on your skills. If you were a child in the group you might spend some time helping your mother or father feed the animals. Later you might tag along with a favorite adult for a while, then go into the schoolroom to watch an educational film, and still later end up helping in the central kitchen.

"If you were a teen, you would see very little difference between your life and that of most of the adults except that you would spend time with one or two mentors developing your ability to plan and execute a useful work or research project.

"As part of the group you might attend family meetings, celebrate the birth of a child, prepare for the passing of a beloved old one, or enjoy an impromptu picnic on the porch. You would be committed to open, honest, and loving relationships, and to helping one another nurture the development and gifts of your human potential.

"Over the next fifty to one hundred years there may be times when you are tempted to look at the world and see only violence, destruction, and suffering. We would ask you to see correction instead. You will not be able to see these changes as corrections unless you are correcting your own life. The violence, the suffering, the destruction—all are results of your former way of life and the breakdown of the connections and com-munications *within* the human, *among* humans, and between humans and nature. This must be corrected or you will not survive."

The little men paused and we looked at each other for a silent moment. I wondered if they were waiting for me to ask a question or acknowledge the information in some way, but before I could come up with even a nod, they remarked in a very pointed way, "And we most definitely want you to survive. That is why we are showing you these pictures of the future. Again, if you do not have some concept of a better future, a clear picture of what you are moving toward, then you may not have the strength to carry on when the troubles are at their worst." With that, they were gone. 📖

13 📖

SEX, BIRTH, AND HUMAN DEVELOPMENT...

THE small vegetable garden planted back in early spring was growing beautifully and on a hot, humid afternoon in late June, I was puttering in it, an activity and pleasure that gratified my soul. Because I had planted things so early, the pole beans were ready to eat and I was picking some of them for dinner. When the bowl was full, I set the beans aside to look for other vegetables that might be ready. As my hands groped under and around leaves and stems, my mind wandered here and there, turning over vague, disconnected thoughts about 'the Robes.' I hadn't seen the little monks for weeks, and although part of me accepted them as a regular feature of my experience, the rest of me continued to struggle with both the fact of their visits, and the information they kept showing me.

At times I tried to talk with others about the difficulties I had seen without mentioning any little men in brown robes, but my remarks about severe weather, political upheaval, a disrupted distribution system, and shortages of food, irritated friends and bored Ben. When he threatened to make a huge sign proclaiming "The End Is Near!" and hang it on my back, I was embarrassed and made a conscious effort to be silent on the subject.

With a sigh of pained resignation at the apathy of friends, I stood up to stretch away the stiffness in my lower back and legs, and there on the porch were the little men!

They looked at me evenly for a long moment then said, "Greetings! You are doing well... and we have pictures that will help you to do even better. Would you like to see them?"

I nodded, half-amused at the sameness of their visits, the way they always showed up when I least expected them, and their cheerful insistence that the pictures they showed me would help.

Taking the bowl of beans into the house, I washed my hands then sat down at the table. Qietly I leaned   back in my chair, and allowed their pictures to unfold across the screen of my mind, where I found myself immersed in a very familiar present. People were going through the routines of the Everyday. Adults went back and forth to work, children went back and forth to school, and rising tides of change went unrecognized or unacknowledged.

Whether they lived in cities, suburbs, or small towns, everyone seemed to be pretending or hoping that life would remain normal and proceed according to an assumed routine. In the corners of my own mind the same hope flickered, a hope that stood in sharp contrast to the dread I felt about the things I'd seen coming and the uncertainty I held about our ability to respond wisely.

Then the little men began.

"As the breaking up of the first world nations begins, there will be a general atmosphere of 'eat, drink, and be merry' and your entertainment industries will be running full steam. Even so, the first warning signs of transition will already be showing up.

"As we have already seen, appearing in unwelcome places will be individuals, or even groups, who shoot schoolchildren or set off bombs among shoppers. Jail and prison populations will begin to compete with school enrollment as large numbers of people attempt to alter perception of their unhappy reality with drugs. Law systems and rule-making will run rampant in an attempt to control the delinquent, and use of those plants that were meant to expand your awareness, take you into other systems of reality, anchor the rituals that bring you needed insight, as well as keep your human development moving will all be banned.

"Springing up here and there will be cases of the old plagues along with the rise of strange new ones; diseases that kill even more quickly and mysteriously than the old ones once did. Accompanying these will be the discouraging increase of cancers, diseased hearts that pump blood painfully, and digestive systems that no longer digest. Worse, difficulties and diseases that you once thought were only the problem of the very old will begin to appear in the children and you will ache to see your babies suffer horribly. However, the most frightening and frustrating of all will be the disease of alienation in your young. Nothing will cause as much heartache as the misshapen, misaligned minds of young people who attack one another or their elders with vicious and destructive intent. Without respect for life or patience for law, they will express with their lives the symptoms of a population that has not only stalled in its evolution, but has begun to slip dangerously backwards.

"Many factors will play a part in the destruction of your young and we hope to point out some of the important lessons that can be learned from this, as well as make clear the extent of the changes that must happen if you want to correct things. The first of these changes has to do with your ideas surrounding the reproducing of human bodies.

"For hundreds of years your churches have been preaching the idea that the sexual act is for procreation only, and that sexual experience must be enjoyed only by those who are married, preferably those married in a ceremony performed and recognized by that particular church.

"Like most power structures making rules through which they can control people, these teachings about sexual experience are misguided, useless decrees. They were proclaimed by humans who had no real understanding of what sexual experience was about or what it was for.

"To deal with this teaching, a primary change will be needed. Their insistence that you are essentially bad, and therefore condemned to hell if you do not accept their dictates as your own, is not true. You are essentially good, and your existence in the physical dimension is designed to expand your ability to create wisely. As you continue to evolve, you will come to recognize that any power structure that attempts to control the *inner* life of the mind can be much more damaging and insidious in its ability to derange development than those who try to control the *outer* life."

In a remark addressed to me personally the little men said, "You, personally, have already experienced the awakening of consciousness that is encoded into every human being and accessed through the sexual experience. In time, you will come to understand the deep implications of this awakening, and it is our intention to assist in this understanding, for this is part of your personal destiny—to discover the keys to the health, development, and evolution of body/mind systems, whether the system is plant, animal, or human, for all forms here on your planet are composed of both body and mind."

With that announcement, they presented a series of pictures involving a string of sexual encounters. In one, a young woman traveling alone on a ship was making love to a man she met on the trip. In another, a woman was making love to a stranger in an alley somewhere. In a third, a pregnant girl with bright red hair who couldn't have been more than twelve or thirteen was involved in a court case seeking an abortion and continued to have sexual encounters with several older males. In a fourth situation, a young married couple was enjoying some wildly passionate sex, and in a fifth, a sickly woman with absolutely no hair, who was obviously at the end of a pregnancy was making love to a man who appeared to be her husband.

Then the series shifted back to the first woman, the one who had been the traveler on the ship. She was expecting a child, was still single, and looking forward to it with a mix of excitement and apprehension. The woman who had been making love to the stranger in an alley was also pregnant. The thirteen year old was delivering the child that had never been aborted, the young married couple was expecting their first child with a mix of anxiety, helplessness, and uncertainty, and the sickly woman had delivered a healthy baby boy and was now dying.

In the next set of scenes all of the women had given birth, the sick woman had died, and all of the young babies seemed to be in distress. The young single woman was never there for her infant because she had to work. Each day she was exhausted when she finally picked the child up from the day care center. Once home she was too tired to do more than go through the motions of feeding and bathing it.

The child born to the woman I had seen in the alley seemed to have something seriously wrong with it, both physically and mentally, and the problems were made worse by the mother's neglect. The thirteen-year-old had enjoyed the excitement of her child for a few weeks and then began to ignore it in long bouts of pouting, petulance, and anger. Her mother tried to force her to take care of the child but the only result was more anger and tension.

The young married couple seemed caught in a tense, endless fight. They were struggling terribly to adapt to the demands their unwelcome child had placed on the relationship, and neither was able to hide the resentment they both felt. The child whose mother had died was colicky and cried continuously, irritating the babysitter during the day and the father at night, neither of whom was able to deal with the sense of helpless hostility each felt toward the tiny human.

"We could show you hundreds, thousands of births," the little men said, "and every one of them a tragedy, each in a unique setting and each of them the result of the same problem—the mindless, unprepared reproduction of bodies.

"In every case we have shown you here, no thought was given as to *what* was being created, *who* would take up residence in the physical body being reproduced, or whether that entity was appropriate for the family group it would be born into.

"In every case the bond of oneness was broken. This bond is essential in human development for two reasons. The first is because it literally sustains a new *energy body* in the making of a strong, clear, complete physical Self. The second is that when this bond is broken and not repaired, the new human *mind* develops a core of fear that forever retards its growth and handicaps its development as a full, creative, and powerful human being.

"Within the bond of oneness is the connection to your source. In that source are found joy, peace, and health; through it creative genius is activated along with the ability to generate the entire frequency-set of love. You now have a whole planet full of humans suffering from the handicaps created as each child's bond with the mother or father was broken and never repaired, resulting in the loss of connection to your source and its replacement with fear."

I sighed deeply, wondering if anyone I knew could be categorized as a fully developed human, but the little men interrupted my thought to emphasize what they had already said.

"We realize that we are contradicting some of your most established religions but the sexual experience is *not* solely for procreation. It is not even *mainly* for procreation. Its primary function in the human is to regenerate the wave matrix that maintains the physical form you think of as your body. In everyday language, the primary purpose of sexual experience is to maintain the physical form, good health, and long life.

"Let us look at this from the beginning. Your physical body is a three-dimensional matrix of energy waves. Each wave in the matrix has a particular frequency. Each frequency carries a certain kind of information, which carries out a particular cycle of activity.

"On a similar but very small scale, an atom of matter consisting of protons, neutrons, and electrons is the result of a tiny matrix of wave frequencies located in space and time. This matrix of wave frequencies not only holds the protons and neutrons in place, it is the 'set of tracks' around which the assemblage of electrons moves. The electrons ride these waves. Depending on the number and arrangement of particles, you can have an atom of hydrogen, or carbon, perhaps oxygen, or some other kind of matter.

"Each of the particles within the atom is similar to a small magnetic sphere; and each sphere has both a north and south pole. The orientation of these poles in relation to the wave matrix allows the information carried in the wave to pass through the particle, and allows the particle to stay informed of what is happening with all the other particles in the matrix.

"The human body is a collection of these particles which have organized themselves into atoms. In turn, the atoms have collected and organized themselves into forms called molecules. From the point of view of an atom, a molecule is a highly advanced form of cooperative intelligence. From the point of view of a molecule, a human cell is an even more advanced form of cooperative intelligence containing many wave systems of information that have decided to work together. And so it goes up the ladder of complexity all the way to a functioning plant, animal, or human being, the important factor being that each form—from particle to atom to molecule to cell, and so on, has a north and south pole *and* the need to maintain that polar orientation in order to stay in contact with its fellows.

"Within each body, whether plant, animal, or human, the matrix of energy waves is what holds the physical form together and also provides the communication framework for the atoms gathered there to work together. However, in the course of daily living with its continual disruption of the frequencies of the basic wave matrix, one or more of these waves can suffer from destructive interference of its frequency and go slightly out of alignment, out of tune. If this is not corrected, the atoms lose their orientation, their source of information, and means of communication with one another. As a result, physical problems such as illness or disease show up in the body.

"To help continuously align and re-tune the wave matrix of the human body, the sexual experience has been designed as an automatic, self-correcting mechanism through which the body cycles regularly, approximately every one-and-a-half to two hours. At the start of each of these cycles, the body is prepared for the possibility of full correction via partial erection in both males and females. When full sexual orgasm does not occur, there can be either dissipation of the arousal, or perhaps a mini-correction of the energy matrix. During this mini-correction, the electrical system of the body discharges in a brief series of very low amplitude waves. If full sexual orgasm has occurred recently, there will most likely be dissipation of the heightened electro-magnetic charge. If it has been a long time since full sexual orgasm, you may notice the faint sensations of discharge during a mini-correction. And if it has been a long time since full sexual orgasm, there can be full spontaneous discharge during either waking or sleeping.

"If there is a full sexual experience, one which is characterized by orgasm, a broad set of powerfully amplified tuning waves specific to each individual body is generated and moves through the body, correcting the polar orientation of your cells, returning many wave frequencies back to their original phased settings, and generally improving overall function of the body/mind system.

"The fact that you have constructed a myriad of inaccurate perceptions and concepts about the sexual experience only serves to impair its effectiveness. In the perfect sexual experience not only does this amplified set of waves move through you, restoring and renewing body and mind, the waves also move directly up the spine to the brain, connecting you to your Source, and opening you to the experience of oneness and bliss in the Godhead. This then stabilizes the frequencies that hold your physical self together, reminds you of the dimensions that exist side by side with the physical realm, and expands the brain's capacity to operate over a wider range of frequencies, allowing you to perceive beings and events going on in other dimensions of existence.

"Sadly, the prevailing concept of oneness is a degenerated picture of two people having sex and temporarily 'joining to become one body'.

"Another version of oneness is 'getting married' and becoming one societal unit. This concept of marriage frequently destroys the evolution and development of both partners. Originally, the concept of marriage came from the practice of husbandry, which was based on a commitment 'to nurture' and 'to raise to fullness.'

"Later, the term 'marriage' was used to denote a person's decision to remain in relationship with someone who was a positive, creative, nurturing force, someone who supported the ongoing development of both people. Marriage in that sense did not demand that the two people live together, that they become lovers, that they be male and female, or that they stay together for life. It asked only that the relationship be creative and nurture personal growth.

"Today, marriage as it is practiced in your world generally demands so much attention on external appearances, that the focus on internal development is lost and the whole concept has become pointless and destructive. As such it is unnecessary.

"The second purpose of sexual experience is to function as a bridge of awareness between your physical body, which is made of Earth and minerals, and your eternal Self, which is made of mind and characterized by peaceful bliss. Mind is the basic medium in which the energy waves and bodymind matrix are generated. Through the action of the force you refer to as 'love,' mind gathers together the particles that then become a body in the physical realm of time-space. Together body and mind make up the bodymind system, and although you inhabit a body only temporarily, your existence in the world of mind and intelligence is eternal. The fact that you have decided to focus yourself in a physical body, however, does not mean that you cannot know your eternal side. The sexual experience allows you to do so by accessing the oneness and bliss that reveal your Source.

"This Source or condition of oneness is sometimes called The Void because it is empty of all things with which you are familiar. Plants, animals, other people, or material forms—these things do not appear in the blissful state of oneness. There is only *awareness*, a brilliant awareness that you exist. From this place of awareness you can shape yourself into any form that can be imagined.

"This place of oneness is also known as the *I Am* state and is overflowing with a love so complete that nothing else is needed, hence the lack of material things. The sexual experience is a blessed gate that opens the connection to oneness, which then reminds you that bliss is your basic nature, and love is the force that literally holds your particles together.

"Love is the basic force that transforms the intelligent awareness of mind into consciousness and at the same time, organizes consciousness to become a living cell, then pushes that cell to become aware of self and communicate with others, thus making whole intelligent systems possible.

"The third purpose of the sexual experience is to extend life to others. This should be used only with much preparation, careful intent, and only after great deliberation. It is a purpose that should be much more rarely tapped, for creating another human is serious business and requires careful, long-term commitment.

"A wise, personal rule of thumb for creating other humans during the decades of transition would be that no new bodies be created until the group that will be responsible for the new human understands in depth what the responsibilities of the task are. They must be ready to commit the time and energy required; and they should be able to do the required parenting. That is, they should have the skills, qualities, and characteristics desirable for such a task because these very things will be duplicated in the new human, impressed into the new matter like a hot iron in wax.

"The thinking of many people at this time is that children are born complete with personalities, traits, and a mind of their own. You observe that they have bodies, they have individual temperaments, and you think they have a sense of self. You think that all a parent needs to do is provide food, shelter, and clothing, wait for the child to learn to walk and talk, then send the little one off to school to be educated. Soon, you believe, there will be a fully-grown adult who will go out into the world and function at least as well as everyone else.

"Unfortunately your perceptions of babies are not accurate. Babies have enormous amounts of free intelligence waiting to be developed. If they show signs of individual spirit and personality it is because some of the spirit and former personality of the entity has come to live in a body again in order to be re-shaped, literally re-made by the new experiences the new body offers. When you neglect this re-making, you slow down the impact and re-shaping that a new physical body and its experiences offer to an entity. The result is that the entity living in the body ends up repeating the same experiences that it came here to change, much of which is complicated by its state of underdevelopment.

"At this time the best you are able to say of the results of your reproduction is that you have thousands of humans with underdeveloped intelligence who try desperately to find happiness, who sell their lives and their souls short to get others to love them because they are not connected to their own oneness or inner Self, and who then end up accidentally and/or unconsciously creating another body, which also remains undeveloped, perpetuating the whole circle of disappointment.

"It will become clear that it is time to break this circle of disappointment when you find that many are unable to conceive or bear a child at all. It is normal and natural for a healthy human to be able to reproduce other bodies, although it is neither necessary or expected that you must do so. But when you have ignored the basic laws of nature for too long and the human form degenerates below the excellent reproductive standards set by nature, reproduction shuts down and all energy goes into survival mode. This will be a signal that it is time for you to begin focusing on personal growth and development, not finding shortcuts around these blocks to reproduction."

The little men stopped to give me a chance to digest what they were saying, and then continued.

"Returning to the rule of thumb for creating that was suggested a moment ago, we would like to emphasize one point. The idea that 'no new bodies should be created until the group responsible for the new human understands its responsibilities in depth' is a most important one. Note that we did not say 'parents,' neither did we refer to a 'new mother and father.' This is because it is time to evolve beyond the belief that the woman who gives birth to a child owns that child, or that the nuclear family of 'mother and father' is the ideal setting into which a child should be born.

"In the years to come, everyone will become singularly conscious of population numbers, even though there will eventually be far fewer people on the planet. The decision to have a child will become a group decision and once born, the child will belong to the entire family, although the physical parents will take responsibility for the majority of care. There will be careful preparation for the birth physically, mentally, spiritually, and emotionally, and unplanned pregnancies will be rare.

"Why? Will there be some kind of law that forbids having children?" I inquired.

"No," they replied, "nor will women or men take the kind of birth control pills you now take, use contraceptive devices, or have operations that will sterilize them. In the beginning, most women will drink a special tea made from a natural bush and this will prevent pregnancies for long periods of time. For those who do not want such long-term protection, drinking several cups of another kind of tea for two or three days every month will result in menstruation and few un-wanted pregnancies. Later you will learn to practice birth control with your mind, but that is a subject we will not go into now.

"When they do occur, unplanned pregnancies will be cause for a meeting of the entire family. During this meeting, the family will ask many questions. They will ask the prospective mother and father if precautions were being taken. They will probe deeply into the question of whether or not they really want to take on the responsibilities of raising a new child, and who, in addition to the mother and father, will join in this work. Occasionally the family will decide that it is not a good time for a new member and the pregnancy will be ended. In these cases, there will be careful attention to the emotional condition of the would-be parents.

"There may be times when the prospective mother or father did not intend to create a child and do not want this responsibility. They may decide to end the pregnancy, but must consult with the entire family before doing so, in order to make sure they have enough nurturance and support to avoid suffering any serious physical or psychological reactions to the ending of the pregnancy. In this kind of situation there will be a careful study of the chemistry of both partners to determine why the natural forms of birth control were not working. In addition, there may be the requirement that both undertake new programs of self-development that lead to deeper insights into the responsibilities of creating.

"If the prospective mother and father did not intend to create a child, do not wish to raise the child, yet are not comfortable ending the pregnancy, someone in the extended family or another family may sometimes raise the child. In such cases, the Bio-mother or the Bio-father will be honored and celebrated as an important part of the child's effort to come to Earth.

"In no case will a mother, or even a mother *and* father working as a unit, be left to decide on their own whether or when to create a new human. In terms of developing human potential, the single-parent family is about equal in effectiveness to the two-parent nuclear family, and both arrangements create serious imbalances in the lives of everyone within the family. The task of creating and shaping a new human is simply too demanding and will quickly deplete both the single mother as well as the two parents found in a typical nuclear family.

"Who will feed and nurture the single mother if she gives all her time and energy to the process of creating a child? Even when there is a mother and a father, there is seldom enough energy between the two of them in your current social and cultural structures to create a child who does not have a core of fear. They lack energy because they are not healthy enough in the first place. The job is made infinitely more difficult because they are underdeveloped themselves and are forced to deal with a child who will likely remain underdeveloped as well.

"At present, if the mother stays home she often stays undeveloped. If the father goes to work, he ends up in a rut and his development stalls. If they both work, the child develops by default in an insecure, lopsided manner, with too many biases and too little understanding of other people or the self.

"At this time you do not have a realistic idea of what is needed to create and nurture a human that could easily, and earlier, tap the hidden potentials of the human body/mind system. The idea of creating such a child, one that is perhaps wiser, more powerful than you, is something you all fear. You would be surprised at the level of commitment it would take, the time and careful attention needed. Yet even a few basic changes would make a huge difference overall.

"At the very least, such a child would be extremely healthy, very intuitive, a rapid and natural learner, with a peaceful nature. Multiply this by thousands, or perhaps millions, and you would have a different world, one whose people had little need for huge medical systems to tell them how to heal, public school systems to tell them what to learn, over-reaching industrial complexes to tell them what to do with their lives hour by hour, or wasteful and competitive wars that feed their illusions of power and righteousness.

"Of course, mindful creating demands dealing with the difficult issues surrounding birth and raising children. As pointed out a moment ago, questions of growing difficulty will be found in the issues surrounding population. These include the issues of abortion, issues that deal with who has the right to conceive and bear a child, who has the right to stay home and care for that child, and who is truly fit to raise a child.

"The subject of abortion alone is many-sided and already causes much grief. Some believe abortion is never acceptable, that it's a terrible sin because their religion has said so. Their argument is that the fetus is a living thing, which it is, but this is only one aspect of truth, and the real truth has little to do with the religious institutions that have grown to power in your time and place.

"Another aspect of truth is found in the example of a woman who needs to end a pregnancy as a correction of a previous lifetime in which she neglected or abused her children. In this case, the law that condemns abortion interferes seriously with the higher law that demands her personal growth and soul development.

"Some try to split hairs on the subject of abortion. They say that abortion can be performed before the new human is technically able to breathe on its own. From this perspective of truth, abortion is declared technically acceptable up to six or seven months.

"Some say that abortion is acceptable up until quickening, the time when the mother can feel the new life moving about within her. Again, this is acceptable for those who believe in this fashion. But if you were sensitive enough, you would feel life and movement from the very moment of conception, even before. You would feel the egg being released from the ovary and beginning her journey though the tubes. You would feel the sperm aggressively struggling to penetrate the egg, you would feel

the implantation of this new life in the wall of the uterus and the movement within the berry-sized collection of cells, later the pulsing of a
miniature heart, and still later the fluttering of extremely tiny arms and
legs.

"Others say that abortion is acceptable until the new and growing
human can live on its own, in which case the abortion could be performed
either before the birth, or after the birth. It could even be interpreted to
mean until the age of three if you define 'live on its own' loosely to mean
'understand that it is part of the group and can contribute to the group,' or
possibly up to age twelve, if you define 'live on its own' more strictly to
mean 'protect, defend, and supply itself with food, clothing and shelter.'

"Some demand laws that attempt to define the moment when the
fetus becomes 'legally alive.' They want to use this as a guideline for
deciding whether and when an abortion can be performed, declaring all
later abortions as murder. This is also an acceptable alternative for some,
although it is confusing in view of the fact that both the egg and the sperm
are fully alive before conception ever takes place. You could never get a
live fetus from either a dead ovum or a dead sperm. To argue as if there is
a 3- or 5-month pause in life during which abortion could be performed
because the new human is not alive does not make any sense at all.

"Then there are those who take this same premise—that the new
human is alive from the very start, that it has a right to live—and declare
that abortion is never acceptable, that it is always murder. The problem
with these people is that they have taken what is right for them and are
trying to push it onto others. Allowing a new body to be born may *not* be
right for the baby, the parents, or the family group; and humans who push
their ideas onto others often have more of a problem with issues of power
and control than they do with abortion or murder.

"Complicating the issue is the mix-up in who has the right to tell
you what to do. Through your line of popes and priests you have totally
misinterpreted the words of your last Christ-figure who is reported to have
given Simon Peter the power to make decisions for others when he said,
'Whatsoever you bind in heaven shall be bound on earth, and whatsoever
you loose in heaven shall be loosed on earth.' The Christ did not mean that
you should create a new power-figure at the top of a new church which
was to be patterned after the old decision-making power of kings and
princes claiming divine right, but since that was the only way people could
imagine structuring power at that time, that's exactly what was done.

"What the Christ intended was to give you an important message
about understanding yourself so you would have a tool for further self-

development, as well as encouragement to nurture wisdom by nurturing inner authority. What He actually meant was that whatever you believe in the realms of your own mind and heart is what you must honor as you create in the physical realm. Whatever you do not want or can't believe in, you must not attempt or commit to do because you will be going against your own self. You will not be able to create it. It was meant to be a lesson in the congruency of the mind and the body and the use of power. The Christ could just as easily have said, 'What you see is what you get!' or perhaps, 'What you think is what you will experience.' Other teachers have said similar things, as Mr. Cayce often remarked, 'Mind is the builder!'[5]

"These words and others like them contain the message that you must act in the physical according to what you believe. Nowhere is there permission to make others do as you believe. Let us say we have a man named Martin. Martin believes that abortion is wrong. This means that abortion is wrong *for Martin* and he should concern himself with making personal choices that will *not* lead to his becoming involved in situations that lead to the question of whether or not to have an abortion.

"Further, if Martin tells himself that he can cause harm or bring pain and grief to others because they believe abortion is right for them, he is deceiving himself. If he does end up hurting others, what he is really demonstrating is his desire to control others and his willingness to hurt them in order to make them do as he wishes. In this regard, he may be more destructive than the individuals who consent to or perform an abortion, for they may be doing with great humility exactly what is necessary for their own personal growth.

"You will also find that many people who oppose abortion would not think twice about supporting a war in which they believed they were on the side of righteousness, or shooting an intruder who came into their homes to steal. They would not intercede to save the life of a cow or a chicken, and they would think nothing of going out to shoot animals just for sport during hunting season. They would not hesitate to cut down a tree in the way of their new house, nor would it bother them to tear the ears off of a corn plant to enjoy a corn roast. Yet in each of these situations there is a similar destruction of life and intelligence.

"Life *is* alive and has intelligence regardless of form, and we are all are connected in oneness in spite of appearances of separation. What makes you any different from or better than a tree or an ear of corn? Both

---

[5] A referral to Edgar Cayce, (1877- 1945) a well-known American clairvoyant.

of these also have the ability to extend life, to reproduce due to the fact that they are alive, yet you do not consider it murder to bulldoze the forest or grind the corn and eat it.

"If you hold the coin of creating up to the light you will see that your haphazard approach to creating a new life is matched by your haphazard solutions for ending it. The real and lasting solutions will be found in new forms of consciousness and awareness that you must build, along with a mindful approach to the creating and the undoing of physical form. The truly mature and developed human being knows when and how to create, as well as when and how to destroy. When there must be the undoing of a form, you must, at the very least, learn to ask the intelligent spirit that resides in the form to leave, and as we have pointed out, to do this requires a whole new level of human development and consciousness.

"As the changes in your civilization escalate, a practical approach to birth control using the many natural means afforded by the plant world would be a wise practice. This will come about as you give more and more consideration to creation of true freedom, and concentrate on developing greater wisdom. At the very least, we hope you will become hesitant to introduce more bodies to the slavery of money, the bondage of ill health, and the misery of underdevelopment.

"Over the time of the earth transitions, those choosing to create new bodies will suffer greatly in their efforts to feed and shelter these new humans. The result will be a steep decline in the number of new bodies. However, once a self-sufficient, well-developed group has decided to add a new human, this decision should be recognized as only half the task. The other half is to find a tenant for the new body, and this should be completed before the new body is conceived. To do this there should be the careful attempt to contact what you now call a 'soul' that would be suitable for the group and for the new body, keeping in mind that the purpose for life experience is both creative expression and soul refinement.

"To contact souls on what you think of as the 'other side,' you will need to develop your inherent abilities far beyond the hunches of simple intuition. When you develop this ability, you will also be developing your ability to see and hear and feel in all directions—past, present, future. And once you do this, you will accelerate the changes in your world.

"After the group has contacted a soul that seems to fit them, the prospective soul can give important input as to who in the group is most suitable as a biological parent. You might be interested in knowing that to some degree, this is similar to the way your last Christ child was born, the highly developed master now known as Jesus. In this case, Mary understood herself to be the best biological mother, and even though she had previously decided to remain celibate and unmarried, when she discovered she was pregnant, she agreed to carry the child, and this was approved by her group.

"When a compatible soul has been found, preparation of the biological parents should begin. This should include meditation, physical exercise, and an abundance of healthy food. It should also be a time of careful re-examination of motives, mental readiness, emotional stability, and regular contact with the soul that will live in the body. Only when these preparations are complete—perhaps six months to a year later—should the blocks to conception be removed and sexual experience be celebrated as an event meant to extend and create new life.

"Once the new life has begun it should be monitored with the same care and attention that characterized the pre-pregnancy period; with healthy food, exercise, plenty of rest, meditation to maintain mental and emotional balance, and occasional contact with the soul waiting to be born. If it happens that the newly developing body has become deformed, or is weak, there might be the decision to terminate and start over. If the soul that intended to inhabit the new body changes his or her mind, there may also be termination of the pregnancy. Again, in order to stay informed of these kinds of changes, a whole new level of development and knowing is required. This cannot be over-emphasized.

"If there are no interruptions to the pregnancy, when the child is born there should be the greeting and welcoming of the new human by everyone in the group, including touch, voice, and eye contact, even when the group is large. It need not all happen on one day, but this should be an important ritual, one never to be missed.

"After the birth there should be a well-planned, well-organized routine of care and support for the new human, the biological mother, and the biological father. In no case should they be allowed to become over-tired, irritable, or negative about the work of shaping a new human, for the first few weeks of life are absolutely critical in establishing the electromagnetic and bio-chemical operations of full body/mind function. Without the correct frequencies and chemistry to drive perception, the entire effort to shape the human becomes remedial. When it is done correctly, however, the unfolding of the human and his or her potential is spontaneous and nearly effortless, requiring only the proper stimulation at the right time."

"The period of time from birth to about age two will be the time when the child will establish within the body/mind system the foundations of your spacetime reality. The more he or she is allowed to observe, touch, and experience life, the more clearly defined and responsive to reality and human potential the child will become.

"From their earliest days, children will flourish best if they are part and parcel of the family. Because of lessons learned from your own difficulties in surviving the coming changes, from the time they can walk, children's primary education will consist, first and foremost, of learning the skills of survival. They will take part in all of the small chores that contribute to growing food, creating or repairing shelters, healing techniques for people and animals, and practices that help maintain the land.

"From age three to around age seven, the child will experience and express a belief system that is based on a framework of 'anything is possible.' At present, you do not acknowledge this important stage of human development and thus do not model what is possible. Sadly, you treat this stage as a time for the child to be taught that his or her belief system is not correct. You act as if it is time for the child to 'get realistic' and to be introduced to the limitations of reality.

"Never do you ask with true curiosity or serious inquiry why all children pass through this stage. It has never occurred to you that 'anything *is* possible' yet if you were a fully developed human in your own right, this would be the stage in which your advanced abilities of mind would be demonstrated and given simple, basic explanations because the magic inherent in the young human was ripe for strengthening and developing. It has never occurred to you that this time of open belief and the sense that anything is possible is the time when the skills of mind-to-mind commun-ication are best learned. It is the time to demonstrate how to move the physical body from place to place without external means of transport, it is the time to teach the skills of communication with plants, animals, and even inorganic substances, for it is in this stage that the ability to use the skills of mind-over-matter are first anchored.

"The tragedy of this stage is that instead of reinforcing the possible human, the child is rigidly forced to accept an entire array of limits on everything from physical matter to mental ideas, from personal creativity to behavior and verbal expression.

"After age seven the new human is ready to be fully involved in the processes of the Everyday, and indeed this is one of the most creative periods of the entire life. The child, now involved in the tasks that sustain life and allow self-expression, yet without having been over-exposed to routine, can often come up with a fresh approach to an old task. Even when the approach is not faster or better in the old sense of economics, it is often unique, more fun, more challenging, and thus can be a source of enjoyment in its own right. And sometimes it is a very valuable alternative.

"The tragedy of this age is that young humans are sent away from their family to sit uselessly in schools where the majority of their creativity is destroyed and involvement with important models of adult thinking and creative natural behavior is cut off. As we have already pointed out, since children learn and grow mainly by observing and copying other people, when they are trapped in schools with only other, immature children as models of behavior, they answer their own inner questions of 'how should I behave' by copying the behavior of other children. Thus their behavior decisions are often inappropriate and problems are compounded ten thousand times. Many of them emerge from the process of schooling incapable, insensitive, confused, and generally useless.

"By age twelve the new human should be completely able to be self-sufficient, self-supervising at his or her tasks, and well integrated into the family group. As they grow older, entry into family business will be considered the focal point of their higher education. They can become familiar and proficient with the technology used by the family to produce their products, educate themselves, and develop their human potentials.

"By this time, the clear emergence of individual gifts, interests, and abilities should begin. These form the basis for any decisions about embarking on more formal education. The new human should have gradually become a self-directed learner who now pursues information and experience in his or her own way. He should be able to arrange this knowledge in ways that are personally useful, and apply it uniquely. This is the time to acknowledge the child's gifts and natural interests, and for several people to take on the job of mentoring and guiding emotional development in the young human.

"Sometime after the age of twelve the stage of puberty will be reached and if you are wise, you will prepare and plan for sexual initiation rather than leave this to chance, or more foolishly, pretend that you can deter the child from this natural development. Sexual experience is far too important to be delayed or allowed to go awry. Even if the child has been masturbating quietly for years, the first formal sexual experience should be a rite of passage meant to open the heart, teach gentleness, sexual manners, and especially, expand the frequencies at which the brain/mind operates.

"It is at the beginning of puberty, that humans should begin the practice of moving sexual energy up through each energy center, all the way to the brain. Here, it becomes the catalyst that transforms the overall frequency of the body/mind matrix and results in greatly enhanced consciousness and compassion, the perceptual base known as intuition, the skills of clairvoyance, telepathy, teleportation, and so on.

"Only *after* the young human has been successfully moved through the sexual initiation should there be the consideration of education on an apprenticeship basis with other families. Even then, the mentoring of emotional development must be continued, for a human with highly developed abilities of the body/mind syst em can lose them or twist them destructively until emotional maturity and enhanced perception are stabilized, a process that takes place slowly between the ages of fourteen and thirty years of age.

"During this period, there can be a tendency for young humans to become unbalanced in their sense of when and where to use their powers, as well as occasional difficulty in staying centered. Steady contact and close mentoring, along with highly evolved models who are powerful in their own right are necessary both at home, and in the apprentice-family if the young adult goes away to learn special skills.

"At the beginning of puberty, neither sexual experience nor further formal education should be pushed or discouraged. Rather, there should be close attention to personal self-development. By focusing on self-development, the sexual and the educational aspects arise naturally and can be handled wisely.

"At present you seriously discourage sexual experience while seriously enforcing formal education. These attitudes range from counter-productive to outright destructive. On the one hand, discouraging sexual experience makes as much sense as trying to push a river uphill. You are working against the natural unfolding of life as a human being, as well as the health and well-being of the overall body/mind system. In addition, you disturb the connection to oneness, thus leaving yourselves with another adult that could be considered permanently disabled, forever immature.

"On the other hand, you often put too much emphasis on formal education, which is like trying to plant seeds on bare rock. Information must be relevant to the personal interests and developmental path in order to be grasped and integrated into one's life.

"Timing is of the essence in all learning. That is why your schools are so unproductive. You send children away to schools to learn, but all you are really teaching them is that children are not important and should be sent away. When they grow up, they send their own children away to school all day. The end result is that few people either want or even know how to deal with children any more. The natural flow of information about sustaining life that should move from the land to the adults to the children is disrupted, then lost.

"As a result, children live without security and self-esteem, then become adults without security or self-esteem. Their natural intelligence, creativity, and expressions of love are spoiled, and it is easy to see why few people have the time and patience for children. Children remind adults of their own unfilled needs and unexpressed behaviors.

"To cover your errors and your guilt, you create a lot of un-necessary clatter around school clothes, sports, and schedules. Each of these is an attempt to distract the child's attention from the pain of being sent away to school each day and the destruction of their inherent learning abilities.

"Homework is another harmful intrusion into family life where adults fuss and fume when information does not flow from the book to the child. If the parents could just get that text or that teacher to make information flow into the child's mind, then the adult would not have to bother and would be free to relax after a hard day's work for money, itself another error!

"While the child suffers his way through school, the adults offer platitudes and meaningless rewards to push them toward graduation. Or worse, they punish the child.

When the child becomes a teen and ends up antagonistic to the family, rude to younger siblings, and treats even friends thoughtlessly, he is simply modeling the behaviors he experienced in the first dozen years of his own life.

"When this young man or woman then selfishly demands things like money, clothes, use of the family car, special favors, and permission to run his or her own life, all the while refusing to take responsibility for the results of running his or her own life, you have the natural outcome of events that follow the break in bonding with oneness, the teachings of limitation, the sending away of children, and the absence of human development.

"In the end, the child grows into an adult with no real power, no useful sense of self, and no inner authority. Without inner authority, which is simply the activation of natural intelligence, he will wait for someone to tell him how to think and feel, what is allowed, and what he must do.

"Sensing that something is missing but unable to figure out exactly what it might be, the human lives out the entire life in a crucible of fears and the emotional conflict that fear generates. Unwilling or unable to transcend the broken bond of oneness with the Self, the human shuts down whole areas of brain function and feeling and becomes far less capable of intuition and the creativity of self-expressive thought and action.

"Emotional development, or *feeling* is at the core of human development and the wise utilization of intelligence. Throughout the universe, every waveform with its encoded information also carries the kind of information known as 'feeling.' When the matrix of waves that *is* the human being has been adulterated with fear, there is a serious interference with the body/mind system's ability to observe, experience, understand, and respond to the many kinds and degrees of intelligence that abound in the universe of patterns. Instead of reaching out, the human contracts in fear, afraid that what it will feel will be painful. When the connection with oneness is broken, intuition, clairvoyance, telepathy and other abilities built-in to the human system become dysfunctional or inaccessible, all because of fear.

"Advanced perceptual development is normally triggered into action by the combination of early human bonding, stimulation of the stage-specific forms of awareness built-in to every human, and the sexual experience which stimulates ongoing increases in the range of frequencies at which the body/mind can operate comfortably. With a steady hand to guide emotional development, these three factors of bonding, stimulation, and sexual experience become the basis of being able to utilize the skills of advanced human development. These skills make every task easier whether you are locating lost objects, communicating long distances without machinery or technology, or exploring the vast ranges of space and time.

"These skills are also the basis of spontaneous healing, the force behind the ability to move objects without touching them, the ability to travel without the assistance of cars, horses, and planes, or the skill of speaking with a beloved grandparent who is deceased or waiting to be reborn into the family. Most importantly, it is the foundation of the ability to regenerate the forces of love that maintain the physical body.

"Love is not the expression of romantic uproar many people think it is. For a large number of humans, all that romantic uproar is merely an excuse to throw off the yoke of personal responsibility and claim that someone else is responsible for how they think and feel for the moment. An opportunity to throw one's self into the arms of romance is an opportunity to blame fate for the outcome of a situation.

"We are not suggesting that romance be discarded or that you should not enjoy moments of romance whenever they invite you to. We do suggest that love be more clearly defined and that romance not be confused or mistaken for love. A romantic dance that leads to a sensuous sexual experience between two strangers is a romantic episode and should be treasured in the memory as such. It is not love.

"Love is a particular type of force in the universe. To begin to utilize the most basic form of love here in this dimension, it is at least necessary to be able to tune into the frequencies of the wave matrix that literally hold your physical form together. This will allow you to know your Self.

"Committing oneself to love is not a commitment to a husband, a marriage, a wife, or a child. It is a commitment to a *way of life* that expresses peace, joy, health, and the creative power of the self. Using basic expressions of love, you can develop the ability to extend this power to other beings while at the same time responding to the presence and behavior of those beings, regardless of which realm they are in and what they are communicating.

"Love is a steady force which can be used to express many feelings, but it is not an emotion in the way you generally experience an emotion. Emotions go up and down with your food, your mood, or your hormones while love is a Way of Being based on attunement to a specific form of energy. Love is a constant awareness of oneness, and brings with it the power to communicate in ways that far exceed your present abilities. Advanced expressions of love go much further and are able to generate particular energies and forms.

"It is our hope that through these teachings the humans of your planet will continue to evolve and develop, bringing love to your world once more." With that they were gone. 📖

14 📖

ON THE PRECIPICE...

OF all the visits so far, this had been the longest, most intense, most challenging. For the rest of the evening and days afterward, waves of emotion washed through me each time I thought about the things the little men had said.

As a result of my Catholic education and upbringing, early on I had come to believe that sex was tinged with something unsavory, a sinful, difficult business woven right through us, an impossible-to-ignore trapdoor to hell that lurked in our very essence.

The little men had plopped the subject right in the middle of the table and blithely discussed it as if we were talking about the practical aspects of buying new shoes. In less than one afternoon, they had contradicted everything I had been taught about sex, relationships, giving birth, and raising children.

Much of what they said was still a tangled lump in my mind, but I could not deny that what they said and the way they presented it struck deep chords of truth and common sense in me. Still, I agonized about whether to believe and accept what they were obviously trying to teach me. What if I ended up going to hell? What if I took the attitude that sex was neither sinful nor shameful and acted... acted... my god, how would I know how to act regarding sex? Who or what would control my behavior?

I had been struggling terribly with the sexual and sensual after-effects of kundalini for two years. Kundalini generated extraordinary states of sensitivity that rolled over into states of whole-body sensuousness, which blossomed into nearly uncontrollable sexual desire. Spontaneous orgasm, which traveled up the spine to the brain, had at first frightened me, then confused me. Wasn't sexual experience supposed to happen in bed while making love? What sin was I committing when it happened in the middle of living room while dusting furniture? Or in the grocery store? What explanation was I to give to myself or anyone else when I had to flee to the restroom while eating dinner at a restaurant because of spontaneous orgasms? Was I guilty of something bad when I had to pull the car off the expressway and into the rest stop for fear that I would not be able to maintain control of my driving because I could not control the seemingly independent sexual activity that flowed through my body?

"Could two thousand years of church teaching be off course," I asked myself, "telling us that sex was bad unless you were married and intended to have babies? What was the church planning to tell us about sex when the world got too full of people? Probably that we should stop having sex altogether! That would be typical... but how could they tell us to stop something that was so much a part of our human nature... although certainly they had laid the groundwork for such a prohibition by declaring that our basic nature was bad. Once they got us to believe we were intrinsically bad, then they told us we needed a church and a savior to save us. Wasn't that a neat piece of salesmanship?!"

I had been hiding in my house for nearly two years, trying to get control of my mind and my body. By every rule of the church and the family I had been raised in, I was surely hell-bound. I was living with a man, loving him desperately, making love to him daily, often several times a day, because it was the only way I knew of relieving the intense sexual pressure that dogged me. My grandmother had banned me from her home. My parents refused to come and visit me. One or two family members had written vicious letters, accusing me of being evil, of being a whore, of liking the city, of thinking I was better than everyone else in the family, of giving the family a bad name, of being selfish, of being a terrible mother who did not deserve her children.

From my point of view, I was experiencing something that neither I nor my family had ever encountered. I didn't know what was causing the strange sexual experiences. Nor could I explain the sudden psychic abilities either. If I couldn't explain it to myself, I certainly could not explain it to family. As for the steady flow of wide-ranging information from other places that passed through my mind continuously, until I could learn to manage my perception again, I was too embarrassed to talk about what was happening to me.

Another thing I could not explain was the love. For the first time in my life, I was truly, totally, unconditionally in love. The problem was that I refused to deny it, or color it ugly because it did not fit the rules and expectations about how it was supposed to happen or work out.

On top of the love problem, I suddenly felt I had to honor what I was feeling, come hell or high water, or I would never again be able to look myself in the eye and trust what I saw there. True, I had not planned to live with someone, but I was trying to get him to keep his word about marrying me.

For the time being, the only thing I was convinced of was that we didn't know enough about the subject of sex, and most of what we thought we knew was what someone else had told us. To make things worse, we'd been told that the subject was taboo so it was hard to discuss.

My personal experiences over the past two years had raised dozens of questions. What, exactly, was happening to me? Why was I having periods of intense sensuousness leading to the unexpected, spontaneous sexual experiences? Was it just coincidence that I began to have the sexual experiences at the same time that the psychic experiences began? What did it mean that I could not get the sexual experiences to stop when I wanted them to? Was there something in the body working according to its own needs and timetables? The little men had hinted at this, but how did it work, and why?

Their statement that the sexual experience was a health maintenance mechanism designed to refresh the entire field of energy that made up the human body certainly rattled the cage of my assumptions. It also stripped away the sheen of guilt, leaving the issues of sin and temptation somewhere in an irrelevant dust. If sex was the doorway to our eternal self, this was a one-hundred-eighty degree reversal of sex as the trapdoor to hell. Who should I believe? Obviously someone—either the church or the little men—did not have their facts right.

As for marriage, was it necessary or not in its present form? What would getting married actually do for me besides make it easier to get a loan? I did want the social approval for the sexual relationship with Ben, but what was this lost or missing thing called 'oneness'? Was that what I was chasing... or was I running from something? I already had one failed marriage, why did I want to try again?

Reflecting on how I had entered my first marriage, how I'd managed my life, I felt a keen anguish that cut through my soul, dragging me back in time and pointing an accusing finger that said, "You knew, why didn't you listen to yourself?"

And I did know. I knew as I stood at the altar that I didn't love the man who stood beside me the way he seemed to love me. I knew that I wasn't committing to a lifetime with him. While mouthing the marriage vows I was thinking, "Well, probably not, but I don't have any other choice... we'll see what happens..."

Now I could see that it would have been so much easier for all concerned if I had just been honest about what I was feeling... except it had never been okay in my life for people to be honest about what they were really feeling. Earlier in the relationship I had tried to break up with him time and again but he wouldn't give up, wouldn't go away, threatened to kill himself. Full of youthful ignorance, I began feeling guilty for rejecting him, and since 'guilty' was what my religion was always telling me I should be, I felt right at home. I took on responsibility for his very life. Here was someone who loved me... I should be grateful... He was rescuing me from the ignominious dungeons of lovelessness that women were cast into when no man came along to claim them or their love. I should be ashamed of even thinking of hurting his feelings by telling my truth... Besides, I was carrying his baby... I had to get married... Abortion was out of the question... It was too difficult to figure out by myself what I was going to do with a baby.

So I took what I thought was the easy way out, which turned out to be not so easy. In fact, it had been extraordinarily painful and heart-breaking for all concerned—him, me, four children, and the parents on both sides. Now I could see that I'd had no guts, no strength; I had ignored what I knew in my own heart, and continued to ignore what I saw and felt in other areas of life as well.

When my first daughter was born I was determined to do a better job than my parents had done. This daughter was not going to be wild and willful like me, she was going to be calm and quiet, polite and thoughtful, well-behaved and sweet. And she had been! The second daughter had not been quite as cooperative but she was bright and sunny. My son had been gentle and loving from the start, and my last daughter, had been calm, quiet, and particularly attached to me. I had birthed them all in less than six and a half years; only one of them was planned, none of them really prepared for, so they had suffered my mediocre motherhood and grew while I finished growing up.

When I sent my oldest daughter off to kindergarten, she came home one day and said, "Mama, what does 'fuck' mean?" Horrified, I asked where she heard it and she replied, "The safety-boy on the corner says it."

I could not believe it. I was twenty-four and still didn't feel old enough to swear. With a sinking feeling, I realized I had no control over what went on in school or on the way to school.

And sure enough, one by one, as my children went off to school, they changed dramatically. Once playful, creative, and happy to spend hours with one another, they were now competitive and aggressive. They worried about whether they were doing things correctly, constantly told each other what to do, made endless judgments about one another, seemed impatient, insecure, and disdainful of other children.

I had known in some deep intuitive way that something awful was happening with them since I began sending them away during the day. At the time, anxious for my children to do well in school, I had overlooked the truth that my heart was telling me. Something beautiful in their hearts and minds was slowly being destroyed. But they *had* to go to school, didn't they? Everyone had to go to school. It was the way things were, and the concept of not going to school did not exist for me in that place and time.

Nevertheless, somewhere in that period of time after my children began school, I received a book titled *Blackberry Winter* by Margaret Mead. In it she described her early years, how her grandmother had tutored her at home at least half of her life instead of having gone to regular public school.

Once I had read it, I put it on my bookshelf with the kind of romantic sigh reserved for appreciation of things that could no longer be. However, with all that the book contained, the two things I recalled were that Margaret had not gone to school continuously, and that she had been an extraordinarily intelligent woman. I didn't know how that could have happened because in my mind, school was what made us intelligent.

Again I ended up ignoring something I knew because it flew in the face of what the established authorities were telling me. Sadly, I reflected on the unhappy path that stretched out behind me. I had sent my children away, they were caught in a system that ruined their natural learning abilities along with their relationship to the family. Now they were like me and everyone else, remedial beings who had been birthed and not nurtured well.

Tangled in conflicting emotions, I looked back at how intuitive I had been and yet how immature. Eons ago I had taken my shrinking self to marriage counseling with a wonderful woman named Mrs. Monks. When I was strong enough, the marriage finally broke up. I then took myself and my four children through months of intense family counseling which healed many things, taught us listening skills, and how to show we cared for one another.

Later I embarked on two other brief, counseling-based journeys into myself, one when I was at Chrysler for the purpose of developing what I called "my womanpower," and the other for the fun of working within a group. I thought I had grown a lot until I began dealing with the little men in brown robes and the way they looked at the world. Viewing my own world through their eyes, I could see that I had created a mess, all of it the result of my own gutless choices that shrank from difficulty. Acutely disappointed with myself, I was sorry I had caused everyone so much pain. Why had I done everything the hard way? How had I gotten to be the way I was? It was because I believed I was supposed to do what would please everyone else.

I had been educated in and graduated from St. Augustine school in a small town in the 'thumb' area of Michigan. Between a stiff, classical education, a fairly strict father, and an old-fashioned family where men were the bosses, and women did what they were told, I had adopted the idea that a woman should be quiet and helpful, she should overlook her hurts and be willing to sacrifice herself—for what, I wasn't exactly sure.

I believed it was better to turn the other cheek when someone insulted me, to 'put myself down' in humility, to be sweet and undemanding, to not try too hard, not be too aggressive, or think I was too important. A woman's role was to give and give and give, and to do whatever was necessary to take care of others. The worst thing that could be said about a woman was that she was cold, hard, or selfish.

While living in Detroit and hauling my children back and forth to day care twice a week, contradictions to this long-held belief had appeared here and there. I met a woman who was none of the things I was raised to be. Yet I liked her and we had become good friends. As friends, we talked about many things and in some of these conversations I was horrified to discover that when there was a problem, she didn't rush in to fix it, shush it up, or gloss over it.

She had the ability to go right to the heart of a problem and bluntly state what was wrong. Because of her blunt approach, I thought she was cold and hard, and I told her I hoped I never got that way. She defended herself declaring she was a feeling, caring person who was only taking responsibility for herself. Since she *was* that way most of the time, I was never able to pinpoint exactly why I thought of her as having a cold, hard core. It didn't dawn on me that people who were willing to take responsibility for themselves were often people who were able to see what was going on at a lot of different levels, able to speak their truth, and then stand behind it. It was something I had never learned to do, and *I* was someone I had never learned to be.

Surveying my life from a calm detached place, I realized I was very close to my bachelor's degree and still didn't know who I was or what I was going to be or do with my life. About a year earlier, I had gone visiting among the various departments at Wayne State University in Detroit. I had made appointments with the chair of each department and at appointment time had inquired about the kinds of possibilities that would be open to me if I left engineering and transferred to their department.

The chair of psychology had been openly irritated with my questions regarding the mind and the possibility for unexplained perceptual phenomena also known as psychic phenomena. I left knowing that a degree in psychology would leave me hamstrung and questioning my own sanity even more so than I was already doing.

The chair of English had told me flat out that making money as a writer with four children was a pipe dream and the best I could hope for would be a position as an English teacher *if* I could find a job.

The chair of communications had gotten into an argument with me when I began asking if there was a place in communications to explore the possibilities of the human's built-in communication system. We ended up in a shouting match and I stalked out, as frustrated and insulted by his rigid ideas and superior attitude as he was with my upstart insistence that such things were possible.

When the chair of the school of education droned on with a list of intolerably boring possible paths, I ended up making an excuse to be elsewhere and left without further promise or commitment.

The result of these visits was the decision to leave engineering anyway. I had been forced to officially declare "no major" because I did not know what I wanted to be. Shortly after this I heard wonderful things about WSU's College of Lifelong Learning and decided to finish my last year there simply because they understood and were organized around the concept of integrated learning. They celebrated using all you could know, and focused on teaching us to see how inter-related things were in both cause and effect. This sounded like something I needed, and once enrolled, I loved it.

Now there were only a few credits to go. I would graduate with a degree in humanistic studies, although I still had no idea of what career path to take. Certainly I could continue teaching an intuition class here and there if I needed money, but where was I going?

My picture of the future was disturbingly hazy and unstable. In unguarded moments I pictured myself as a doctor of the body/mind system, teaching people how to stay healthy and understand their own mind... perhaps opening their consciousness so they could continue to develop themselves... or getting them to bring their special form of love and gifts into the world... but I had no idea of how to actually do any of this or where to begin.

Over the last year I'd looked at dozens of careers and none of them had job descriptions that even came close to what I kept thinking I'd like be involved in. If the world was going to change as much as the little men said it would, people would need help to make a lot of transitions. Maybe there was some way I could help them through those transitions... but nothing definite came to me as the days and hours passed.

Putting on a light jacket one evening I walked down to the edge of the bay and sat staring at the water for a long time. Shards of awareness poked at me, and question after question rolled through me. They were deep, unfathomable questions. "Who was I... what was I doing here? What was the point of my life... what was happening to me... why was it happening... how could I stop being afraid that life would turn out to be too painful, stop being afraid that unpredictable experiences would continue to happen and I would not be able to deal with them?"

There were no answers, only more questions, and when the clouds came and covered the sinking sun, I walked home, oddly peaceful for having allowed myself to ask such questions. Instead of breaking, I felt like something in me was turning cold and hard.

To my surprise, the ability to ask the hard questions and see things this way brought a sense of power, the kind of power that comes from knowing *what is*. This brought a sense of truth, the kind of jarring truth one experiences when looking an attacker in the eye just before being pushed over a cliff and into the sea far below. It was a knowing that life was taking an unexpected turn that could not be stopped. For the moment,

I could only struggle on, hoping to regain my footing. As darkness slowly fell, I walked home, precariously suspended. 📖

15 📖

FOOD, MOLECULES, AND MEDICINE…

STILL on the edge of that precipice and struggling for balance a few days later, I was weeping in frustration when the little men' appeared. Using a most polite and gentle attitude they said, "We are sorry that you are confused. We have hoped that the things we showed you would help you through this transition toward doing what you came here to do. And we have more pieces of information about the things to come. Would you like to see them?"

"Why not…?" I said, sniffling with a 'poor-me' attitude, then went into the living room, sat down on the floor in front of the sofa, and leaned against it with a sigh. Once my eyes were closed, reality shifted sharply and without delay I found myself in what was obviously a jungle. No people were in sight so I looked around. The trees and plants were growing densely and flowering vines wound upwards. There was an open space just a few feet in front of me and in the middle of that space a few stalks of corn were growing tall and spindly. After a minute of quiet, I wondered what I was supposed to be seeing.

In answer to my thought, the little men began.

"You are seeing exactly what we are hoping you would see, the corn in the midst of the jungle. Although you and the rest of your people do not acknowledge the presence of plants in the way that you acknowledge the presence of animals and other humans, be aware that plants are most definitely aware of and acknowledging you! In fact, we would like to ask you a new question with an old concept behind it. 'Is a corn plant still a corn plant if there is no human to celebrate and eat it's gift of corn?'"

They paused briefly while I was busy in my mind, trying to translate my understanding of the old question, 'If a tree falls in the forest, and there is no one around to hear it crash, did it make any noise?' I struggled for a few moments, but had never known how to think about the tree riddle, so I couldn't quite grasp how to think about the corn question either.

After a brief, polite wait, the little men continued.

"The answer is *no*. The intelligence that is corn has no need to become a corn plant that will nourish human life except in response to the need of the human to have something to eat. You and the corn are part of a oneness in which the need for food is one side of the equation and the appearance of corn is the other. For all intents, you cannot have the corn without the need to be physically nurtured, and you cannot have the need for physical nurturing without the corn.

"At any one time and place, plants, animals, and humans here on Earth are perfectly suited to meet one another's needs. At all times plants, animals, and humans are changing; you all come into being, develop, flower, and decline in response to one another's presence. During the time of the dinosaurs, plants were much different. Yet these plants and the dinosaurs around them were perfectly suited to support, nurture, and shelter one another.

"For example, as the human began to evolve, flowers with brightly colored petals and the ability to help develop human emotions began to appear. The early human experienced a visual delight at the sight of a flower, while the unique and subtle chemistry and color frequencies of each blossom had profound effects on feeling and emotion at the very time the emotional centers of the brain were developing further. The appearance of flowers not only helped the early humans to learn to recognize emotions and the changes in behavior these emotions brought, they helped develop the ability to concentrate attention, which made many other kinds of perception and feeling possible.

"Other plants had other effects, but just like the corn, every single plant upon the earth developed in response to your needs and the needs of other animals. In a perfectly functioning world system no need goes unfilled, for the plants maintain a constant awareness of the animals and humans around them and respond intuitively to every possible condition. Their whole existence and purpose is to be there for you in every capacity, as food, as oxygen source, as companions, as artwork, as medicine, as spirit helpers, as protectors, to assist in your evolution, to open the connection to oneness, to smooth your births, to carry you out of the body when you choose to leave here, to facilitate communication with other forms, to remind you of your creative skills, to become your tools, and to be useful to you in ten thousand other ways.

"Plants, fellow travelers also sojourning on earth, are responsible for maintaining your life, and you cannot, under pain of death, ignore this or pretend otherwise. As human development is rekindled, you will see that you cannot decide to make and eat substitutes for plants, legislate the restricted use of plants, or mindlessly destroy the environment that you and plants thrive in. When you do *any* of these, you will experience disease and pain, joy will turn to sorrow, and peace of mind will dwindle. Without a strong and ongoing connection to the world of plants, you will live with a sense of anxiety that swings between irritation with your self and outright war with others. Your creative abilities will run amok, leading you to destruction and death."

Suddenly speaking directly to me, the little men said pointedly, "Although you, personally, are highly biased against those you dismiss as ecological fanatics, you will come to understand in great detail this network of intelligent life that connects all, that holds and heals all. When you understand that you cannot be healthy without a direct relationship to the plants that are meant to be your food and companions, you will have come a long way toward becoming the doctor you have always dreamed of being, one who heals truly. By the time you have come to grips with all of the information we are showing you, you will have learned a great deal on your own about plants, food, health, joy, and healing. In addition, you will have learned to see and understand things in a global way and it is our hope that you will share both the knowledge and your perspective with others, along with the information that we are showing you."

Abruptly they returned to their narrative.

"To better understand the nature of healing, it will be helpful for you to know something of how plants, animals, and humans affect one another. The earth, its plants, animals, and people are living beings composed of billions upon trillions of atoms and molecules. As we have already pointed out, each molecule is a wave of energy flowing in a unique pattern and repeating itself as a unique set of frequencies. Think of each molecule as a tiny tuning center, much like a string on a piano or guitar. Each tuning center vibrates at its own perfect pitch, generating a host of subtle sub-tones, and this basic-frequency-plus-sub-tones is the set of frequency waves used to trigger chemical reactions. When the body is healthy, all of its molecules are 'in tune' and maintain a wide variety of functions with little effort.

"Now, let us say the body is not healthy. In actuality, what has happened is that one or more of the tuning centers have gone out of tune. It is no longer vibrating at the correct frequency. If this is allowed to continue, it will trigger a host of unhappy physical events, but by eating a selected plant with the correct complex of frequencies in it, you can tune up the out-of-tune molecules through the principal of resonance.

"For example, when you eat a carrot or a cucumber, some parsley or a potato, your stomach and digestive system immediately set to work to tear down the physical structure of the plant until all that is left are the pure mineral elements and their frequencies. These elements might be iron or calcium, magnesium or potassium, for these are a few of the building blocks that plants use to build themselves up in the first place.

"Once the carrot or parsley has been digested and separated into its basic elements, these elements and their frequencies are carried by the blood to all parts of the body where the action of resonance between the two sets of frequencies—the human's and the plant's—will bring the frequencies of the human body back in tune and thus back into correct function.

"Simply stated, when a human being eats a plant, what he is really doing is attempting to keep the body operating and 'in tune' by exposing it to the frequencies that were used to create the carrot, the parsley, or the potato. The healing happens due to the processes of constructive inter-ference. Each kind of food contains a unique mixture of substances and thus each kind of food does a certain kind of re-tuning.

"The individual intelligence of each plant expresses its purpose by creating a fruit that contains a particular combination of substances with unique capabilities. The kind of energy in the food produced is modified in various ways and these modifications show up as differences in size, shape, color, and density. Each fruit or vegetable has singular sensitivities and specialized abilities designed to work with human molecules by recognizing and communicating with the molecules within the cells of the human body.

"The minerals, enzymes, and vitamins associated with a given kind of plant develop in response to the total complex of frequencies they find in their daily external environment. Thus the Vitamin A from one carrot is not the same kind of Vitamin A from another carrot grown in another part of the country with a different environment, and both of these are different from the Vitamin A found in a sweet potato or a peach. Once eaten, the individual frequencies and sub-tones of each plant's version of Vitamin A will enhance, change, or moderate the cellular frequencies they encounter inside the body in their own distinct ways.

"Keep in mind that the frequency pattern of a food plant helps determine both the path and the action of molecular and cellular energy as it moves through the body. By learning to trace wave actions forward and backward, you will learn to see how the energy of the wave helps create form.

"Once created, any form works by channeling some energy through itself, and other energy around itself. This makes certain kinds of cyclic functions possible, depending on the routes and repetitions of the cycle. The cycle of these functions, in turn, affects the flow of wave energy in and around other forms, sometimes modifying those forms further, sometimes stabilizing them. Thus, in a simplified way, you can see that frequency arrangements end up determining form, form channels energy, energies have function, and function has the capability of altering form in an endlessly unfolding circle of creativity.

"What we would like you to see here is that your current system of chemical medicine is doomed and there are several reasons for this. These chemicals have lower levels of living intelligence simply because they have not been transformed by time spent *inside* plant intelligence.

"A useful analogy here would be to say that when a mineral or chemical element spends time inside a plant, it becomes somewhat educated. In a sense, it learns to read its environment and express itself better. It polishes its communication skills, and adapts to working with other elements in a highly productive fashion. It learns how to build living systems, discovers how to identify problems of poor construction at the molecular level, and how to correct them by coordinating all available resources at its disposal. These resources are the unique mix of compounds, minerals, enzymes, and vitamins that are found in the soil, water, or air, as well as those that can be created within the plant itself.

"When a raw mineral or element has been educated by time spent in a living, organic plant, it will join with neighboring elements to create a strong and unique symphony of frequencies and sub-tones.

"When this symphony is introduced to a human body having a set of molecules whose frequencies have gotten out of tune, the plant frequencies will set up a consistent resonance, gradually bringing those molecules back in tune and thus into a state of health.

"There will also be restoration of neighboring molecules that receive directions from the group that was out of tune and sending badly garbled messages, as well as those whose job it was to send messages *to* the molecules that got out of tune. These neighbors may have exhausted themselves by either trying to understand the garbled directions, or by sending enough messages to get the renegade molecules to follow the communications being broadcast.

"The chemicals used in medicines of today, have no helpful assistance from intelligent, educated frequencies that nurture a return of the body to correct form and function, and worse, the subtle, supporting sub-tones are absent. There is no help from intelligent assistants, living enzymes, or vitamins, and you are rewarded with disastrous side effects tantamount to removing a wart with a sledgehammer.

"The chemical or drug ends up working in a sudden and heavy-handed fashion, destroying the molecules causing the problem, yet failing to restore them. The symptoms stop but the problem does not go away because the chemical does not contain the corrective frequencies that will guide molecules in the body back to a healthy, productive course of action. The destruction caused by these chemicals seriously interferes with whatever functioning the body does manage to maintain.

"The human being is a sophisticated association of molecules governed by a delicate balance of wave frequencies. There will come a day when you will look back on your twentieth century medicine as barbaric. You will ask yourself how you could have thought you could pour poison into a body and hope it would heal, or subject it to the frequency of the x-ray and think you were helping. You will wonder whatever made you think you could chop off an ailing part and not address the cause of the problem in the first place.

"The cause of illness and disease in your time runs very deep and people are overwhelmed in their efforts to assess the causes and correct them. With typical tangling of issues and illusions you have come to the point where the majority of your corrections are incorrect. Why? Because you have lost your connection to the earth and her plants. You have ignored the basic laws of nature, forgotten the basic knowledge, and this ignorance alone is enough to threaten your continued existence, notwithstanding all the other factors that can disrupt human lives.

"Your medicine people and scientists are blaming bad genes for the diseases you cannot heal. Your genes are not really the culprits. Each gene is actually a small, encoded and enfolded form of intelligent wave energy. It is triggered into action by exposure to a specific, pre-set frequency having a set of sub-tones which together act as the keys to unlocking the sequential actions encoded in the gene.

"These specific 'key' frequencies are found in the plants and foods you are meant to eat. When you eat the correct range of foods, the gene is triggered into action and its function unfolds beautifully and effortlessly, creating a whole cascade of healthy effects in the body.

"When the gene is present—but never stimulated—its protective or maintenance effect is never generated. At best, the human will continue to live, but at a reduced level of health and performance. If this human reproduces itself in a new infant, the new baby may have the same reduced level of function. Yet with the correct stimulation, both could have some chance to awaken the neglected gene and thus benefit from some of the protective effects of the gene. Or, both parent and child may die prematurely, ignorant of the fact that the solution to the problems was inside them.

"If this line of humans with a none-functioning gene continues to reproduce without ever triggering the gene into operation they can reach the point where the gene no longer forms at all, or forms incorrectly, and you have the reality of an inherited defect. From this point forward, humans born into this family find that they lack a certain kind of protective function, a specific immune response does not occur and they are more at risk for a given disease than those who live in other families.

"If the gene is present yet poorly formed, and happens to be triggered into action, the malformed gene can create a stream of malfunctions in the body. An unfolding cascade of effects occurs, but the frequencies are out of tune, rhythm, or sequence, and the effect on the body is devastating, even destructive, instead of protective. These defects are tragic mostly because they are unnecessary.

"Slowly you will come to see that the problem of poor health, sickness, anger, depression, disease, and disfigurement is really a problem in the relationship between humans and plants, between humans and the Earth.

"If you are wise, you will come to realize that a good relationship with the Earth and plants will be needed if you wish to survive. This realization will be delayed if you are racing off to an office or a factory every day in your struggle for money, thus inching yourself closer to disease and destruction. You and your children will continue to be unhappy and antagonistic until you once again connect yourselves to the flow of information that is meant to move from the land to the human by way of plants.

"By reflecting on all of this you will come to realize that most diseases can be undone, sometimes immediately, sometimes within a generation or two, by the correct combination of plants and foods, and many can be prevented altogether.

"As time goes by, you will come to learn more and more about frequencies. The only thing to beware of is the mistake of thinking that you can forego your relationship to plants and use technologically generated frequencies to eliminate disease and dysfunction. On a small scale, you will be able to accomplish some healing using frequencies from such things as music, lights, and frequency field generators. But these are stopgap measures in that they do not have an intelligent group of frequencies at their core, and often the correct sub-tones are missing. The basis of all health will be found in the plants that thrive in your local environment, and until the human has evolved beyond food, or you are able to instantly generate a living plant using frequencies alone, you will not be able to say that you understand frequencies, or that you know how to use frequencies for healing.

"Having said this, we would encourage you to continue your research into the nature of waves, frequencies, and wave fields of varying kinds. Eventually, with careful study and experimentation you will find that any life-threatening disease, from cancers to AIDS and beyond, can be quickly and completely healed by careful exposure to the correct frequencies. However, once returned to health, you must maintain this state by feeding and maintaining yourself with food from plants until you have evolved much further.

"In fact, a state of extraordinary health of both body and mind is a basic requirement for further human development. If you are healthy, you will be better able to perceive and manage your knowledge of frequencies, not only for healing purposes, but for other things as well.

"You will find that by using certain frequencies, even the dead who have not suffered too much destruction of tissue can be brought back to life without damage. You will be able to construct transportation systems that move people and objects almost instantly. Even a simple form of frequency knowledge would allow you to build cars and trucks that refused to bump into one another just like two positively charged particles refuse to come in contact. You would be able to develop communication systems that would allow concept communication between people who do not speak the same language. You would be able to communicate with people from the past, and people from the future, as well as those from other realms and star systems.

"You would be able to disintegrate dead bodies instantly without need for caskets and funeral stones, to disintegrate old buildings, or when more practical, to renew them by performing instant rejuvenation of their materials. You could erect barriers and security points without physical walls or humans to patrol them. You might learn to apply frequencies to fields and forests, recreating the giant plants and species of the past, increase the size and yield of plants in your fields and gardens, or grow luxuriously healthy and nutritious plants in your basement throughout the year. You would be able to warm yourselves in winter or cool yourselves in summer, enjoy the possibilities of creating new forms of plants, new minerals, metals, fabrics, and many other things using frequency manipulation. And these are elementary operations.

"Of course there are obvious possibilities for mischief in bloodless wars, or the use of wave frequencies to disintegrate a life form, whether human or otherwise, but the benefits for a healthy, balanced human are nearly unlimited. You will find that the more you try to reach out into the universe, the deeper you will have to reach into yourself. The more you try to manage the things around you, the more you will have to learn to manage yourselves.

"What we hope to do here is teach you to see your selves and your world, including plants, animals, people, and their support structures, as one continuous system, dependent on one another in the most intimate of ways. All of this information is geared partly to lead you toward a deeper understanding of health, which is necessary to help you re-ignite your development and evolution. You can only be motivated to take on the challenges of your situation when you can see clearly *what is* now, what is meant to be, and get some encouragement to begin the changes you are headed toward."

With that, they nodded goodbye and faded away. 📖

16 📖

EVOLUTION, TIME-SPACE, AND FREQUENCY BANDS...

BY the end of July, the visits of the little men were taking their toll. The information and perceptual experiences they shared left me in an increasingly awkward position. Getting my degree seemed pointless. Going to work for someone else felt like a mistake in direction. Working for money appeared senseless, like a scam designed by the government to get me to pay income taxes and force me into a system that was about to disintegrate.

I had no career goals left, no money, no job prospects, and a huge, two-year gap in my career history that could not be explained away by the fact that I was still working my way toward a degree at the university.

I didn't know what I wanted to do with my life, didn't fit into the ordinary world any more, and didn't want my life to be driven by the clock, the job, or the paycheck. When I thought about starting a business of my own, I was afraid that it would not support me on a long-term basis. Worse, I couldn't think of anything to do, and was sure it would fall apart when the world rolled over. I was overwhelmed with too many changes in too short a time and caught in feeling sorry for myself.

In direct contradiction to the morass of self-pity I wallowed in, there was something in the back of my mind, or perhaps my heart, that was so powerful even touching the edges of it frightened me. It was a deep, tender, unshakable, sometimes sensuous, sometimes motherly, occasionally fierce, love. As if it were a seething volcano of liquid fire that rumbled constantly in the background of my consciousness, I skirted the edges of this great love gingerly, content to leave it out of my daily affairs. Paradoxically, I would fret about it, then turn around and touch it just to reassure myself it was still there.

"What am I going to do with all that love?" I asked myself, mourning the emptiness and disintegration of my life and goals. Afraid the fire of that love would consume me, afraid of its powerful compassion, afraid other people would see it or sense it and be as frightened as I was, and having nowhere to spend it, I hid it, keeping it under rigid control. Stupidly, it didn't occur to me to lavish it on myself. Love was reserved for others, especially for that special 'other.'

📖

One night, released early from class at WSU, I went with five or six other students to sit along the shores of Lake St. Clair in Grosse Pointe Woods. Someone was just spreading a blanket on the ground for us to sit on when one of the men in the group said in a sharp voice, "What's that?!"

We all looked up toward the water where he was staring. There floated a large silver craft about five hundred feet above the waves. The craft had a large dome sitting atop a wide, flat deck, and mounted on the outside edges of the deck were four rows of lights that revolved around the deck. A slanted break in the positioning of the lights made it possible to see that the lights were revolving.

As it hovered there, we all stared. No one said a word; perhaps everyone was holding his or her breath. I gazed at the craft, struck by the thought that this craft, a typical flying saucer, was there specifically for my benefit and that someone or something was trying to break my entire perception of the world.

Without a sound, the craft swirled to the north and in the space of a blink, was hovering over Grosse Pointe Yacht Club about half a mile to the north. We continued to stare at it. After a brief pause, it drifted further out over the water, then suddenly shot up and out of sight, disappearing into the heavens.

For a minute or so we stood there, frozen, and finally someone said, "It's a good thing we didn't open that bottle of wine yet or I would have blamed what I just saw on the wine!" Laughter followed and we sat down, speculating on the flying saucer for a bit; but when talk turned to other things, I could not get comfortable with the conversation or the people I was with.

The conversation was shallow, the points of view expressed from minute to minute had no depth, the jokes and banter felt cruel, and I kept having the impression I was sitting on the shore with a group of hollow people whose emptiness clanged in the silence that filled me.

Ashamed of such perceptions, I blamed this new and unexpected incompatibility on the little men in brown robes, then the effects of kundalini, then the fact that I had been so isolated for the past two years. None of this blame for the cause of my discomfort served to lessen the gulf that stretched between myself and the rest of the group, and finally, chilly and tired, I got up to leave.

All the way home I examined the evening. I had lost some essential ability to connect to people in the ways I had always found so natural. Other people were the same as they had always been, but something deep, something in the core of my being was different.

I didn't see the things they saw any more, or hear what they heard, and I didn't think like they thought. What was more difficult, I didn't feel about myself, my life, or their presence they way they seemed to feel about themselves, their lives, or my presence. It was like watching myself walk along the bottom of the ocean while trying to maintain relationships with people who were splashing and swimming on the surface. Communication suffered from all the attendant distortions of water, waves, and the differing angles of refracted light. I felt I was living in a new and different medium, one in which I should have had great difficulty breathing and navigating. Instead, I was having difficulty in my old medium, the one that had once been so familiar and comfortable.

At home, the house loomed dark and lonely. Reaching inside the front door I switched on the light and found the little men in brown robes standing in the living room.

They greeted me with great energy saying, "Good evening! How wise it is to get out and stretch yourself in the company of others."

This comment reminded me that they knew what went on in my life and how I was feeling without me telling them, and for the first time, this seemed not only normal, but natural, even desirable.

Reflecting again on the events of the evening and the glaring absence of that connection to people I had always felt, it dawned on me how much time I spent trying to communicate my thoughts and ideas. Even more time went into listening to people trying to tell me their thoughts, ideas, and problems. Too often I knew what they were going to say before they said it, but given our culture and the manners I had been taught, it would have been impolite to interrupt and say, "I know... I know... I know that already." The awareness that people weren't looking for a solution also bothered me. They didn't want brainstorming, insight, or ideas. They wanted to talk on and on about what they were going through.

Gratefulness washed over me that I didn't have to explain what I was thinking, feeling, or going through to the little men. There was no need to cover it up either. They knew, I knew that they knew, and it suddenly seemed like a waste of time and energy to communicate the way humans had always communicated.

This train of thought was interrupted by the little men who remarked, "Yes, it is more time-consuming, but it is the way things are done here, and it is our hope that humans will soon come around to doing things the old way."

"'The old way?" I asked. "You mean we used to communicate telepathically and lost that ability somehow?"

"Yes, and although you believe you are the most advanced creatures ever to inhabit the earth, you are children compared to others who have been here and gone in earlier civilizations, or those here on the planet that you are unable to see at all! Now, in the hope that your civilization will survive and prosper with its continued development, we have more pictures to show you if you are willing."

When I had agreed and seated myself on the sofa, their pictures and sounds, surrounded me, filled me, and within a short time I was in a totally unfamiliar environment. Blackness was everywhere. Here and there, out of the blackness, a light would come toward me, bringing a distinct set of thoughts complete with sensations and emotions. These thoughts, sensations, and feelings would envelope me briefly, there would be the sensation I was being explored, then it would all disappear. What seemed like minutes later, another light with a different set of thoughts and emotions would surround and fill me, explore, then leave.

One such set contained the thought, "You are an excellent student with all the right questions. Never stop pushing for answers and you will reach your goal."

"What goal is that?" I wondered, thinking the message had something to do with my college degree.

"To gather your selves back together and return to your source, which will then be the end of time."

This was not what I expected to hear, and I assumed it was some kind of religious message with an unintelligible prediction for the people of our planet, but before I could ask for an explanation, the little men began their narration of what would turn out to be, for me, the most difficult yet fascinating of their visits.

"Although you do not yet understand the how and why of our communication with you, or the many varieties of perception and knowing you have encountered over the past two years, do not be concerned about this. You will understand completely, but not for some years yet.

"Since you have now had many experiences out of the body or in other dimensions, it should be clear to you that reality is far more complex and has many fewer limitations than your culture teaches. Common points of your old belief system include a god in heaven encouraging you to be good, and a devil in hell tempting you to be bad.

"In truth, there is no heaven, there is no hell, there is no god of righteousness waiting to judge or punish you, there is no devil trying to entrap you into his fires. These are only belief systems, similar to your concepts of Santa Claus and Easter Rabbit, useful for those who have not discovered that the god power they seek is inside them. These people struggle because they refuse to integrate their inner authority or accept responsibility for what they are creating. They use whatever authority they do have to declare the authority of *outer* gods and devils and do not recognize it is their own *inner* authority that is declaring this to be so!

"The human being is here to immerse the Self in experiences that will advance evolution within and toward the Godhead. Simply stated, the main purpose for your immersion in the time-space world of planet Earth is to enhance your ability to create life.

"Everything that you see, hear, or feel on Earth, from the human form to the stars and the galaxies, is constructed using a selective band of frequencies. Space is an ocean of frequencies, time is the perception of frequencies, and the task of human life is to explore the possibilities and the limitations of these inherent frequencies. You are here to experiment with shaping these frequency waves in new and creative ways, then to observe the effects and retain what is good or useful for your ongoing evolution and development.

"The goals in creating are, first, that your creation must be life-extending, and second, that it be life-sustaining. Although you are free to create anything you choose, these are the basic laws of creation and you would be wise to hold them as your main rules of thumb when creating anything.

"By definition, to create something that is life-extending means that it must exhibit the properties of life. These basic properties are intelligence, the ability to reproduce, and the ability to generate love. Intelligence is a form of self-knowledge, reproduction allows you to copy yourself, and love is a formative educational force characterized by the ability to communicate and evolve without limitations.

"To create something self-sustaining is to instill the ability to repair and renew your form endlessly using the natural laws of regeneration, transformation, and evolution.

"You will know that you have created something *without* the basic properties that all true and eternal creations must have when the things you create do not have these abilities and take unending amounts of time and energy to sustain or re-create.

"At this point in time, humans here on the planet are life-extending in the sense that they have intelligence and can reproduce, but they have not yet learned to generate love. And strictly defined, they are not yet life-sustaining. All human forms eventually die, partly because you have decided this, and partly because the form itself has limited eternal value until you learn to self-sustain. However, it does have great intrinsic value as a vehicle for adding to your power and wisdom in creating.

"Because the current form lacks eternal value, those who are responsible for creating and destroying in the greater scheme of things beyond time-space have no particular qualms about the death of human beings, especially since death is one of your own created decisions. However, because of your capacity to evolve, humans are observed and nurtured in the hope that the evolution will continue. If it becomes clear that this is not going to happen, nurturing will be withdrawn and destruction of the form will be allowed to occur. We do not want you to feel abandoned or fearful about this, we simply wish to acknowledge what is at present.

"Having said this, we also wish you to know that as human beings, you have not been destroyed by what you think of as your maker for several reasons. One is that there is no maker as you visualize one. It would be closer to the truth to say that you are self-created, and if you are destroyed, it will be due to self-destruction.

"Another reason is that you have the ability to reproduce your-selves, and because of this you provide a continual supply of opportunities for beings to enter the time-space continuum and to experiment with the many expressions of life available here.

"A third reason is that the Earth is a very useful, powerful place to learn unique approaches to creating under severe and limiting conditions. And a fourth is that you will either end up destroying your own selves, or you will learn to go beyond your present crisis, re-create yourselves, and leave as a group.

"Even though humans are not yet fully life-extending or life-sustaining, the general practice in the universe of creator beings existing outside the time-space continuum is that once a new kind of living form has been created, it is best to leave it alone enough to allow full discovery of the adventure and laws of life. These beings keep watch until the new form comes to the great fork in the road, and then nurture it carefully in the hope that it will make the right decision—which is the choice to align itself with either creating or destroying.

"Regardless of which system they exist in, many beings choose to align with creating. To align with destroying always, and we do mean *always*, leads to destruction of the form and whatever that form has created. Alignment with creating allows for the continued evolution of the form until it either becomes fully life-extending and life-sustaining, or is incorporated into a being that already has those capabilities.

"Frequently there is some resistance or unwillingness to shoulder the responsibility for making such a choice. However, the choice must be made, will be made, whether by intention or default. If the choice is to align with destruction, and you are already on that path, nothing more need be done beyond what is already being done. The destruction will proceed naturally.

"If the choice is to align with creating, then adjustments must be made to shift into frequencies that remove certain limitations and allow for expansion.

"If you choose to align with creating and are *not* already on that path, then very careful attention must be paid to the processes of the shift. It is during the shift that stability as an organism is most vulnerable and most likely to fail or disintegrate. The individual or group must have access to wisdom that provides reliable information and guidance, and they must learn to see backward and forward in time so that all possibilities and outcomes are examined and accounted for.

"All other beings in the universe who have evolved beyond you have faced the same question, 'Shall we align ourselves with creation, and learn to use our power to create even further... or is this enough and we are satisfied with what we have created and with where we are in our growth and development?'

"Only those beings who deliberately, consciously, choose to align themselves with life and the creative, then base all further action on that choice are given the secrets to the deeper powers of creation... and only *after* they have dealt with all those in their group who are not interested in alignment with creating. This includes dealing with those who don't want destruction but don't want change either, those who cannot seem to recognize the need to make a clear choice, and those who recognize the need for a choice but who sit, undecided, on the fence waiting to see what happens to others before they make a decision to join them.

"Many beings, including humans, want a 'sure thing' or a guarantee of what they're getting into. They don't realize until too late that it *is* too late, then they suffer unnecessarily or give up in pain because they did not allow enough time to make the required changes. Others cling to old ways and cannot get their minds around the totality of the changes coming at them. They fall further and further away from the energy of the group, lapsing into helplessness and becoming a burden for the whole group until they die and pass away. Therefore, it is not unusual for several generations to pass before the shift is complete.

"To emphasize the importance of what we are saying here, we would like to repeat. Because of the properties of life itself, every form of humanity that has ever been on this planet has eventually come to the choice between creating or destroying. You and your entire group of fellow humans are at this point now.

"Because it is important to grasp these concepts so that human evolution can continue, we will present them now, planting them in your consciousness like seeds in the hope that they will sprout and grow when the time and conditions are right.

"You have not even begun to imagine your potential as creators, yet the evolution toward this function continues. After you have made the choice to align with creating—but before you can go much further—you must begin to explore and discover the wholeness of which you are a part.

"The portion of you that remains outside the spectrum of physical frequencies during the life of the human form maintains full memory of who you are, how you are, and where you come from. This greater part of your Self is able to communicate instantly with you, with all of the humans it has currently seeded, and with its other beings, whether these are in or out of the physical time-space system.

"Through the subjective, intuitive side of your mind you have full access to the greater being that you are outside the time-space system simply by shifting frequency sets. Should you go exploring and connect with this part of the Self, you will find a fountain of wisdom and guidance for yourself.

"The connection, which is through inner channels of communication, would allow you to discover all that you have ever been. All of the physical personalities you have developed, lived, and learned from, as well as the experiences you have had in other frequency bands, create the *whole* self which you are continuously building and shaping, moving toward full creator status.

"It is possible for you to remember who and what you are, but to do this you must be able to understand and utilize mind and perception differently than you have in the past.

"Most of the difficulties that you, personally, have had since the awakening of your mind involve the uncontrolled shifting of your brain into and out of other frequencies, presenting you with information and experience in a variety of places and times all at once. You were unaware that frequency zones exist, and are now discovering these and the information they carry. You are learning to tune into these experiences at the same time you are having experiences in your normal physical reality. This ability is considered normal in other realms.

"Generally, people do not have a clear idea of how the brain works to create perception or access memory. The brain is a collection of nerve cells and each individual cell is attached to frequency receptors. Each receptor is attuned for the whole of its life to a singular wave frequency. Whenever you tune into a pattern of frequency waves, each individual wave in the pattern triggers a 'recognition response' in the particular receptor within your brain that has learned to respond to that unique frequency. Thus, what you experience as perception is really the act of tuning in to a familiar pattern that exists in the ocean of frequencies that surround you, usually because you have been taught to do so.

"Familiar patterns will be recognized and interpreted instantly, often before you are conscious of perceiving them. Unfamiliar patterns may be perceived as foggy or confused, and some of them are disregarded even when fully present. When you wish to learn new patterns that are constructed with unfamiliar frequencies, your brain will adjust gradually and, if necessary, will dedicate new cells to aid in their recognition.

"Cell receptors also respond to unfamiliar patterns that have characteristics *similar* to a pattern they would normally recognize. This response makes some understanding possible when novelty is encountered, and creates 'layers' of symbolism, which allow for increasing complexity.

"Perception is dynamically created moment by moment as the brain constantly scans the fields of frequencies surrounding you and responds to what it finds there. A reality is stabilized by tuning to the same patterns again and again, experiencing what is available there. The evolution of a reality becomes stalled when you tune in to the same patterns too often. When this occurs, you are not creating perception, you are stuck in memory.

"Memory is not as you usually think of it. There is no such thing as a location in the brain in which memory is stored. Because of the nature of time-space, all that has ever happened or ever will happen is happening at one time. When you want to 'remember' something, what you are essentially doing is tuning your brain cells to the same frequency pattern that comprised the original event. Doing this will actually re-display the entire event—which is an ongoing event within eternity—and you are able to perceive the experience all over again. You can re-perceive the event with the same sensations and emotions or, if you wish, from an entirely new perspective.

"This is what makes it possible for a hypnotist to take someone back to the scene of a crime or an accident and allow them to recall many more details than they at first noticed. It's because it's all still there and able to be examined in greater detail. This is also the basis for Freud's psychotherapy. The events that proved to be stressful or so unbalancing for an individual are still going on. That fact will not change. But the way the events were perceived and the decisions made during the experience can be expanded or contracted; and the entire event can be re-experienced and re-worked in every way.

"Thus you see the potential for re-creating yourselves, even though most of you put great energy into maintaining and defending the way you were yesterday or last year. You are meant to evolve! In the time-space realm, the only thing set in concrete is cement itself, and even cement is temporary in many cases.

"To further your evolution, mind is both the material to be worked with, and the tool used to do the work. The objective side of the mind is a wonderful instrument for creating once it has been seeded by the visions that are accessible through the subjective side of mind. And the possibilities for creating are endless, unless a reality becomes stalled.

"As humans you regularly become caught up in the sensory input coming from your immediate physical environment and do not pay attention to information available from other frequency bands and their patterns. In addition, you do not understand *how* to shift among the many available frequency patterns and end up believing that your small reality is all there is.

"You have heard or read that the human uses only a small percent of the brain and there has been much speculation as to why this is so. The reason is because from the time you are young you learn to recognize only a small band of frequencies, then use them repeatedly. The remainder go unused, but they are not meant to sit idle.

"Some are to be used for perception of other frequency bands. Some are to be used for transmitting messages over long physical distances, while others are for receiving messages over these same distances. There are frequency groups meant to be used as modulators for perception in other realms altogether. A few can be used as generators of frequencies for assembling or disassembling physical reality. Some are useful for communicating with the whole Self, including the greater you who waits outside the physical frequencies for your return. Know that there are other uses besides these, but these are some of the basics.

"Due to the cyclical nature of time-space, all civilizations move back and forth between subjectivity and objectivity. Subjectivity allows the visions necessary for creating. Objectivity allows for the actual, hands-on work. A return to subjectivity allows for further visions, as well as evaluation and correction of what has been created making sure that you are still on the path to creation rather than destruction.

"Your civilization has been engaged in objectivity for some time now and is about to cycle into subjectivity. At the end of the last cycle of subjectivity, you had become mired in superstition. At it's beginning, however, subjective reality was carefully explored and constantly compared to outer reality in an effort to determine the laws of life. Things that happened in close sequence in your mind were categor-ized as 'cause and effect.'

"Subjectivity became corrupt when those in power began to insist that the subjective events going on *inside an unwanted individual* were the cause of unfortunate or disastrous events taking place in the outside world. Subjectivity became an excuse to harm or get rid of others.

"As you swung round to the objective end of the cycle, subjectivity came to be viewed with contempt. It disappeared into a cupboard labeled 'uncontrolled, unreasonable, and unverifiable.'

"At present you have over-subscribed to objectivity to the degree that it has become uncontrolled, unreasonable, and irrelevant. Science is disdainful of subjective experience because it cannot be dissected, it doesn't lend itself to endlessly repeatable experiments, and they do not know how to analyze the deeper expressions of it. Making this situation worse are the scientists who do not trust their own experience because they have no inner authority and have never learned how to use subjectivity.

If subjective reality functioned the way science wanted it to, you would all be robots, endlessly repeating the same behaviors, the same words, regardless of effect or affect. Without subjectivity, you would go on ignoring the question of whether your actions and responses were appropriate or inappropriate. You would be heedless of what you caused or how you were affected by what you created.

"In your objective rush to scientifically explore and explain the universe, you have begun declaring all sorts of laws and rules that too quickly dismiss the subjective experiences and observations others may legitimately have. This runs counter to the reason for your being here in the first place, which is to learn and modulate creating! To make matters worse, you claim that all these rules and laws are 'scientific' truth.

"As we have pointed out in an earlier visit, science, once a great and revered way of discovering the hidden laws of the universe, has become just as corrupt as subjectivity once was. It has been used in many ways to maintain and control the present structures of power, and you are now ready for a new cycle of subjectivity, hopefully one that is balanced with objectivity.

"The thing to watch for in this cycle is not superstition or the attempt to blame external troubles on the inner workings of individuals, but the tendency to over-focus on the subjective experience. The adventure within brings a fascinating spiritual awakening, and you can end up losing connections with others who are important to your physical survival. And attempting to produce a continuous string of subjective experiences just for the sake of the high levels of excitement they bring will be like dragging the repeatable, mass-production aspect of objectivity into the realms of subjectivity.

"The real goal, the required goal is to rest comfortably in suspension somewhere between subjectivity and objectivity. Where to rest, and how to express yourself from that resting point, is a very personalized choice.

"The properties of the subjective self are creative, perceptive, mutative, and cannot often be seen by others. Neither can this subjective self be measured with the physical instruments you have available. Subjectivity is based in the deep pools of potential that spring continuously into existence either through the thought and intent of your whole self, or as a natural response of the self to the existing forms and frequencies it encounters!

"The properties of the objective self are of a more concrete nature. They *can* be seen and heard by others, as well as measured and enjoyed with the physical senses. Objectivity is also based in the deep pools of potential that spring continuously into existence through the thoughts and intent of your whole self and is often expressed through the mental and manual skills of its own human form!

"It is only by reaching into the deepest part of the subjective core for ideas and visions, then going back to express those visions in an objective way that a good balance of creative power can be maintained.

"The challenge is not in trying to prove that one side of yourself is better, more real, or more necessary than the other, it is to discover the high levels of creative expression that are possible when there is a balanced relationship between the subjective self and the objective world it is creating. To overlook objectivity or negate subjectivity leads to an incomplete, eventually dysfunctional reality. To weigh and measure objective reality, yet neglect to assess and evaluate it subjectively, is to miss half the reality. The equation can only be fully understood and developed when both the observer and the observed are taken into account. And development of yourselves as creators can only be advanced when you understand the true nature of the expressive relationship between the observer and the observed.

"Each individual is a unique filter of the frequencies that surround the human body/mind system. Each human brain is a radio receiver responding to the matrix of waves and energy flowing through and around it.

"The brain's job is to help the human body respond appropriately to the ocean of frequencies it lives in, and be a tool by which you explore those frequencies and the possibilities within them. To do so is literally to explore the possibilities of the Self. The process is meant to be shared with others in the way you used to share when you were children by saying, 'Hey, look what I found... Hey, look what I can do... You can probably do it too.'

"Instead of asking others what they see or what they have found, you have all gotten off track and into the habit of trying to *tell* others what they see, hear, feel or have found! Rather than exploring the nature of the way you filter and interpret these frequencies, you spend your time arguing about who has the correct interpretation of them, who has the correct version of reality. There is no attitude of delighted discovery and gone are the challenges you used to present to one another when you were six or perhaps ten years old and shouted freely, 'Hey, can you do this…?'

"The truth of the matter is that each of you has assessed and interpreted the reality correctly, but this interpretation is correct only for *you*. Others may or may not filter and interpret the reality in quite the same way. Perhaps they can if they want to, but it isn't necessary. If two or more of you end up with very similar perceptions of reality, then you have the possibility of sharing something for a while.

"The most important goal is to explore the reality openly, to stretch deeply into yourself to find things that you might be interested in experiencing, to create those experiences and evaluate them, then bring all that you have discovered back into the whole self who waits for your return and joyously accepts the gifts of wisdom and knowledge that you bring.

"Therefore we would ask you to consider the following: What do you suppose the results might be if, instead of negating subjectivity, you used it as one of your most powerful variables in scientific searches and applications? What do you suppose you might learn about yourselves, your world, and your reality? What might you discover about the hidden or unexpected capabilities of some individuals? And how might you use this new knowledge or these skills to continue exploring and moving toward your own evolution, and acceptance of yourselves as full creators?"

Leaving these questions hanging in the air, the little men faded and I sat, silent and in shock.

I ran their pictures through my mind again and again and again. I wasn't sure exactly what I had seen… scenes that looked like people going in and out of bodies, other scenes in which people did not have physical bodies yet conversed and interacted with one another easily. There were beings who were immense in size and made of light. Some who had been able, merely by gazing at a form or structure, to willingly alter that form or structure. And in other scenes it appeared that two, three, or more people were housed in one body. I tried to get my mind around what they had said, put it next to what I had been discovering via the gifts that came with kundalini, and make it fit together inside myself, make it fit with what I had always known.

But what I had always known didn't seem to fit together any more either. The reality I thought I had all figured out when I landed the job with Chrysler Engineering only three years earlier had been slowly disintegrating ever since. From my relationships to my career, from my perceptions to my emotions, from my values and ethics to my activities and plans—how had I come to so seriously miscalculate life?

Everything had been so sweet just a little while ago. I could recall as if it were yesterday the feelings I had experienced that first day when I started in my new position as tool and process engineer at Chrysler. It was March, 1978, and I was headed home in late afternoon, crawling slowly through the traffic jam at the interchange of I-75 and I-94.

The sun was bright and the cab of my truck was warm so I opened the driver's side window and rested my left arm on the edge of the opening. I was wearing a long-sleeved white blouse and when my eyes rested briefly on the white-sleeved arm resting in the sun, I thought perhaps I should pinch it to see if it was really me here on this magic highway to success.

Suddenly my sense of excitement and joy became a gigantic, explosive euphoria. Looking out over the hundreds of cars in the interchange, all trying to get into the same place at the same time, I felt huge and special and loving and so grateful to be part of such a wonderful traffic jam, and such a wonderful life. For two days I had floated on that carpet of euphoria, and since then I had seldom been bothered by traffic back-ups.

Now here I was in July of 1981, frequently out of the body, with a roving perception that seemed prone to entering other times and places for no practical reason that I could discern, and being visited by a group of little men in brown robes who were seriously upsetting whatever shreds of reality I had managed to cling to.

It was all too much... flying saucers, little men, hollow people, empty heavens. I went to bed and cried myself to sleep. 📖

17 📖

POPULATION, FAMINE, AND TRADE...

THE day was warm and sweat dripped while I cleaned house. Ben and I were splitting up and selling the house. I had no idea where I was going or what I would do, but I was cleaning with an eye toward getting rid of the things that no longer seemed to fit my life. When the vacuum finally went back in the closet, and the dust cloth and window cleaner went back under the sink, I went out to sit on the dock with a cool drink.

I was quiet and felt detached from everything as I listened idly to the sound of breezes, the birds, water, the traffic going by in the front of the house, the sound of someone's boat starting up for a Saturday afternoon excursion onto the bay. I would miss living on the canal.

Lately, whenever I was alone, odd observations went through my mind. Repeatedly I traveled back to my childhood, trying to remember what or how I thought my life would be when I grew up, but even with great effort, everything beyond "happily ever after" was vague and undefined.

From my earliest memories until the time I was twelve I dreamed of being a doctor. Talking about this dream elicited no particular response from my family until one day, while I chattered on about becoming a doctor, my mother looked at me calmly and said, "Why would you go through all that trouble to become a doctor when you'd just have to give it up once you had children?"

I can still remember standing there, next to the kitchen table, dishcloth in hand, literally hearing the sound of breaking glass, seeing the whole dream shatter and fall to the ground in irretrievable shards. Implicit in her words were powerful messages, messages that said I should want children, that I would have to have children because they were inevitable, that women didn't have careers—they had children, and that my dream would have to be given up.

My mother was wonderful. She didn't mean to send these messages, she was simply telling me what was true for her, but I was too young to separate my truths from hers and so I adopted hers, then cast about for something that required less commitment than medicine.

Eventually I decided to be a stewardess so I could travel the world. After a few years I could retire, get married, and have the required children. My bedroom walls and the ceiling over my bunk bed were plastered with posters of airplanes, cruise ships, and exotic places. This dream lasted until I was about sixteen when I discovered that a stewardess couldn't wear glasses and had to be at least five feet, five inches tall.

By this time I had begun to write – poetry, journals, short stories – and loved it. I would become a writer. When I heard someone refer to "lonely writers starving in cold attics and never making any money" the dream withered and I went back to my original dream for a time. Later, I combined the previous plans of medicine and travel, then added the component of writing back in. I would be a nurse, a missionary-type nurse, so I could still travel and see the world, helping heal people in primitive, far away places, while writing about my adventures. I worried about whether I would be able to quit this career in time to have children, and deep inside my being, began to think that perhaps I should have the children and get this out of the way before I really got started at any kind of career. It would be too distressing to start the career and then have to give it up.

With no one to discuss my career and provide encouragement or a reality check, the dream became more complex and less realistic the closer I got to graduation. By the time I was eighteen I was adding and subtracting components such as interior designer or fashion designer, journalist or architect, to the doctor-traveler-writer goals every other week. As the dream became more complex it also became more confusing and further out of reach.

When that first love came along and offered me a diamond ring, a chance to marry, a chance to have those children early, and relief from the confusing disappointment of my own dreams, I took the offer and married the month after graduating from high school, the first child already on the way.

Although submerged, the dream of going to college, getting a degree, and having a career carried me forward through the dark days of the marriage. As in high school the dream had a variety of versions, the most common one being the desire to go into medicine. I felt as if I were waiting... waiting... waiting for my life to begin. Eventually the drive for a career pushed me out into the world of work. My husband violently objected to a wife that worked and when he eventually insisted I choose between a career and him, the marriage came to an end.

Once divorced, I enrolled immediately in the pre-med program at Wayne State University. Just as immediately, the realities of a university program and the impossibilities of being a single mother on welfare in a pre-med program, with four young children in various elementary and nursery schools, became apparent. The urgent need to get through college quickly so I could make my own living brought a total change of direction.

I dropped the medical goals and went into engineering purely for the money. Even though I had rediscovered my love of writing during an English class, I did not pursue it. I had four children to feed and clothe, and writers were lonely people, cold and starving in an attic somewhere.

Now, sitting on the dock in the sun, my whole life stood out as just one long over-reaction to everything around me. I hadn't done anything I wanted to and my excuse was that there was always some difficulty in the way. By looking for the easy way out and running from difficulties instead of facing them, I had only created more difficulties. Like someone who took one too many detours in an unfamiliar landscape, it wasn't long until I finally lost my way altogether.

"Has it ever occurred to you that you might finally become the healer-traveler-writer after all?"

I jumped, snapping out of my reverie and turned to find the little men in brown robes standing under the tree just off to my left.

"No," I stammered, deeply embarrassment at the excuses I had made for not reaching any of the goals that interested me. Then, foolishly worrying that someone would see me talking to such strange visitors, or worse, think I was talking to myself, I got up, folded the lawn chair, and went quickly back in the house. The little men reappeared in the living room and stood quietly.

"Hello," I said sarcastically "Did you like the pictures of my life I was showing you? Did they help you understand how messed up everything is?"

As soon as I said it, I was sorry, but the little men seemed not to notice or take offense. "You should look at your own pictures more often!" they said. "You will learn something useful each time you do. Our pictures are meant to release you from some of the traps you feel caught in at the moment. While you may not want to see why things are happening as they are, it is as we have pointed out many times, the life you have tried to set up is not what you came here to do."

"Well what is it then?" I asked, not really sure I wanted to know.

"We'll get to that in a later visit when you are more ready to see." they replied, "First we would like to address several things that we have already covered in a partial manner and want to add a little more detail regarding general developments. Would you like to see?"

There was a long pause that ended with a sigh on my part.

"I guess..." And still feeling slightly sarcastic, I sat down on the sofa and closed my eyes dutifully.

For a brief time nothing happened, I simply stared into the darkness of closed eyes. Then a sense of movement swept me up and up, and the next thing I saw was the surface of the earth from what looked like several thousand feet in the air, far enough away to get a good perspective, but still close enough to see many of the details on the surface.

In the scene that appeared below, a large city sat on the edge of what I assumed was the Pacific Ocean. Trolley cars went up and down hills, heavy cables and wires stretched everywhere throughout the city, and the impression from above was one of looking at the city through an unevenly woven screen of wires. The longer I looked at it the more certain I became that it was San Francisco, and just as I came to this conclusion, the whole scene changed. I was looking at a different city, also on the water, and with wires running in every direction imaginable. I had just determined this to be Chicago when the scene changed again, this time to Detroit, then in succession to New York, Miami, London, Paris, Tokyo, Hong Kong, and finally Los Angeles.

In each city I noticed masses of cable and wire running everywhere and assumed that we were looking at times that had already passed, since I did not know of any place where trolley cars, buggies, wagons, and carriages were still the dominant form of transportation. From above, each city looked quaint and quiet in its own way, a nice blend of urban and pastoral landscapes, with only the masses of wires to mar the picture. I decided this must be a lesson having to do with wires.

A second round of visits to these same cities began, but this time the number of cities expanded to include Singapore, Sao Paulo, Rio de Janeiro, New Delhi, Calcutta, Cairo, Mexico City, and Moscow. The period seemed to be the present and there was a bit less wire apparent, some of it having been run underground.

Compared to the cities in the first round of visits, these cities had grown in height and the number of skyscrapers that poked up from their midst, as well as the amount of land inundated with people, houses, roads, factories, parking lots, and shopping centers.

The conditions in these cities were also shocking. I knew that population was growing steadily, but until that moment, I had no picture in my head of the tremendous outward oozing of humanity across the land. At this point, I decided the lesson the little men were presenting must have something to do with population instead of wires.

Moving into the future, a third round of visits to all the same cities revealed even more changes. I was about to ask the little men how far ahead we had moved when they said quite simply, "We are in the next century."

San Francisco seemed intact but smaller, Chicago was half its original size, Detroit was practically gone, and while part of New York City was gone altogether, the rest was under several feet of water. It was not enough to submerge the city but it was certainly enough to make it uninhabitable and as I looked at it I thought how much it resembled pictures I'd seen of Venice.

Miami was smaller but no longer at the very edge of the water, as if the land offshore had risen a few feet, London seemed not only smaller but to have been divided by a widening river or perhaps a bay of water. I was shocked when we came to Paris, it was decimated, as if a war had taken place there and everyone had fled, the same was true of Hong Kong, and Tokyo was not there at all any more.

Los Angeles was smaller and parts of it were destroyed, although it was hard to tell if this had occurred because of an earthquake, fighting, or some other reason. Perhaps it was all of these. Mexico City was a mere fragment of its original self, appearing to have been partly swallowed by the earth, and to have lost a huge number of people as well.

In Sao Paulo and Rio there were far fewer people than I had seen in the previous round of visits. Again this seemed due to a combination of troubles—disease or epidemic, serious fighting, and natural disasters that involved earthquakes and what I thought was once a large dam.

In Calcutta, and through the entire eastern side of India, along with coastline portions of Burma, Thailand and Cambodia, the aftermath of all these factors—disease, internal fighting, extremes of weather and changes in the land due to earthquakes and floods—had devastated the cities. In the north of India the country had been split several ways by what appeared to be small civil wars and New Delhi was no longer a capital city.

Singapore, a clean sparkling place in the first visit, seemed deadened and dusty with a sparse population. The buildings were intact, showing no signs of internal strife or overwhelming natural disaster, yet it was a ghost town. I had the impression that travel into its domain had been seriously restricted because of disease or other factors.

Cairo had first impressed me as a place that was sprawling, active, and mysterious, but was now shrunken and deserted, with small groups scuffling through its ruins. The impression of mystery was gone, in its place was an aura of pathos, and I had the impression that something of a terrorist nature had occurred in Cairo.

Moscow was another ghost town with no more people than a large village might have. It appeared that the population of Moscow had moved south into Kiev and the Odessa region because of drought or some kind of water problem similar to what happened in Egypt.

In the last round of visits, I again asked the little men how far ahead we had moved and their reply was "Another century or so." This time, in each of the cities, there were not only further reductions in size and population, there was an intangible air of something that was difficult to characterize. It wasn't just the obvious demolition in some, the deterioration in others, or the fact that miscellaneous groups had taken over small sections of city, barricading themselves in, away from violence and the outside world. It was the disappearance of the rings of suburbia that had enclosed many of them. It was something to do with cohesiveness or identity. Whatever it was that once held people together in these huge cities was now gone.

What I was seeing now began to sink in. The cities and suburbs were slowly being replaced by the large *families* as the dominant units of structure in society. Here and there across the land, the compounds built by groups of people who thought of themselves as families dotted the landscape.

With great curiosity I watched the scenes in several of these compounds and thought there was an intense concentration on the land and great effort by each family to support and nurture the small ecosystem of their own acreage, be it mountain, seashore, desert, or plains.

There was strict adherence to the guideline that each family was responsible for cleaning up any waste created by the family business, and surprising lack of tolerance for families that did not. There was no such thing as living in a clean, fancy suburb and driving to a polluted industrial center to work. The work was in the home and people quickly discovered they had to live in the mess or the paradise they created. There was no expectation that it was someone else's responsibility to clean the air, the water, or the soil. When a family could not or would not take responsibility for cleaning up their wastes, no one would trade or communicate with them.

Once again I noticed the absence of many roads and remembered their absence in earlier visits. How did people get around? There seemed to be small narrow roads that connected some family compounds to others in their region, but not to everyone and not to the remains of the cities!

The little men interrupted with an answer that did not really address the question in my mind.

"What you are seeing is the slow, gradual shrinking of population due to earth changes, violence, and severe shortages of food and drinkable water. As you have seen in earlier pictures, your lives and daily routines will become more and more disrupted by the growing ineffectiveness of governments, by changes in the large corporations, and by extremes in the weather. As we have already pointed out, these weather extremes are very much the result of your removal of trees and plants. Of course, the removal of trees and plants is due partly to the ever-increasing number of people who need to be housed and fed, and partly to the system of agriculture that you have developed to feed them.

"In your current world, the belief circulating among many people goes something like the following, 'Don't worry about producing food for feeding yourselves, that is someone else's job. You do your own job, collect your paycheck, and don't try to do someone else's.' The result is that millions upon millions of people alive today no longer know how to grow food to feed themselves.

"As floods and droughts become severe, as winter freezes become prolonged and the summer sun dries everything to a crisp, it will be more and more difficult for those who have produced large quantities of food to continue to do so.

"As the production of real food slips further and further below the demand, those nations that have so anxiously hurried to convert themselves to capitalism with the intent of getting a better position in the world marketplace and then importing necessary foodstuffs will see increasing death from starvation. The machinery of their industrial revolution will not be running smoothly and they will realize that the cost of this conversion was seriously underestimated. The common people caught in the crossover will suffer immensely from the broken dreams of a few greedy individuals striving to channel money and power to themselves via the industrial pathway. Too late they will see that they would have been better off skipping the industrial stage and going directly to the markets that have grown up via the large global network. Too late they will see that this would have put them a step ahead, whereas the industrial path will have put them two steps behind.

"At the time that third world nations are floundering in their mistaken hurry to catch up with the first world, those in the first world nations will not be aware of the growing problems around food. These problems will be covered over by the appearance of more and more artificially manufactured foods in your grocery stores, along with restaurants that spring up everywhere, offering quick meals for those who are no longer centered around hearth and home.

"Just when you need to be paying more and closer attention to what is happening with the food supply, the illusion will deepen that food is everywhere, that it is cheap and available around the clock, that you do not even need to do much to prepare it any more, and if there is a problem, the scientists or the governments will deal with it. And perhaps they will for a while, but artificial foods will not support human life.

"As those who have been bred, birthed, and raised on such foods begin to suffer from multiple health problems at earlier and earlier ages, you will have the burgeoning of the health crisis that both complicates and spurs the break-up of those nations that have considered themselves most advanced.

"You will see growing health problems at all levels which not only cost increasing amounts of money, they will disrupt the fragile functioning of your nuclear families and the rigid, corporate, lockstep lifestyles that have evolved. Following this there will be an increasing rate of death and a decreasing rate of healthy births, both the result of poor health, which stems from the malnourishment caused by eating artificial foods that are empty of much needed nutrition.

"As awareness of the food problem grows, the demand for real food will increase exponentially, but this demand will come at precisely the wrong time for two major reasons.

"The first will be found in the extremes of weather that seriously disrupt food production. The second will be the fact that your farming practices over the previous century will have destroyed both your soil and the once widespread knowledge of how to find, produce, and prepare nutritious foods that will sustain a human body.

"Adding to these difficulties, you will find that you cannot reverse these agricultural practices without first dealing with the large corporations and the new power structures. Even if you should begin the reversal process immediately, it will take nearly a decade for results to be achieved, and you will not produce nearly as much as you formerly thought possible.

"As the prices of food go up, they will become a significant percentage of the average income. These rising costs will put a heavy burden on those who continue to try to work for money, pay for taxes, take care of the sick and dying in their family who cannot afford medical care, raise their children, make their house and utility payments, afford the clothing, the nursery schools, the cars, and all of the little extras that are necessary to make their jobs bearable.

"As the price of food continues to climb, the uproar in the developed nations will climb with it, and as the shortage of food deepens, it will soon be apparent that a major crisis is occurring, not only for the nations, but for families and individuals.

"Either you will have to grow your own food on a year-round basis or face starvation. The tragedy is that a good many people will starve simply because it will not occur to them that they *could* grow their own food; others will attempt this but begin too late to save themselves, or will not know enough to guarantee a harvest. Still others will only be able to grow a few things like peas in spring and tomatoes in summer, leaving themselves open to hunger and sickness when the growing season ends.

"Compounding these problems, many will have lost altogether the art of preparing nourishing food 'from scratch' as you call it. More will starve because they no longer recognize basic food items. Those who do recognize basic items will go hungry because they have no idea of how to turn that item into nourishing food even if the item were handed to them. Thus, some will die from the diseases that result from years of eating artificial foods, ignorance about food, and hunger outright.

"It will be difficult for those in the developed countries to face the fact that such a situation is occurring. They will think they are long past such calamities and only the poor, living at subsistence levels should have to worry about hunger, malnutrition, or starvation.

"As food production drops and the death rate rises all over the world, population will diminish. Of course not everyone will die directly from starvation, some will get caught in the fighting over food that results from the shortages everywhere. Others will exit the body unexpectedly when they try to push a formerly sedentary self to do the amount of physical labor required to grow food and harvest it regularly. Some will leave when their genetic weakness is triggered into action as a result of insufficient nutrition, and some will give up in despair, unable to believe they are capable of surviving without someone to feed them.

"Among those who survive will be the obvious need to change life styles. As we pointed out earlier, people released from their corporate positions early on will have the greatest opportunity to do this.

"Those who do not waste time and effort complaining about being shut out of the good life will hopefully have made some of the basic changes necessary, such as learning new survival skills and reducing their dependence on money. If they are wise they will make serious efforts to reduce the amount of manufactured food they eat, learn to plant, care for, and harvest an extensive garden, and how to use the large communications network for finding what they need. Some will 'retire' early, and perhaps some will have even moved into versions of the large extended families to be near people of like minds, to grow excellent food, and live in a whole new manner.

"As food prices continue to rise dramatically, the governments—still slowly collapsing—will make a temporary and half-hearted effort to place more and more controls on food and its prices. Unfortunately, those who know how to grow foods will be unable to do so *and* survive to make a living wage unless they are allowed to charge what it really costs to be a functional and productive farmer. Thus the government will have to choose between letting people go hungry, and letting those who know how to grow real food charge real prices for their work.

"Other factors will also work against government interference. Those who have been growing food outside the system for some time will no longer have any need to depend on government help, support, or guidance. They will simply ignore government.

"People will flock to those farmers producing high quality foods in spite of government efforts to discredit them or control them. The continuing die-off of those who eat artificial foods will lead the public to ignore governmental spokesmen, agricultural experts, many scientists, and the large corporations.

"Mounting evidence of the power of high quality food to heal and to maintain health will become a powerful statement of truth. And freedom from the taxes and schedules once required by corporations will be a powerful elixir for those who abandon commercial foods and begin growing their own.

"At this point governments will be faced with several realities. Even with sums of money in public coffers, food, water, land, and energy will be major problems. Tearing up farmland to build houses will increase the difficulty of maintaining enough good land to grow food. To avoid public uproar, government will end up encouraging people to grow their own food. The shortages of potable water will bring worse problems. As people begin to understand the extent to which their water has been poisoned, wars in the courts will proliferate. Energy shortages will encourage implementation of once suppressed sources of energy for heat, lights, and transportation. And there will be the first consideration of the proposal that those on welfare be given tracts of land that is theirs to live and survive on if they will take responsibility for themselves.

"A truth that has never changed will again be affirmed: The laws of nature remain steady and constant, and for all civilizations that pass through the earth system, none will survive who do not discover, accept, and live in accordance with those laws. Although this may seem like a para-dox that forces you back to old ways, the truth is that this is the only way to advanced evolution of the human being.

"Thus a number of troubling forces will be working at one time. The shortages of food and water, decreasing health, continuing cutbacks in traditional corporations, the wobbly ineffectiveness of government, lack of energy for the distribution system, destructive weather, and changes in the earth will take their toll.

"Increases in local fighting and small civil wars will add to the tension, as will the destruction caused by international and home-based groups. The refusal of more and more people to pledge allegiance to the flag in whose territory their home is located, or to a nation of any kind, will confound everything. All of this, combined with the inability of the large governments to legislate these problems away, and the growing power of certain businesses, will bring about the slow, bankrupted collapse of the large national governments everywhere.

"As we have pointed out earlier, this will be accompanied by the rise of business to power for a short time. But shrinking populations and changing life-styles will work against their ability to maintain this power, for a shrinking population means a shrinking marketplace. Add to this the factor of growing independence from regular paychecks, coupled with a mushrooming desire to be free of both government and the 'rat race', and you have the recipe for massive changes in the structure of daily life and family function around the planet.

"As the number of people living on the earth drops, people will band together for safety and survival. At first many of those who have banded together into families for survival will bring their cars and vehicles with them, refusing to let go of this former symbol of freedom and the good life. Gradually, as fewer and fewer people drive to work in the city every day, to grocery stores for food, to schools or nursery centers, to the shopping mall, the restaurant, or the theater for an evening out, the demand for mass produced goods and cars will drop to a fraction of its present demand.

"In the same way that people no longer shop the way they used to, there will be a serious drop in travel due to the danger of random acts of violence or sabotage on ships, trains, or airplanes, and fears of becoming the hostage of a group demanding food or vengeance of some kind.

"Without revenues the collapsing governments will be unable to repair and maintain the system of superhighways for the handful of cars still traveling these roads. You will see a scattering of money into various areas of transportation in the hope of somehow making these systems work well enough to keep things moving. But once they are unable to guarantee the safety of those who use these roads by providing police to monitor the traffic, the use of cars will drop even further.

"In spite of increasing efforts to plug the gaps in dikes designed to maintain the ways of the past, the waves of change will wash over all. The most serious obstacle to dealing with all of these changes will be the habit of looking back at what used to be, trying to maintain or restore the past. No one will be looking at what is actually happening, or trying to work with the possibilities for a new future that are presenting themselves.

"In spite of the efforts to retain or restore the past, there will be the gradual disappearance of cars, buses, trucks, trains, and airplanes as you know them. Changes in peoples' lives, their belief systems, health, schools, institutions, and the fact that governments and businesses are either unable or unwilling to pay for an aging piece of the infrastructure that they have no use for, will all come together to carry you past the age of the automobile.

"For a while, families will make an effort to maintain one or two vehicles for varying purposes and these will be owned and used jointly by all. As they become more self-sufficient, there will be less need, and even less desire to go outside of their local region for much of anything. Later vehicles will go out of use for want of repair and the simple fact that they are not needed.

"In spite of these changes and the disruption of trade at a number of levels, for a while the need to ship at least some things here and there will not disappear. If the rise of the huge planetary network is not interrupted too much, it will help to shape new methods of trade among the families that are themselves being re-shaped.

"For instance, let us say that in the area of Pennsylvania there is a family whose love of books has led them to preserve the library concept by collecting and caring for older, printed versions of information even though all current, useful information can be found in the global network. Having recently added a few new members to the family, they need a few new pieces of chinaware. They put a notice on the network that they are in need of dishes, and are keepers of old books and printed information.

"Now, let us say that in the area of New Mexico there is another family who makes chinaware, painted with unique and beautiful designs and colors. A man in the New Mexico family has the desire for a particular book, old and rare, that he has heard about. This man's sister, also a member of his 'family,' decides to find a copy of this book and give it to him as a gift. She searches the network for a family that has old books and needs dishes.

"The two families find one another and agree to trade the book for the dishes. Together, they put a notice on the network that they need someone to carry the book south and bring the dishes north. Two offers come their way. One is from a former truck driver in the Niagara Falls area who has developed several rugged-terrain vehicles. He is planning a trip and offers to carry the book south. He will bring dishes north if he can get a set of three large, white serving bowls for his family.

"The other offer is from a family in Pennsylvania that has four members making a trip to the New Mexico area to collect a particular kind of rock which they use in their business. They are not making their trip for at least two months, and when they do, they will be gone for an additional two months, but they will carry the book south and bring the dishes north for free. The two original families settle on the former truck driver and the book is exchanged for the dishes.

"In your current ways of doing business there is a myth that you cannot make a trade agreement unless you feel you are getting the best of the bargain, which often translates to getting more out of the deal than the person you are dealing with. In fact, many feel satisfaction only when they think they have cheated or gypped the other person in some way. Notice that in this agreement, no money changes hands, there is an attitude of helpfulness on the part of everyone, and the 'deal' is not exactly 'fair' in the ways you have come to expect. The family in Pennsylvania that had the book and wanted the dishes did not have to 'pay' the man who brought the dishes north. But the family in New Mexico who made the dishes and wanted the book was asked to make three large bowls for him. The fact was, they had extra bowls, felt they could easily give them to the truck driver, and so the bargain was struck. Everyone was satisfied.

"Now let us look at the case of a small family today, perhaps one where a woman likes to make chinaware. In your world of mass production, it is very difficult to buy manufacturing supplies without buying and producing in huge quantities. It is seldom economically feasible to buy just enough to make what you are interested in making. Our china-maker must buy large quantities of tangible supplies such as clays and muds, glazes and paints. Additional expenses include a potter's wheel, a variety of molds and mold-making equipment, a kiln for firing, as well as the background business items such as a desk, chair, bookkeeping system, telephone, file cabinet, business cards, and a variety of paper and forms to produce paperwork.

"Once all these are collected, there must be a place to carry out the work of making china. Now she must choose between converting a bedroom or a garage, both of which are considered unprofessional, or renting commercial space, another financial difficulty.

"When the dishes have been made, it is difficult to sell them without a store front. This is so costly in terms of overhead, time, and effort that the poor chinamaker will barely make a living if she rents a store. Yet if the storefront is out of the question, the chinamaker's choices are few. She could get dressed in good clothes, put the china to be sold in a family car or truck, and drive around to a number of stores that might be willing to sell some of her dishes. This can turn into deep disappointment when she discovers that the stores want to be able to tell her what to produce, when to produce, how many of each to make, and how much she will be paid for them.

"If the store exacts a promise of unlimited pieces of her work on demand, she may be forced to rent a bigger shop, hire other people, adopt complex tax and bookkeeping schemes, and go into serious debt, all on the store's promise of a big sale and her need to fill minimum orders over which she has no control. If these sales go through, she will likely have money rather than the pleasure of her work. If the sale doesn't go through, she will suffer the losses and her work may well be discounted as a hobby by the tax people.

"Her other option is to become more of an artist, creating specialty pieces and going on the road a good portion of each year to display them at various art shows where she will have to pay a good-sized fee to get into the show in order to display them. It will be impossible for her to compete with the big pottery houses churning out hundreds of pieces of cheap china every day, and it becomes necessary to charge a high price for a small, unique set of dishes. She will also spend considerable amount of time delivering her work to specialty shops in vacation resorts and similar places, hoping she'll make enough money in the end to keep going another year.

"As self-sufficiency replaces 'the job,' her relationships with the land and family become the source of needed food, clothing, shelter, entertainment, personal growth, and meaning. Her work becomes less something done to survive and more an expression of her inner self. Our chinamaker can make a set of dishes for herself, another set for someone else in the family, and perhaps another for a neighboring family. When she is tired of making dishes, she can switch to vases perhaps, or landscape containers, or take up the sculpting of nature forms if she wishes, trading them to others over the network who have items she might need. And as trade evolves, another form of transport will also evolve."

Now I was looking at something I did not immediately recognize. It was a single rail track that ran between some of the larger family business neighborhoods. Along this track a large, closed box whose shape resembled a small truck moved quietly and with considerable speed. The "truck" had no wheels, a very small cab with a single, dark window in it, and something that looked like a typewriter underneath the window. Through the window, words and instructions could be viewed when the right buttons were pushed on the typewriter, and these same buttons also caused the back of the box to open up, allowing someone to take out whatever had been sent to them.

"You are looking at the intermediate shipping system that will evolve to take the place of trucks, trains, and many other vehicles. As your cars, trucks, and roads fall into disrepair and then ruin, a new form of infrastructure will emerge. This will consist partly of the extensive communications center in each family compound by means of which you make trade agreements. The other piece of this system will be this single-rail, electronic transport network that at first connects only the larger families to one another, and is extended later to all but the smallest of families. When a family orders something over the network, the item will be delivered to them promptly. If they are not connected to the delivery system, it will be sent to a nearby family that *is* connected, and all that will remain is to go and pick it up."

I watched, fascinated, as someone opened the truck-shaped box. He took out something thin and rectangular which had been suspended in a mass of threads resembling a complex spider web and which must have been to prevent damage from bouncing around during transit. Then several small boxes and what looked like a curved piece of glass were placed among the threads dangling in the truck-box. The door was closed, the typewriter was used to type something, and the box slid away silently and at great speed, evidently heading toward a new location to deliver its contents once more.

The little men continued their narration.

"In the coming years as population dwindles and the market scatters, trade will slow dramatically. Some of the huge ports will close, as will many warehouses. Stores and your beloved shopping malls will have difficulty. As people stop going out for things, these will shut down.

"On the brighter side will be the savings of fuel, electricity, and human and economic energy once expended in these forms of trade. The Madison-avenue-style advertising needed to maintain the one-size-fits-all mindset will slowly disappear. The making of useless articles, the waste of paper and other resources, the stress of unnatural schedules, and the tendency to cluster unhealthily into gigantic cities will come to an end.

"As the large global network continues to grow, its nearly unlimited freedom to communicate will lead to new forms of trade and the growth of close relationships among humans in varying places around the planet. As a positive side effect, there will be an undoing of the past efforts of national governments to paint the humans in other nations as bad, threatening, or both.

"You will discover that people in other places are simply other people trying to deal with their own lives and the challenges that living brings. Since communication leads to knowing, and knowing leads to love, and love is an unfettered response to another being, there is the possibility that love will come to the world finally. And this, quite honestly, is what we are hoping and working for in our visits with you.

"The old saying 'United we stand, divided we fall' will come to be thought of as a favorite expression of national governments who were aware that if they could keep humans reacting with a 'herd' mentality, the government would remain standing. They were aware that as soon as people were allowed to become separate, individualized beings, responsible for their own lives, their own values, ethics, rules, relationships, communication, means of survival, and trade, the idea of national governments would fall.

"Looking back, it will be difficult for you and your people to decide whether changes in world structure and function demanded changes in you, or whether changes in you created changes in world structure and function. It will be difficult for you to contemplate, even in retrospect, the amount of pain, grief, and suffering experienced by all as a result of the need for change after years of stalled human development, all of which was complicated by the mass production of human bodies.

"In the end, you will come to see the physical problems of over-population as simply another manifestation of imbalance created by industrial mass-production and the mindset of one-size-fits-all. You will recognize that too much conformity shrivels the Self, shrinks human potential, stalls human evolution, and brings about destruction."

The pictures faded and the little men remained for a moment, looking at me in a pointed fashion.

I thought perhaps they expected me to say something but I could not. I was caught up in the picture of the single rail delivery "truck" I had just seen. The thought crossed my mind to ask them if they were ever going to show me anything about my career, but I didn't. Instead, for the first time in all their visits I mumbled a vague "thank-you." Then they were gone and I was left to stew. 📖

18 📖
2413 A.D. ...

AUGUST closed and September opened as I wrestled endlessly with the idea that people could starve to death in our modern world. I wanted to believe the pictures of what the little men had shown me, and perhaps a portion of me did, but I couldn't understand how such an ancient and unlikely problem as famine could recur in such an advanced civilization, especially one with so much technological know-how.

Malnutrition was something that happened in the ghettos of Calcutta or the deserts of east Africa. Here in America supermarkets were overflowing with food. Grocery stores and restaurants threw away thousands of pounds of food every week. Farmers were paid to leave their fields idle.

"If we need more food, we can just grow more," I thought, dismissing the little men's statement that we had destroyed our soil because this bit of critical information meant nothing to me. How could you destroy soil, for god's sake? It was everywhere, the whole earth was covered with it, and I couldn't imagine how there could be a problem with something so plentiful or so elementary. If vegetables and grains were not growing well, we could just put a little more fertilizer on them.

A few days later I was still churning over the possibility of hunger in America. It was a rainy September evening and I was clearing away supper dishes when the little men in brown robes appeared quietly.

"Good evening," they said with a calmness I envied.

"Hello," I returned their greeting."

"We thought perhaps we could clear things up a bit with some information that might help... would you like to see it?" they asked.

Wondering what was wrong with me that I couldn't say no when I was still mulling over the last visit, I agreed; and leaving the dishes until later, I sat down at the table to relax.

Their pictures opened around me and I found myself looking at a hillside covered with green plants, trees, and flowers. Nestled into the side of the hill was a large, glass, dome-shaped building. A smaller building of similar shape, also of glass, was attached to the side, and through the glass of the smaller dome I could see plants growing as if it were a greenhouse or botanical conservatory.

There were no other buildings in the immediate vicinity and I could not tell where we were just by looking around. Finally I asked, "Where are we?"

"The structure you are looking at is in the mid-west of your U.S.A., but there are similar structures in many places around the globe that have cold climates for part of the year."

"What time is it?" I asked.

"If you mean 'what year is it?' it is 2413, roughly four hundred years from your present," they replied.

"Oh," was all I said as I continued to look at the glass, domed building. I had seen a building similar to this one some years ago on Belle Isle in the Detroit River; it was a place where unusual and exotic plants were grown. Although I hadn't gone inside of it at the time, I remembered wondering why anyone would put up a glass building in a northern climate and then try to grow heat-loving plants in it.

The little men interrupted this train of thought with the shocking statement, "We have brought you to this time and place to see yourself in the future and view some of your own work in your next major life experience."

"What do you... mean?" I could hardly get the words out for all the thoughts that came crashing in on me.

"Very simple," the little men said. "You will return for another important experience in the year 2413. This is where you will live," they nodded in the direction of the glass, domed building.

At that moment a man emerged from the building. He was of medium-height, appeared to be in his forties or fifties with dark, graying hair and large black eyes. He looked to be of mixed blood, perhaps Oriental, Mexican, and Caucasian, he was thin and wiry, and he carried a large basket.

Going to a small tree he reached out, touched something mounted on the tree, and to my surprise, birds began singing everywhere. Walking around to the side of the building he turned, went uphill a short distance, then bent over and began picking several kinds of leaves and some small, round berries which he put in the basket. When he had enough, he went back down the hill and into the building.

"You may not be able to immediately grasp everything you will see or be told in our visit this time, but we feel it is important to show you and to help translate as much as possible," they said.

"The man you have just seen is yourself in a the year 2413. You are male, your name is Dennis Sanchu, and your occupation is that of engineer specializing in design and construction of living spaces complete with food and energy systems. Now let's go inside."

With that, we shifted to the interior of the glass building and for a moment I was surprised at the way the interior did not meet my expectations. I had expected it to be full of exotic plants. Instead it was more like the lobby of a hotel. There was comfortable furniture arranged in two small groupings, a desk and chair arrangement in another area, and off to the side there was a kitchen area with a countertop, sink, table, and chairs. Doors led off in several directions. One went into the good-sized greenhouse in the adjoining glass dome, one went down a hallway that lead into the side of the hill, and the other was closed so I could not tell where it went.

It was really bright inside the main dome. When we had been outside only a few minutes before, the day had been overcast and gray. I looked up but there were no lights anywhere. I looked around for lamps but there were none of these either. I looked up again, trying to figure out how it could be so bright without lights, when it was so overcast outside. Gazing at the rounded glass ceiling far above, I was struck by something else unusual, the air or the light in the upper reaches of the dome seemed azure blue and for a moment I thought the clouds had cleared away and I was looking at blue sky.

"No," the little men interjected, "the clouds are still there."

"Then how... why does it look like..." I stopped, unable to decide what to ask first.

"First, the building itself is not really glass as you know it. You can call it glass because it is similar, but it's not quite the same. You could think of it as a kind of glass whose molecules have been mixed carefully and oriented in such a way as to collect light and deliver it to interior spaces. There are several layers of these special glass compounds used together. One layer has a specially mirrored coating allowing people inside the buildings to see out but not allowing those outside to see in. Another layer is filled with minute bubbles of special insulating gasses and is designed to keep homes warm in winter and cool in summer. Still another has fibers running through it that serve as conductors of various kinds of energy frequencies that supply light, heat, cooling, communications, and other energy needs. There are also layers filled with tiny organic sensors that work to balance air combinations for the organisms in their presence, whether for plants or people."

"Pointing up, the little men directed my attention to several places in the glass that had a different texture or perhaps were distorted. Small, multi-colored star-shaped lights could be seen emanating from these areas.

"At those points special arrangements of light come together, similar to laser beams. Some bring light into the home, and some are directed to strike specific places on the floors, which then respond with heat.

"What would happen if I were to stand in the way of one of those beams?" I asked.

"There have been burns in some of the earlier, more primitive systems, but it is unusual for this to happen now. Frequency beams surrounding the main beam act as sensors and momentarily turn off the main beam if someone walks through it. The people who live here are very sensitive to changes in the various energy frequencies that move through a given space. They move around these beams of energy the same way you would be aware of and move around a coffee table so you don't bump your shins."

Next, we moved into the smaller glass building filled with plants. The room seemed bigger than it had looked from outside. It was perhaps forty feet in diameter and easily twenty feet high at the top of the dome. The variety of plants was utterly amazing. Every summer of my life I had worked in our large family garden and this was reminiscent of that garden, but with much greater diversity and many plants I did not recognize.

"This is the cupboard garden," the little men continued, "the family grows all their food here on a year-round basis. These are the staples of the diet and most things are eaten fresh. If you look around, you will see a combination of vegetables, small fruits, herbs, grains, and flowers. Other plants grow outside and provide even greater variety as well as seasonal changes in what is eaten."

I looked around at the plants growing so vigorously. They were planted quite close together, there were vines that grew upward in a number of places, and there were two small trees—I assumed they were fruit trees—growing on the far side of the room.

Suddenly curious about the small kitchen area I had noticed in the larger dome, I went back to look at it once more. There was a counter-top area about ten or twelve feet long with a large sink in it, cupboards above it, and cupboards below it. Something that might have been a single stove burner was embedded in the counter top, but there was no evidence of a refrigerator, oven, dishwasher or any of the other things that were common in present day kitchens.

"There is a refrigerator in one of the lower cupboards although it is much smaller than the gigantic appliances you are familiar with. The oven is in one of the upper cupboards, and dishes are rinsed out then hung up in the upper cupboards to dry under special lights," the little men remarked.

"If these few cupboards are taken up with refrigerators and ovens, then where do they put their food?" I asked.

The little men nodded back toward the greenhouse area. "It grows in there. As we have said, most food is picked and eaten fresh. There are no grocery stores or their boxes, jars, and cans of artificial food."

Questions were crowding in and I wanted to ask about things like bread or toilet tissue, but instead I asked, "How many people live here?"

"There are eight living here at this time," they said, "two couples, three single adults, and one child. You are one of the single, male adults."

I hadn't seen anyone other than the man they had told me was my future self, and I wondered where everyone was. My mind skipped to the family compounds I had seen in earlier visits and I wondered if they no longer existed.

Reading my thoughts, the little men responded saying, "Yes, they still exist and this home is part of a family compound. Population is still dropping, while homes and food systems, manufacturing, and energy production have evolved a great deal. There are some wires still around, but not many. Most energy comes directly from the sunlight and space. Let's go for a walk."

"Could we see where people sleep, or do you think that would be too nosey?" I asked.

"Sure," the little men replied, "Let's go this way."

We went down the hallway I had noticed when first entering the building. There were three doors on each side. Entering one took us into a suite of rooms. The largest room was the bathroom. It was spacious like the bathrooms I had seen in my first glimpses of family compounds in an earlier visit, with a few astounding differences. Instead of a bathtub, there was a high wall of rocks over which water trickled down to a large pool easily ten or twelve feet in diameter, and big enough for several people to sit or soak in. Plants grew here and there along the edge of the pool, both in and out of the water.

A table—I assumed it was a massage table—stood in the middle of a slate floor, draped with finely knitted or maybe cotton jersey sheeting. There were two fixtures that looked like toilets but neither had a tank on the back or the familiar handle for flushing. The wall opposite the rocks was mirrored from floor to ceiling, there was a countertop along a section of it with a large sink in it, and I was reassured to see a good, old-fashioned hairbrush sitting on it. Next to that was a floor to ceiling closet that I assumed was for linens.

"Stand here and look in the mirror," the little men pointed to a place on the floor.

I moved over to the spot they had indicated and stood facing the mirror. To my great surprise the image in the mirror was not the human form I was expecting. Instead I saw clouds of color and waves of energy interspersed with masses of twinkling lights, tiny shooting stars, and funnels that appeared to channel lights in an orderly manner throughout the form I was looking at. The entire form blinked and then sort of mushroomed outward momentarily, matching the wave of surprise that turned my stomach around.

"You are in a special high-frequency zone that allows you to see the energy system of the body," the little men told me. "It is used to keep an eye on health and to correct problems before they get into the body."

I wanted to stay and examine the clouds of color and lights that made up my physical self, but the little men moved away, motioning me to follow them. We moved into the next room, which was clearly the bedroom. It was smaller than the bathroom and very simple, with a large bed in it, and a narrow closet. As in the bathroom, there were no windows, curtains, or lamps anywhere, but there were thick woven rugs on the floor. The light was bright and the rooms had a fresh clean smell even though I did not notice vents or grates that might be part of a heating and ventilating system.

In the last room, which was even smaller, there were two chairs that looked like expensively designed La-z-boy chairs. The chairs were of an unusual design in that the head of the person sitting in them would rest in a small cavity or indentation to which were attached something that looked like headphones along with a wide head band that slid down over the forehead and eyes.

I ran my fingers over the headpiece on the chairs, wondering what it was for, when the little men supplied an answer, "For frequency modulation in the body-brain."

That didn't tell me much, but I didn't ask any more, simply because I didn't know enough to ask anything else.

Although the hallway continued onward and I could see a door to the outside at the far end, we went back down the hall the same way we had entered, and out through the main door of the building.

"The entire hill is man-made. It was constructed over a site that already had several natural warm springs," the little men said. "It is very common for family sites to be constructed to take as much advantage as possible of natural energy systems."

We started down a broad path covered in pea gravel that wound its way around the hill, which was covered with berry bushes. On the other side of the hill were several other glass, domed buildings of varying sizes, all connected by long, narrow, glass-covered hallways.

We went into one of the larger ones and from there into what I assumed was the communications room as there were five or six people sitting at what I thought were television sets. A couple of the screens had a picture of another person on them and it looked and sounded like the person on the screen was talking to the person watching the screen. One screen had a lot of numbers on it, two had blueprint designs on them, and another had pictures of homes blinking by in succession.

The little men motioned for me to follow them to a small room at the far end of the communications room where there was a glass enclosure about four feet square. As we watched, something began to materialize in the enclosure! It was some kind of long, thin object that looked as if it was made of the same glass the buildings were made of. To my surprise, Dennis got up from one of the television screens and took the object out of the enclosure, telling the man next to him that he would "check the structure." Then he disappeared into a small, dark room.

We did not follow. Instead we left that part of the building by walking through one of the long connecting hallways, passing a section that had good smells. It was the first indication of cooking and for some reason I felt reassured, but we didn't follow the smell.

Instead we went into a room that had a pyramid-shaped structure in the middle of it, and standing in the middle of the pyramid was a table resembling a cross between an x-ray table and a massage table. An eerie feeling of deja vu came over me and the little men added to the feeling with their comment, "Remember this? It was used in an earlier civilization for healing purposes. The afflicted person lays on the table, a schematic of their individual meridians is inserted into the table, and correcting frequencies of energy, heat, and light are routed along their energy meridians via the fibers that run through the table."

For reasons I couldn't explain, I had a clear and complete picture of exactly what they were talking about. It was a healing system based on the principle of simply returning the body to its original healthy condition using light. Certain colors and frequencies of light were used in specific diseases and would quite successfully reverse any disease processes that had started or taken hold in the physical system. When the little men had first talked about frequencies, cellular tuning centers, and healing, I had struggled to grasp what they were saying, but inexplicably, this was as clear and familiar as a cup of tea.

The little men motioned to me to follow them and at that point we went outside and walked around while I looked at the grounds, the unusual way that food plants seemed to grow everywhere in a profusion of what appeared to be unplanned, almost wild-looking gardens.

It was quiet as we walked and I realized how accustomed I had become to the traffic that moved along Jefferson Avenue all hours of the day and night in my present life. Enjoying the quiet, I stopped and looked up into the overcast sky. The clouds were in the way of seeing any airplanes or vapor trails, but in the silence I had the feeling that there were no airplanes up there any more.

"There are a few antiques around," the little men said suddenly, "and there are several new means of transport, but a fair number of goods are shipped by sending the instruction codes for materialization in chambers like we just saw. There's no need to be hauling things around."

"Then trade has been resumed like it was before?" I questioned.

"Yes and no," the little men said, "It is trade, but not like it was before. Population has continued to go down and will continue to do so for another thousand years. At that point, the few people left here will begin planning their move as a group to the next place in the universe where a different set of lessons in creating can be learned. They may not leave here for possibly another two thousand years after the planning begins, but population will go down in preparation for the move, and trade will continue to change accordingly. It will metamorphose into the sharing of ideas, challenges, and goals in which everyone works together to discover solutions to problems. When an impasse is reached, there will be the passing around of all relevant information on the problem until someone solves it. The solution will then be passed out, after which everyone continues to work toward the next goal or challenge until it, too, is solved and everyone moves ahead again."

"What sorts of problems are they working on?" I inquired absent-mindedly, stopping to examine some flowers that were beautiful and delicate but unfamiliar.

"Some are problems having to do with creating in the sense that you used to think of as manufacturing, but most are problems of human development," they replied. "Frequencies are the key to everything and exploring the various frequency bands is and has been a key part of the research. Mapping the various dimensions is essential if you are to learn how to move about in the universe of realities that exist beyond your own.

"Once a useful or interesting frequency is discovered, the reality that exists there is explored and rough-mapped by primary researchers. These are people who have been taught to shift their brain-wave frequencies in order to be able to enter and operate within that reality. Once learned, this skill becomes automatic. New frequency dimensions are being explored all the time. The work of the primary researchers is documented and sent to secondary research groups who usually both confirm and expand the discoveries. The work of the secondary researchers is sent to specialty groups who compile and cross-reference all information related to a frequency band. They carefully document the experiences available there, the forms that exist there, the kinds of communication that might be useful, as well as the possibilities and the extant abilities inherent within that reality system. After that it goes out to everyone in general, via the planetary network."

Thinking that this would mean a lot of cooperation and tremendous expense for the few people who might be interested in such a subject,

I asked the little men, "How many people are interested in this stuff, how many are we talking about here, I mean... well... how many people are there... people still living on earth?"

"There are a roughly between nineteen- and twenty-thousand families still left," they said.

"Twenty thousand!" I gasped, "with two hundred people in a family that's only four million people! There were almost five *billion* people here... what happened to them all?"

"Why are you so surprised when you have already seen so many of the troubles coming? As we have pointed out, some were lost to hunger, some in fighting, some in disease, but the truth is that very few people have children any more. The population count is actually somewhere between thirty and forty million at this point, as many of the families have more than the two hundred people you were using as an average. In addition, there are a number of rugged individuals here and there that prefer to be alone and are not part of a family business system."

I was distressed and speechless. What was happening to us on earth? How could we have developed so far only to offer the improvements to so few people?

"Do not be upset," the little men chided me, "for you do not see the greater purpose in all that will occur. You cannot continue living the way you are trying to live for too many natural laws are being violated. You are flying in the face of laws regarding health, those of reproduction, those having to do with the frequency bands of your planet, as well as the laws of soil, plants, water, and wind. The natural laws of creation have been reduced to mechanical invention, you are seriously overpopulated, you are lagging behind in development, and no alignment has been chosen. At times, you can get away with ignoring one, maybe two, laws for a while, but you cannot expect to violate all of this and continue to survive.

"Those who experience the coming difficulties will learn some very important lessons about natural laws. When they return for a new life after many of the difficulties have passed, they will have integrated these lessons and will quite consciously seek balance, health, and higher development. It will not be one hundred percent, and some of the families will function better than others, but overall, you will find an amazing level of peace and contentment everywhere. People will not go to work to make a living, struggle to pay taxes and bills, or suffer the diseases and painful deaths that you now take for granted.

"They will find the bottom line is simple. You cannot belong to a family if you do not work to contribute to the health and well-being of the entire family. The goal in life is not getting through college to get a well-paid corporate job with benefits so you can start moving up the corporate ladder while collecting the things considered necessary to join the middle class or above. Rather, the goal has become discovering what it is you like to do and can do well so you can use this skill to make life in the family and for all humans better, easier, healthier, wiser, and so on. Most personal goals will be focused around advancing in wisdom, the power to develop your own self, developing your ability to get things done, or creating in ways that are harmonious with nature. Money is not in the way, land ownership is no longer a problem and, the family commitment to its members is a striking contrast to your present day fracturing of families."

I wasn't quite reeling, but my mind was beginning to skip a beat here and there. Mentally I subtracted thirty million people from five billion.

"My god, that's four billion, nine hundred seventy million people dead in only 400 years!"

A little rough division using the 400 years and rounding off the people to four billion eight hundred million brought me to somewhere around twelve million deaths every year for four hundred years, and that was only if there were no births to replace those dying. If others were still being born, that would mean the death rate was even higher.

"Actually," the little men commented, most of them will leave in the first century after the beginning of the millennium. It will be easy and quick for most, with a minimum of suffering."

This was even more shocking. When I shortened the time span to one hundred years, the number of deaths per year became overwhelming. I had no idea how many people normally died in the course of one year but it couldn't be anywhere near the forty-eight million I calculated or I'd be spending a lot more time going to funerals.

"What about the babies?" I asked. "Isn't anyone going to have babies any more?"

"We have touched on the handling of pregnancy in an earlier visit, setting the stage for your understanding of this issue, for one of your tasks this time is to help the people of earth understand the need to stop giving birth to new humans and begin giving birth to your evolved selves and new ways of living.

"That aside, we do not wish to sound critical, for there is much that you do not understand yet about reality or the place of your universe within the dimensional systems of reality. When creating babies is the only way to use your power, you will of course make babies. When the effects of physical orgasm are the closest you can get to the ecstasy that is normally available by tuning in to a particular frequency band, then you will continue to engage in physical sex. When your most powerful religions tell you that sex is for procreation only, then you will continue to have babies.

"When you have grown past all of this, you will express the drive to create much differently than you understand it now. Your ideas about sexual experience and your belief systems will be replaced with an entirely new system of awareness based on spiritual experience rather than religious dogmas."

"We do not wish to push you beyond your level of tolerance. Indeed, in the most negative of ways you have pushed yourselves far beyond what you can tolerate already by continuing to ignore the pain of your own existence, and pretending you cannot see the future. To some extent, you really can't see it; your true destiny as humans has been well-concealed from you because the alignment has not been chosen. But make no mistake, it does not include such inconveniences as poverty, sickness, or war.

"Built in to each human is the ability to extend life, and to create new forms other than physical machines and human bodies. To do this with any efficiency you must learn to tap and direct the energy generators in the body/mind system, create the appropriate pattern, and then sustain the pattern until the form unfolds and stabilizes in the frequency continuum you have chosen to work within.

"Once you learn to do this you will no longer need to produce babies or engage in the clumsy, wasteful, and excruciatingly slow processes found in manufacturing across the planet. And this is only the first step toward what you can do. Beyond this lies an entire universe of forms and intelligences to explore and learn from.

"To begin this exploration, you must reach a basic level of human development that integrates intuitive awareness into everyday function. Next, you must make the decision about alignment. Then you can begin to experiment with the subjective capabilities of individuals, weaving them into the objective world you are building.

"You are all constructed using the same basic arrangement of energy waves. But flowing through each of you is an immensely wider band of frequencies that can be tuned to, explored, and utilized in a myriad of individual ways!

"Let us review the basic information regarding frequencies we gave you in an earlier visit. Every frequency wave in your universe carries a unique form of information. Like snowflakes, each wave is different. Think of this information as a type of intelligence that knows it exists, knows what is happening to it, knows where it is in relation to other wave forms, and is open to communication. This means that you can communicate with any wave, particle, molecule, or group of molecules anywhere in the universe, and beyond. This includes communication with any group of molecules that exists in your body/mind system.

"Once communication is established, the two forms of intelligence can exchange information—and sometimes function—with one another, at times even creating a new wholeness, sometimes with a new form and way of being. In schools of higher learning, this process is often referred to as 'lesson number one in the practical applications of the law of oneness.' It demands strength, trust, the willingness to be flexible, and perhaps to change at some very deep levels.

"The concept has been taught in many of your religions as 'the willingness to die to one's self and be reborn in the spirit,' however, it has been seriously distorted. In many cases it has been re-interpreted to mean that you should ignore your human wants and needs, sacrificing them to those in power as a penance for 'sin,' then expecting to be rewarded for such sacrifice in an afterlife called heaven.

"Unfortunately, emotions end up strangled, something that greatly interferes with human growth and development. This interference sets the individual back, sometimes for dozens of lifetimes, because your human wants and needs are designed to generate and release emotional power. This emotional power is meant to be used in conjunction with mental ability to communicate with waveforms of energy, moving and shaping them into new configurations. When emotional desire is repressed, scattered, or wasted, little is accomplished, the human remains frustrated, and human development is retarded.

"When you have mastered communication, the next step is to understand and utilize *intent*. Every waveform of intelligence has a property called *intent* and thus, you can be informed of every event and potential event simply by reading the intent carried by the frequencies found in the form. The most basic property of intent is a characteristic that can be described as either alignment with the creative or alignment with the destructive. We have encouraged you to choose an alignment, hoping you would choose to align with life and the creative. Among natural laws, one that governs attraction and repulsion dictates that you will attract energy beings and forms whose intent is creative, when you are aligned with life. And you will attract those whose intent is destructive when you are aligned with the destructive. Although this will occasionally happen even when the alignment with life has been chosen, there are laws that can be utilized to avoid catastrophe and we will get to these shortly.

"When you have determined the alignment of intent in a waveform or energy being, then you can determine the basic utilization of that intent. This could be described as a propensity for a certain kind of 'awareness in action.'

"A loose analogy of this awareness in action might be found in the simple act of running. You know how to run, you know the repetitive pumping movements of the lungs and legs that are required to run, you know what it feels like to run, you know that respiration speeds up greatly, and when you run you are intuitively aware of action going on at many levels within you. The intent carried within each frequency is very similar to your ability to run. Within all forms of energy there is an innate awareness of a certain capability, there is an awareness of the actual movements inherent in that capability, and there is the recognition of both *being* that action, *carrying out* that action, and the *results* of that action at many levels.

"The things that *you* supply in your own running—which are direction and meaning, in other words, a reason to run, a goal, or a destination to run to—are the same things that you must learn to supply to the potentials of the intent carried on the frequency waves of energy that flow through and around you every minute of your existence.

"Now, to review what we have said so far. First, there is the need for human development and use of the intuitive abilities. Then you must practice communicating. Next, you must learn to recognize intent, determine its alignment, and read its propensity for action.

"After this you are ready to begin exploring the many patterns and potentials that exist in the universe and beyond. Once you begin exploring, your skills and abilities can be further developed to operate in realities that parallel your own. But be aware that once exploration begins, entanglement is also possible! Especially if you should encounter other forms with highly developed energy structures.

"If the intent of these other forms is positive or helpful, the result of communicating with them can be a good exchange. If the intent of the other form is negative or selfish, then the result of the communication can range from poor, to frightening, to destructive. The experience could become anything from a slight lessening of your power, to a total disintegration of your physical form and/or a usurping of your energy into the more aggressive form.

"This brings us to the need for understanding and utilizing the law we mentioned a few moments ago regarding avoidance of catastrophe. The reason it is critical to chose an alignment *and* learn to recognize the alignment in other forms is so that you will not attract as many negative energy forms. When you do meet an energy structure or form that is aligned with destruction, you must be able to move fluidly into, out of, or among the following conditions. One is the ability to quickly enter a state of absolute stillness. Another involves the capacity to be completely unattached to outcomes while either active or inactive. And a third is the ability to instantly mobilize enough energy to change states of being, dissolving out of one form and into another.

"These are a bit more advanced but not as much as you might at first think. Those who practice meditation often enter absolute stillness, those who are sick or depressed frequently encounter deep levels of detachment, and almost everyone dissolves out of one form and reality into another when exiting a frightening dream.

"Your current problems in dealing with these more advanced laws are lack of control, delays in human development, failure to recognize how useful these skills are or that they exist as part of natural laws. Add to these problems the inability to use intuitive powers, or to recognize and align with intent, and you can see why spiritual development and evolution of the human being have amounted to only scattered efforts so far.

"You are floating in an ocean of frequency waves and it is time to recognize that not only are you one of those waves, there are many others just as intelligent and capable. Learning to communicate at whole new levels will develop whole new layers of operation within the body/mind system. It will also carry you far beyond the one-size-fits-all mindset. There will be the flowering of many new ideas, new perspectives of what reality is, new technologies based on these expanded perspectives, and the evolution to whole new life-styles.

"These new life-styles will be built on family business as the basic unit of relationship in society. Trade will be based on the large global network, with shipping carried out by the single rail delivery system. Later, shipping will be handled by expanded use of frequencies, which will allow you to dissolve an item in one location and re-assemble it in another.

Still later, you will develop the ability to materialize new items directly, wherever you want it and even in many locations at once, if you choose.

"Eventually you will learn to do this with yourselves, meaning with your own bodies, but this may be beyond your ability to believe at this time. Know that there are those upon your planet in your own present day who can do this. They have always known how to do this for it is passed on from generation to generation, and they could teach you a great deal if you were willing to become a student and able to set aside your limited belief systems.

"For now accept the premise that life here is meant to be simple and pleasurable while allowing for the development of mental and emotional power to be used in creative ways.

"To be spiritually creative is to continuously re-create the self within new systems of reality, with new meanings and new reasons for being. To the extent that you cannot do this, you are off track and lost in wasteful constructions and illusions.

"At the moment, humans are still deeply involved in the old belief systems and the race to make a living. This puts you in danger twice. Once from life-styles that have carried you too far from the flexibility that must be maintained in order to survive within the Earth system. If you do not make plans and prepare to correct this, then as changes occur in the planet and current power structures, you will be set back thousands of years and will suffer severely. The other danger is that you will not continue to evolve and may self-destruct."

Finally they were silent.

I stood staring at the glass, domed buildings, hearing what the little men were saying, but unable to respond. The silence stretched out around me and I found myself reaching for the familiar sound of traffic on the highway or the jets that took off from Selfridge Air Base on evening practice runs. Logical thought eluded me, but the words "Twenty-four thirteen... Dennis... " stuck firmly in the center of my mind.

At last, the pictures faded and we were back in the kitchen where the little men said they would return soon because there was only a little more I needed to know. Then they disappeared and I sat at the table in the deepening twilight for some time. 📖

19 📖
A PERSONAL FUTURE...

A few days later I was curled up in the living room with school-books and papers, attempting to get a headstart on my homework. It was my last semester, and I could barely believe I had reached that point. The house was still for sale, I was still cleaning out and packing, still looking for a place to live, and several times I'd come to the conclusion that I should just put off the quest for a college degree because my life was coming apart at the moment.

Instead, something in me hardened. I wasn't giving up, damn it. I was not about to drop out or postpone the semester just because I had no money, no job, no place to live, and no one to help me. My desire for an education and career had cost me everything I once held dear and there was not much else to lose at this point. Putting my head down I turned stubbornly into the wind, consciously refusing for the first time in my life to take a detour just because there was a problem.

It was September now, I would be done in December, only a few months from now, even though from where I stood it looked like an impossible task and a terribly long, lonely time.

"Too bad," I told myself, "you'll just have to do the long, lonely time." I was determined to act as if I would get through it somehow, so I went back to the assignment at hand. I had only been studying for a short time when the little men in brown robes appeared.

"Hello," they said in their usual, cheerful manner.

"Hello," I replied evenly, recalling with a small start of sadness that they had said there would be one more visit. This was probably it.

"You are finishing school," they remarked in a tone that was more of a statement than anything.

"Yes," I nodded, surprised at their comment.

"Good," they replied.

It was one of the few times they had been conversational, or acknowledged anything to do with my private, everyday life. Instead, they always gave me the impression there was something wrong with my life, but they seldom ventured anything beyond the comment that I was not doing what I came here to do. Following this, of course, were their pictures, which they insisted would help.

I never quite understood what to do with their pictures other than worry about whether the things I saw were really going to happen. My other favorite worry was that the presence of the little men and their pictures were signs of insanity or serious neurosis, perhaps products of an over-active imagination spurred into action by some unexplained psychic mechanism.

"Once you have graduated, you will be free to begin your career. Hopefully you will embark on a much wiser path than chasing a bar and restaurant, especially when you don't like alcohol and hate to cook!"

I was mortified by this comment at the same time I suffered a moment of illumination. They were right! What was the matter with my head that I ever thought I could own a bar and restaurant? The incongruity of it filled me with a sudden wonder. That must have been what they meant all those times when they said I was trying to do something other than what I came here to do!

"That's right!" they said, "and we have pictures and information that may help clarify the situation. Would you like to see them?"

I stared at them with a touch of humor. Perhaps I had been too quick to think they were using a different, more personal approach.

"You never change, do you?" I asked them pointedly.

"We have found that with people of your uncertainty level it's best to be consistent. Then there is no mistaking the encounters for simple imagination. Boring perhaps, but more effective. If we showed up in different forms with a different approach each time, you would discard both us and the information as unconnected and unimportant!"

I half laughed. Again they were right. I could not deny the consistency, the coherency, or the common sense of either them or the things they showed me.

"So where are we going and what are we seeing today?" I asked almost flippant in an attempt to cover the growing sense of nostalgia accompanying the thought that this was their last visit.

"We would like you to look at the work you promised to do here and to renew your commitment to this work," they said in a plain and serious fashion.

My flippant attitude melted and I looked at them quietly, wanting to know, and not wanting to.

"Okaaay…" I said slowly, putting my books aside and sitting in a more upright position. It took me a long time to close my eyes and relax; perhaps five minutes went by while I sat, fidgeting, unable to gauge how I might react to this particular topic. I didn't know what I was going to see, but felt as if I was poised on a fence somewhere in time. Perhaps this was the answer to the career question and the lack of finances. Without conscious volition my eyes closed and I stared into the darkness, which slowly melted away into pictures of myself, several members of my family, and some others I did not immediately recognize.

The voices of the little men wrapped around and through me with their peculiar resonance, "In some ways, your real work will not truly begin until everything has fallen down," they began, "in other ways your early work will be a powerful force that will help bring about the healing processes.

"Before you came here, much time and effort was spent watching, waiting, and planning. Many careful agreements were made with other entities who would play a role. Plans were structured, restructured, and back-up strategies studied. Many potential paths and probabilities were examined and practiced so that as many options as possible would remain open once you arrived here.

"Your parents were carefully chosen from among evolved beings you have worked with successfully before. Your father was selected for his great strength of mind, his willingness to stand by his own decisions regardless of pressure. Your mother was chosen for many reasons—for the peaceful ease surrounding her, which she also extends to others, for her willingness to put down farm roots, and for the amount of mental and emotional space she would give to each of her children thus allowing them to develop without negative interference. She also has an advanced natural belief system, as well as a practical, common sense approach to all things that helps to get things done.

"Your father agreed to demonstrate with his life the agony of one who has lost true freedom and the independence of inner authority, yet understood this at levels too deep to express aloud. Once you have killed in the name of a nation that claims to be fighting for your freedom, it becomes very difficult to recognize and sort out just who has the so-called freedom—you or the nation. His message to you, 'Sometimes you have to fight,' is a very important message. And his constant talk about moving to Alaska was not really a desire to move to Alaska, it was an instinctive need to return to a life that was self-sufficient, far removed from the traps of a civilization that left him and his family exposed to the dangers of extinction due to ignorance of the land and laws of nature.

"Your mother agreed to demonstrate with her life the difficulties of one who possessed traces of true freedom based in almost total absence of the need to control others. She was also able to model the gift of listening to others, young and old, high and low, without imposing her own thoughts, ideas, or will on them. Her adaptability, common sense, deep non-conformity, love of learning and freedom of thought, coupled with devotion to family, have been powerfully demonstrated, forming a solid base for you.

"Together, your parents kept you close to the land, the one essential physical bond that was necessary for both a chance at survival and the ability to inspire your teaching and bring healing to others. This connection to the earth, along with the power of the love you are learning to project to your children will become your basic tools.

"Once your parents were chosen and the forms of these basic relationships were worked out, you selected the religious system of Catholicism so that you would understand the power of institutions and be able to grasp first hand how easy it is for human beings to accept the false security they offer in return for authority over you.

"For many people the illusion of security emanates from the teaching that there is a god somewhere who loves you no matter what kind of atrocity or thoughtlessness you might engage in. Not only is this a senseless teaching, it leaves you secure in your ignorance only. Worse, belief in this kind of mindless love allows you to escape from evaluating yourself and deciding what is good or not good.

"There is not a god somewhere who loves you no matter what you do. It would be better to understand God as the intelligent substance of which you are *made*, and thus if you are cruel or selfish, it means you are not expressing your true nature, you have turned away from the intelligent, benevolent force that is you, and thus you will suffer.

"Although the Catholic Church maintains a hint of self-evaluation in the concept surrounding the confessional, the apologies made during confession are made to the church or the priest, never to the wronged person, which is where they should be made. The punishment for wrong-doing is somewhere between wasteful and irrelevant, often consisting of a few chanted prayers, and never requiring worthwhile action or truly help-ful reparation.

"This lack of self-evaluation and escape from responsibility and reparation reduces your inner authority. The loss of inner authority then allows others to step in and evaluate you, deciding what is good and bad, telling you what you should do or not do. And this, in turn, sets up the basic rituals and structures that lead to a situation in which everyone and everything is running your life except you.

"Returning to our focus on your personal life, in order for you to revitalize human development, you needed to live under the umbrella of this kind of institution, then grow beyond it while retaining an inside ex-perience of its culture, attractions, and limitations.

"From here you went on to choose things like locations for birth and neighborhood during childhood, again keeping yourself close to the land. Next, such things as close relatives, friends, neighbors, bosses, teach-ers, lovers, husbands, and children who would influence your development and help push you toward the goals you decided on, goals which are entirely possible given the degree of understanding and completion you have already reached as a highly advanced being.

"What goals do you mean?" I asked, wondering if they were going to encourage me in my budding massage therapy practice or the classes in intuition that I was about to begin teaching in the adult education program at a local high school.

"There are several goals, all related, the first one being to enter into the christ state and begin…"

For a moment I thought I misheard something, then my old fears mushroomed and I heard myself say "What?!" as something in my stomach dropped and rolled over.

"To enter the christ-mind and teach..." they began again.

Confusion flooded me and I stammered at them, "*What* christ-mind? What are you *talking* about?"

"Your goals," they replied. "In order for you to do the work you came here to do, you will need to enter what is known as christ cons-ciousness..."

Reacting with unreasonable panic I interrupted them, "I hope you're not talking about the kind of christ-state that I'm thinking of... the kind that involves saints and Jesus and people like that!?"

"There is no reason to get upset," they said evenly. "You do not truly understand what the term means yet. And you will not be alone, there will be many others who will be entering into this ..."

I didn't want to hear it. Cutting them off again, I nearly shouted, "Oh no, don't say it... I can't even *listen* to stuff like that let alone *think* about it... it's crazy!"

"You don't understand..." they started to say.

"No, *you* don't understand!" I cried. "Look what happened to the last guy who got into that state of mind... you *know* what they did to him!"

"He had different goals, a different personality, and he wasn't really crucified..."

Not listening, I shouted, "What's that got to do with anything? No, no, no! I don't want to talk to you any more. And I don't want to see your pictures, either. They don't help at all!"

I jerked my eyes open. Tears were pouring out of them and my heart was pounding. Jumping up from the sofa, dumping textbooks and papers, I went to get my sweatshirt, then ran outside and down Jefferson Avenue toward the bay, still crying.

It was all a trap. I was sure of it. Some devious, crazed part of my mind was leading me right into the arms of a straitjacket. I had friends who were nurses, psychotherapists, and biochemists. They worked with schizo-phrenics or studied the brain chemistry of psychotics and I was well aware of the grandiose, savior-type personalities that were locked inside their clinics. *No* one in their right mind would even *think* of thinking of the self as a christ-state, a christ-mind, a christ-anything. That was classic insanity.

I didn't want people to think I was weird, I didn't want anything to do with churches, saints, or anything else that might be connected with christs or saviors, and I was perfectly happy just being a plain, ordinary person. I wasn't particularly strong and I certainly couldn't be classified as "good." I didn't even *want* to be good. The kids in school had always made fun of me for being a "goody two-shoes." Now I sat at the edge of the bay crying for a long time; by the time I walked home I was thoroughly chilled but empty of all thought and feeling.

📖

The next afternoon was quiet and lonely. I sat on the edge of the bed putting together some handouts for the class in psychic development I had begun teaching in the local community education program. As I shuffled through papers, a poem I'd written the previous spring titled, *My Arm Hurts When I Don't Write,* fluttered to the floor. I picked it up, read it as if someone else had written it, and then sat staring at the last few lines of the verse which said,

> I am so afraid of jail,
> What happens to people who don't agree?
> Jesus died, alone, on nails,
> I want to live, to fly free.
>
> Who? What? Why? How?
> When? Where?
> Should it be now?
> I think I can, I think I can,
> I thought I could, I knew I would,
> The question is will you, shall we,
> Construct a new reality?

The words plucked at strings of fear that I could feel all the way to the roots of my soul. Suddenly shaky, I set the paper aside and continued sorting through the handouts but my mind kept wandering back to the poem. Why had I written those words? And why did it remind me of the little men in brown robes?

"Because you know deep inside of you exactly what you came here to do." It was the little men; they were standing just inside the door of the bedroom.

I wondered if I should get up and run, or demand that they leave. Instead I sat there, my mind suspended between the poem and the little men, my body frozen in position and filled all at once with an intense awareness of its position and its relation to the ceiling, the walls, and the window. In fact, it seemed that my body and mind had suddenly ballooned outward to become the shape of the room.

After what seemed like a long time I said to them, "I suppose you have pictures you want to show me again?"

"We do, but we don't have to show them to you if you are going to get upset. Just a simple message will do," they replied.

I nodded silently.

"You have prepared long and hard for this lifetime. We are here only to help you succeed. It is essential that the humans here recognize the need to reconnect themselves to the Earth. The structures of your civilization are far too fragile. In the face of ongoing natural disasters there is a danger that all progress will be lost, either through the disasters outright, or through wars over suddenly shrunken resources that create their own disasters. If this happens you will return to severely primitive conditions and may not reach either the group soul or civilizational goals you have all set out to achieve together.

"The pieces you agreed to do were, first, to teach people about the structures of mind and consciousness, helping human consciousness to resume its evolution and development.

"The second piece, is to help bring people together in new ways of living. Mind you, we are saying that your job is to *help*, this means that you will not be working alone. Others will work with you. If you do your pieces, they will be able to do theirs. You will teach love and an understanding of what christ consciousness is, and demonstrate new forms of communication with plants, animals, people, and the Earth. In addition, you will research the structure and dynamics of many dimensions of energy, while creating new ways of feeding, clothing, and sheltering yourselves. In the end, you will help bring the people of the world together."

"What people?" I asked bluntly.

"All people," they answered.

"Can't you be more specific?" I said.

"We would like to be much more specific," they replied, "but we do not want to upset you to the point that you go running out the door again."

There was another period of silence during which we just looked at one another. Oddly calm and clear for a change, and feeling a need to be severely honest, I spoke up.

"I am willing to look at your pictures, but that doesn't mean I will believe or accept what I see. I mean... just because you show me something doesn't mean I'll do it."

"There is no need to push yourself to believe in anything. We are deeply aware of your reservations and doubts about the things you've already seen. Time will show you the truth, and there is no reason to be afraid of truth."

Slowly I set my papers aside, got into a meditative position on the bed, and after closing my eyes, their pictures unfolded carrying me into the future once more.

This journey to look at my future and the work I came here to do was short and to the point. In essence, it involved teaching people about the body, the mind, about the body/mind as a unique system, and how to rekindle the processes of human development. Some of the teaching was with individuals, some with groups, and a great deal was through writing and other kinds of media. Watching myself made me terribly uncomfortable. The path they showed me did not seem to reflect my interests at all. Some of the things I saw myself doing were so unlikely they were difficult to believe. At times, the experiences seemed incredible, other times boring. When it was over I was crying, tears of disbelief running alongside those of doubt.

"I can't do it," I told the little men.

"We are not in a position to argue or try to persuade," they told me. "We are simply here to remind you that you are not alone, you are one of many working to soften the impact of the changes. You will help others find and establish new bearings, re-discover the necessary skills for creative self-sufficiency, and help build a new foundation of security with the Earth. To do this you will work to awaken the consciousness of those on the planet. This is the piece you have agreed to carry out. You can refuse if you like... but we are asking you to renew your agreements."

"But you don't understand," I said, "who is going to listen to me? I am nobody. I just want to be an ordinary woman like everyone else."

"We think perhaps you underestimate what one ordinary person can accomplish," they responded. "And your fears are unfounded. Over time you will come to see and understand much more. As you learn to generate, maintain, and project love, you will come to understand and accept your work. And as you begin to meet and work with the others who are here to help in this transition, you will find not only that they are delightful, but that things unfold quite easily and naturally."

I had no argument for this last statement. Instead, I sat silently with my eyes closed, trying to pretend they were not there the same way I had during their first visit so long ago. What made them think I had made any sort of agreement at all? How could I ever go back to not knowing, I wondered, as I sat in silence, reluctant to renew the phantom agreement yet unable to say no.

When I finally opened my eyes, the little men were gone without the long sought agreement or even a last goodbye. 📖

20 📖
CONTRADICTIONS AND DENIALS...

THE following year was long, difficult, and lonely. The house was sold, Ben moved away, and I moved into the basement of an older woman. It was cramped and cold but quiet and I found strength and healing in the solitude. I concentrated on completing that last semester at Wayne State and was far too busy to think about the little men or the things they had shown me.

Over much of that year I was penniless and unable to make ends meet. More clothing helped to combat the cold, but the hunger was less amenable. Always looking for meals that made use of a few, simple items, I moved away from the heavy dependence on dinners out, and even the expensive meats and desserts that once characterized what little cooking I engaged in. I avoided boxed and canned foods, refusing to pay for a box, a can, or a wrapping that could not be eaten and would end up going in the wastebasket. I discovered it was much cheaper to eat foods made using a few fresh vegetables, dried peas, beans, and pastas.

Experimenting with grains, I added several kinds of homemade whole-grain bread and muffins to my daily fare. For variety, I ate fresh fruits when I could afford them, and made an occasional homemade dessert such as applecrisp or cookies.

I learned to make delicious soups that started with nothing more than plain water and an onion. Gradually I began to understand when to use and how to combine a number of herbs for better flavor, as well as which foods provided what nutrients.

By the end of that year, I had a basic understanding of how to cook or make almost anything from scratch. I had even begun developing my own recipes. I didn't realize it then, and wouldn't for another fifteen years, but over the course of that very difficult and painful year I had taken my first steps into the personal future the little men had shown me.

📖

Over 1982 I worked steadily to rebuild my collapsed life and at the end of that year I met a wonderful man. A year later, in November of 1983, Jim and I were married. Several years after the marriage, I told him that a group of little men in brown robes had visited me, but we never discussed the nature of their visits or what I had seen. I simply said they had shown me some of the work I was to do in my life.

Although I maintained a mental attitude of 'prove it' as far as their pictures were concerned, I alternated between hopefulness that the changes would prove to be real, and a skepticism that wanted to deny their visits altogether. I kept one eye open for signs of what they had shown me, but everything seemed to contradict what they had said.

Instead of falling apart, the U.S. government was experiencing a Reagan renaissance and was at the top of its form. When the government declared AT&T to be a monopoly and the courts issued orders for its break-up, the metamorphosis of a large corporation into a number of smaller regional companies was a direct contradiction to the mergers I was looking for. I decided the little men must have been wrong with their predictions of corporate consolidations and the rise of business to power.

In 1983 I discovered the existence of a computer network called *The Source* that had characteristics of the large global network the little men had constantly talked about. Since Jim and I had several computers, I immediately subscribed to this network and dutifully learned to communicate over it, but nothing was happening in terms of this network that even resembled the broad activities and colorful communications I had seen in the pictures shown by the little men.

Over 1984 I was sure the nomination of Geraldine Ferraro to the vice-presidential ticket was the start of the influx of women into government as the little men had predicted, but she and Mondale were defeated in the November elections. When the defeat was followed by a host of negative investigations and reports regarding her and her family, I found it hard to believe that there would be any influx of women into government. I was sure no sensible woman would want to deal with the rude invasions of privacy that public life engendered.

In early 1986 I discovered someone had started a corporation called *The Education Utility*, a computer network proposing to link elementary schools, high schools, colleges, universities, libraries, museums, and numerous businesses and data banks. The goal was to provide a rich supply of audio, video, and written information from the libraries, museums, universities, and businesses to the subscribing classrooms in the network.

The *Utility* was designed to link classrooms all over the world, making classroom lectures by a special teacher available to students in another region or even another country. It also aimed to provide a tremendous range of information to people of all ages, backgrounds, and abilities, including people at home, in hospitals, or in widely dispersed locations, regardless of the clock, allowing for self-directed, self-paced, life-long learning.

There was an amazing resemblance of this *Education Utility* to the sort of educational system I had seen in the family compounds. Yet when the *Utility* withered into red tape and the jungle of non-standard computer architecture of the times, I decided that the little men and their pictures were a fluke. Finally, I dismissed them completely along with all of the things they had shown me.

Then, one by one, some of the events I had seen, things I had thought were just not possible, began to occur in the "real" world.

It began sometime in late 1986 when I happened to see a photo or a news clip of Mikhail Gorbachev and was shocked by his resemblance to the man I had seen in some of the pictures shown to me by the little men. In the events that I had viewed, this was the man whose love and respect for his mother and her struggle to conform to state rules without abandoning the beliefs in her heart would eventually lead him to live a double life of his own, doing what he had to do to keep moving up, and determined to change things if he ever got to the top.

The closer he got to the top, the more deeply convinced he was that his comrades were suffering greatly, that they had stopped growing and developing as humans were meant to do. He felt that they were becoming dependent, destructive, and needed to be set free with the hope that freedom would prod them into the joy and satisfactions of self-sufficiency once more.

This was the man whose great love and immense understanding of humanity would start the chain of events that would change the entire balance of power in the world. I began to watch Gorbachev and to this day still regard him as the pivotal figure in our times. If he had not played his chosen role, it would have been difficult for the rest of the events to unfold without total destruction.

In October of 1989, I went to Germany for a couple of weeks to visit a pregnant daughter and her husband. They were both in the army and stationed at Wiesbaden. At the time, I thought nothing of this visit and did not recall the prediction of the little men who had said I would go to Europe while I had maintained that if I ever went anywhere it would be to Hawaii or Tahiti.

Back at home a few weeks later, gooseflesh rose from head to toe as I watched television scenes of men and women chipping away at the Berlin Wall, realizing that I had seen this event already, and that not only had the little men said the wall would come down, but that I would be there right before it happened.

When the U.S.S.R. began breaking up I was stunned. I began to think more and more often of the little men and the things they had said were coming. What if all the things they had shown me *were* real and about to happen?

With great effort I soothed my own fears, yet it was weeks before I could go back to my daily routines without a thought about "the Robes" or their pictures. 📖

21 📖
A SURPRISE RETURN VISIT...

VERY late on a frigid February night in 1992, I sank gratefully into bed after a long and tiring day. The clock declared the hour to be one-thirty in the morning, not an unusual time for me to be stopping for the day. Most nights I went right to sleep while Jim lay awake; but this night he went right to sleep while I turned and tossed, unable to sleep. It was already after 2 a.m. and relaxation was just seeping through me when there was an odd sound in the bedroom that startled me wide-awake. Rising on one elbow, I gasped and my heart stopped beating for a minute when I saw several figures at the foot of the bed. It was the little men in brown robes!

"Good morning!" they said, as brightly as ever, as if eleven intervening years since the last time I'd seen them had been but a day.

"Oh! It's you..." I said, relieved, yet feeling waves of surprise wash over me at their unexpected reappearance after so many years. "Yes... uh, good morning!"

Without explanation or inquiries as to health or how I was, they looked at me quite directly and asked, "Why do you think we showed you all those things about the future in our visits of more than a decade ago?"

"You know," I said to them, tangled in blankets and struggling to sit up, "I've been asking myself that same question for a long time now and really have no idea."

"Think about it," they replied. "We will return later for your answer."

With that, they were gone and I finally sat up all the way, staring at the place they had been standing. Many times over the past eleven years I had questioned myself as to why the little men bothered to show me all the things they shared in their pictures. Sometimes the question was "Why *me?*" Other times it was just "*Why?*" Occasionally I wondered, "Who were they... Where did they come from?"

Only a couple people knew of the appearances of the robed monks in my life. I never discussed the things they had shown me because I considered the appearance of seven robed men and the things they presented as too outrageous, too unbelievable.

I lay back down, wondering how many weeks or months it would be before I saw them again. Once more sleep was out of reach. I rolled and fidgeted as minutes ticked by, each as long as a week, while I asked myself over and over, "Why *did* they appear and show me all that stuff?" I didn't ask to see it, I didn't particularly want to know it, and the little men couldn't have picked a more skeptical person.

I was uncomfortable with the idea that I might be "special," and nothing came to me that struck me as the truth, so I just kept wrestling with their question and the fact of their reappearance.

"*Think!*" I commanded myself, but there was nothing that even resembled an intelligent answer. Sometime later, still blank, I tried to focus on asking the right questions, hoping to trigger some kind of insight, but nothing came.

The night passed with exquisite slowness. Several times I tried to go to sleep but I could not turn off my mind and relax. Then, shortly after 5 a.m. I was surprised for the second time that night. There were the little men standing at the foot of the bed again!

"Well?" they asked, picking up our conversation exactly where it had left off three hours earlier. "Why do you think we showed you all those pictures of the future?"

With great reluctance I said to them, "I-I'm sorry, I still don't know. I have wondered why for a long time and I just don't have any idea. I haven't slept all night; I've been trying to come up with an answer but..." My voice trailed away, lost in apology.

Without hesitation or delay, they responded with a tone that was gentle, informative, and highly energized all at once. "We showed you all of that information because you wanted to write! So write! The information we gave you would be quite helpful to those who are trying to survive, those who want to understand not only why things are changing, but what they are moving towards. A book of coming changes could be very useful for quite a few."

"Do you mean you want me to write down some of the things you showed me and give it to other people?" I inquired incredulously.

"Yes!" they replied firmly.

"But... I don't like predictions of any sort... and what if the things you showed me don't happen!" I said, my voice full of anxiety. "I'll look like a fool!"

"It would be nice if some of it *didn't* happen!" they said pointedly. "Perhaps if people realize what is occurring early on, they will be able to make better, less painful choices for the long term. Perhaps they will lose less time and energy trying to hang on to the old. Maybe they will recognize much sooner the need to continue their own human development and can learn to communicate and work together sooner in all areas of life, from family and career, to politics and health. Perhaps they will take up a new vision of the future and simply begin to create it without all the trouble and fuss."

"But I *hate* books full of predictions... and the people who write them usually end up looking stupid," I said obstinately.

"Don't write a book of predictions," they replied crisply. "Just write the things we showed you."

"But it will end up *looking* like a book of predictions... and besides, I didn't take any notes... I've forgotten half of it," I protested.

"Then make it a 'little' book," they said matter-of-factly. "And have no doubt, you will remember all of the important things with no trouble. After all, you've been trying to forget them for over a decade and haven't been able to."

"But how would I translate all that telepathic information into words?" I continued to raise objections.

"Use your own words," they replied. "You have a good grasp of what we communicated and the many nuances of the information."

"Look," I said with a sense of desperation, "after you showed me that I came here to write and teach, I tried to get a book published for over six years. I've given up... it's pointless... getting something published is impossible."

"You're starting in the wrong place," they responded evenly. "You wanted to write. So write the information we gave you. If necessary, publish it yourself and hand it out to people. If you help even one individual, it will be good, but we think you seriously underestimate the growing need people intuitively feel for something that will help them understand and cope with the coming changes. Most humans will appreciate the chance to see inside these changes, and besides, they have an innate need to change in creative ways. The entire earth experience is centered on learning to create. At the very least you would help remind people that creativity, fresh vision, and courage are very useful during times of intense change."

I thought about this for a few moments. After teaching my classes in "Developing and Using Intuition" to hundreds of individuals for over eleven years, I was well acquainted with the fact that the sudden reawakening of human development caused 'intense change' in people's lives. I always warned my students several times on the first day of class, "This class will change your life, and you need to be aware that it could be an overwhelming change, so go slowly, easily."

In fact, so massive were the changes in some people's lives that I had taken to refusing to allow students to go straight through all of the classes! After Intuition 1 and 2, I usually suggested they take a break before moving on to Intuition 3 or 4 and beyond. If they were not open to easy suggestions, I would simply not schedule the class they wanted, or perhaps not inform them of the class, forcing a break for several months at least, maybe even a year.

Sometimes a wife would take the class and experience such tremendous change that her poor spouse would end up coming to the next set of classes, trying to understand what had happened to his beloved partner. Sometimes a mother and former student would send an adult daughter or son to classes, paying their tuition, knowing this would help them continue growing, and hoping they would make better choices in life.

Now I remembered something the little men had said many years earlier, that my "work would help to bring about the healing processes."

"What if I write this stuff down and it *causes* the same chaos on a large scale that I've witnessed on an individual scale? And then, what if people end up saying that the problems are all my fault?"

"Why would you be willing to teach and guide people one at a time, yet be unwilling to teach and guide a group of people?" the little men inquired.

Their casual attitude toward this boggled me and I scraped about for a response. "It's... uh, it's... a... a problem of scale... and... there are usually *several* periods of serious doubt, sometimes even a backlash, an effort to forget everything you know and go back to the old ways.

"*You* should certainly understand the efforts to forget what you know and go back to old ways!" they replied, zeroing in on my own difficulties in understanding and accepting what they had shown me. "Nevertheless, you will eventually come to deal with this quite well. In the meantime, consider whether you think it would be better to suffer *without* vision, hope, or understanding; or to work your way through changes *with* hope, having at least some idea of where you are going, and some understanding of what you are moving toward?"

"Well, I guess some idea of what's happening would be better than none," I said dubiously.

"We will leave you to your writing, then," they said, as if everything had been agreed upon. And when I looked at them questioningly, they asked point blank if I still wanted to accomplish what I had set out to do in this lifetime, and if I would be willing to renew my agreement yet.

Slowly and with great hesitation I made the long-denied agreement, "Well... maybe... yes... I guess I'll... see what I can do..."

They nodded, bowed, paused briefly, and were gone. I have not seen them since. 📖

22 📖
IMPLICATIONS...

THE next morning I told Jim about the middle-of-the-night visits from the little men.

"They want me to write down what they showed me back in 1981 because they think it might help people adjust to some coming changes!" I said with an indignant, obstinate air.

To my everlasting surprise, he thought it was a good idea. When I asked why, he remarked in his practical way that life was always changing and people really did need all the help they could get.

Personally, I thought he was not being realistic. He had no idea of the difficulty in capturing and expressing telepathic information, nor did he have a sense of the magnitude of the changes I had seen.

"He probably thinks that they were talking about a couple of life-style changes," I muttered to myself. To me, the changes were more like an overhaul of the world, and although I agreed to give it a try, after a weekend attempt to get something down on paper, I was overwhelmed and let the project go in favor of other things that needed doing.

Over the next two years, I made a number of attempts to organize what I had seen about the future, but none of what I wrote had the practicality, the upbeat compassion, or the cheery, business-like attitude that the little men had communicated. I would write, stop, start again, get frustrated with the lackluster results, only to run out of time, energy, and inspiration.

Then an unusual blend of experiences came together to encourage me onward. These three factors were arthritis, a medical doctor who was practicing Naturopathic medicine, and a group of elves.

While working in our vineyards early one spring, I triggered a case of rheumatoid arthritis that brought endless pain and fatigue. Being in my mid-forties and feeling much too young for such an infirmity, I began searching, first for relief, then for an outright cure. My regular doctor told me there was no cure and gave me a prescription for pain-killing medicine. I took a few, suffered the side effects, and decided to find treatments that were more holistic.

"There has to be a reason for arthritis," I told myself, "and whatever it is, I'm going to find it and correct it. I did find lots of advice, this herb, that technique, those supplements, but nothing that did the whole job of healing in a permanent way. I wanted to get to the source of the disease, and felt that although my ministrations were holistic, they were still just dealing with symptoms. I wanted a cure.

The search for a cure led me to a young medical doctor who was practicing Naturopathic medicine and was highly skilled in balancing individual metabolism. He was in New York, but I made the trip and was glad I did. He designed a healing program tailored to my metabolism, explained the reasons for each step of his program, and insisted I switch to organic food, regular detox routines, and numerous supplements.

The third factor was the influence of a group of elves who lived on our farm and with whom I'd had an ongoing relationship for several years. They insisted we stop spraying chemicals in our vineyards, and tutored us in the ways of organic farming. Through my relationship with them I had been initiated into the circle of the sacred by learning to communicate with all of life—plants, trees, the wind, water, the Earth. [6]

They kept telling me we were destroying ourselves with our agricultural practices, and when my New York doctor insisted I eat only organic foods, down went the last of my resistance to what the elves had

---

[6] For a full account of my relationship with these Nature Spirits, see *The Elves of Lily Hill Farm*.

been teaching. I took up a much deeper study of soil, agriculture, and food, and discovered that many foods no longer had any nutrients in them. The source of my arthritis was the empty food I had been eating for years. It had no nutrition in it. My body was not getting the nutrients it needed to constantly repair and rebuild itself. The holistic treatments would help with pain, energy, and movement during the time I was rebuilding, but the food was the real source of the problem. [7]

Eventually, due to my doctor's influence, I enrolled in a school offering courses in Naturopathic medicine, hoping to coordinate the dozens of approaches to natural healing in ways that would assist in the rebuilding process. The combination of my own personal healing program, the studies in Naturopathic medicine, and my studies of soil, foods, nutrition, and agriculture proved to be a powerful combination. Slowly I gained understanding along with good health.

Two more years passed and by the spring of 1996, the arthritis was gone, the coursework was completed, the exams were passed with excellent grades, and I had learned more than I ever imagined. When the diploma arrived in the summer of that year, it ignited an inner furor.

As I opened the broad, flat box holding the diploma, the first thing I saw was the title "Doctor of Naturopathy." The words rocked me back to the words of the little men who had told me some fifteen years earlier that I would someday become the doctor I'd always dreamed of, one who "healed truly." Nothing had seemed less likely at the time, but now, here I was holding an acknowledgment of something I had become almost without forethought simply because I wanted to heal my arthritis.

Long at a standstill in terms of writing down what the little men had shown me, I got out the disjointed notes and began shuffling through them. In the manner of all synchronicities, the first thing I came to was their comment about becoming a doctor. Next to it was their forecast that although I was highly biased against ecological matters, I would come to understand the intelligent network of life connecting plants, earth, people, and the nature of healing. Again, they were right. If soil did not have a healthy population of microorganisms living in it, it was 'dead soil.' Plants growing in it would not be healthy. If plants were not healthy, the vegetables and fruits they produced would not have high levels of nutrients in them. If vegetables and fruits had poor nutrition levels, human bodies

---

[7] See *From The Soil To The Stomach,* to learn how to rebuild good health and heal a body caught in catastrophic illness.

would begin to degenerate. The results were arthritis, heart disease, cancers, asthma, and a host of other degenerative diseases.

My journey into healing had taught me much about nutrition and for the first time in my life I understood that having something in your belly did not mean that the body had what it needed to remain healthy. With some surprise I began to understand what the little men had been trying to get across in the visit that focused on the corn plant and its relationship to humans.

For days I contemplated all this with new eyes, wondering once more how much of what the little men had shown me might come to pass. In the midst of this contemplation I happened to hear a news report dealing with welfare cuts and the need for "personal responsibility." I was electrified. There it *was*… the term the little men had used so long ago! That was the term they said we would eventually base our new ideas of self-government on. Were the changes happening… or was it just a coincidence that the term had been used in connection with lawmakers and their endless efforts to cut expenses? I didn't know but the impact of hearing the words was tremendous.

Finally, I sat down to write. Carefully presenting the information from the point of view of an objective, journalistic observer, I kept the material at arm's length and reminded myself frequently of something that happened in early 1980.

During this time I had repeatedly seen a major earthquake and shift of the planet coming to the southeast Michigan area sometime in late 1981 or early 1982. I debated endlessly about what part of the country I could go to for safety, and even warned many of my friends that devastation was coming.

When 1981, then 1982 came—and promised to end with nothing that even remotely resembled an earthquake or devastation occurring in the greater Detroit metropolitan area—I felt like a fool in the face of my predictions. Embarrassed, I swore off predictions forever.

Obviously, I told myself, I still did not know how to handle all the visions, knowledge, and psychic information coming my way and was best off keeping my mouth shut.

As it turned out, the earthquake, shift, and devastation were the *personal* experiences coming to me over 1981-82. The earthquake symbolized the upheaval in my life due to loss of the relationship with Ben and the solid ground of house and home we shared. The shift symbolized a total shift of the work I did to make a living while providing myself with food, shelter, transportation, and other necessities. The devastation was the financial and emotional devastation resulting from all of this, and a total scattering of the self-image I had so carefully assembled over the thirty-three years previous.

The lesson regarding the difference between literal and symbolic information, as well as between personal and public involvement, was well taken. I reminded myself often that what the little men had shown me about the distant future probably had nothing to do with anyone else. Now, here I was, trying to write what I had seen, and violating every rule I had made about predictions or forecasting futures.

I envisioned myself as a mere bystander who just happened to be hanging around when some odd little beings in brown robes landed nearby and started handing out information. Surely the fact of the visits or the information had not affected me personally; it wasn't my message, I was only writing down what I had been told.

Carefully hugging my illusion of impartial, uninvolved scribe, I wrote, working slowly over the rest of that year and into the next. When the manuscript was complete, I gave it to several friends who had always been excellent editors for me. When they were finished reading, without exception, each felt I should read what others had written. They also wanted me to discuss the effects of the information on my own life and the implications of what I had seen.

This was not what I wanted to hear. I wanted to write about the future I had seen without being influenced by what others had written. And the idea of discussing implications brought out all my latent stubbornness. To discuss implications, I might have to say what I thought and felt about the little men and their pictures. I might have to share my own reactions or assess the possibility that these things might happen. I might have to compare what I had seen in the visits with what was happening in the world and make a judgment about how much change had already occurred and where I thought we were going. I hadn't really done any of this and I didn't want to. This was not my area of expertise. Worse, I might have to look at whether or not the information had affected my own life, and this would ruin my attempt to keep it at arm's length and myself in the position of neutral observer.

Instead of taking their suggestions, I polished the manuscript a little more and gave it to my husband, Jim, who was the absolute acid test for all of my writing. The fact that he and I had never discussed what I'd seen with the little men would make him a fresh point of view, and I was certain he would not hesitate to tell me what he thought it needed.

Jim read the chapters a little at a time over the next few days. He was without comment until he came to the one in which I described the families with their main houses and family business neighborhoods. At that point he came upstairs, flopped the chapter on my desk, and said, "Why didn't you tell me we were building a main house?"

I stared at him for a moment, trying to get my mind around the meaning of his words. "What do you mean?" I finally managed to ask.

"This barn we've been building for ten years…" he said, "it's just what you describe in this chapter. So why didn't you say anything before?"

"Say anything?… about what?… I don't understand what you mean… I mean, *are* we?… I didn't see that, or think of the barn that way…" I stammered, but even as I spoke, a wave of shock rolled through me as the implications of what he was saying hit home. The idea rocked me to the core of my being.

We bought the farm in 1987. There were about 57 acres of land, including two small vineyards, an old farmhouse built at the turn of the century, and a small, red barn. The ground level of the barn had once housed cows and horses and still had manure and stanchions in it at the time of purchase. The main floor was filled with old, abandoned farm equipment, and the third floor was a hayloft.

We moved into the house and started remodeling immediately. By autumn of that first year, we began working on the barn as well. Beginning at the south end, we cleared a portion of the main floor and built a comfortable room there. I used it as a combination office and classroom; it was where I did my consulting and taught my small classes in Intuition.

Jim, a construction project manager for Ameritech, built himself an office in the barn which he used as his base when he wasn't in Detroit, Chicago, or traveling the west half of the state.

Next we put in a bathroom so people didn't have to go traipsing across the driveway to the house at break time. Of course, we needed a space to serve coffee and tea during class breaks, or eat our lunch and relax during the day, so we cleaned up a little more of the space, and set up a table to hold coffee pot, teapot, cups, and cookies.

When the number of students in my classes outgrew the original room, we built a new office in the north end of the barn and the old office/classroom became classroom only.

Before long we were desperate for storage space for extra chairs and tables that were not in use constantly, so we fixed up a little more space. Somewhere along the way, we began eating breakfast in the barn while holding our daily planning meeting. Soon we were eating dinner out there as well. When the classes began attracting fifteen and then twenty students at a time, we built a larger classroom in the center of the barn and called it "the commons." With more people coming and going we found we needed an entryway where people could leave hats, coats, and boots. Eventually the old classroom became a full kitchen, which also served as a much more comfortable break room, and allowed me to make some delicious soups and salads during the day while we worked.

While all this was going on, we practically lived in the barn, going out to our offices in the morning, working all day, and continuing to work after supper on the various building projects long into the night. In the wee hours of the morning we would run across the driveway to the house, fall into bed, and get up the next morning to do it all over again.

One frigid winter day, Jim, a dyed-in-the-wool builder-inventor who had always dreamed of having an "attached garage" with enough space to park his vehicles and still have room for his favorite projects, was lying in the snow under the truck, changing the oil. I took him a cup of warm coffee to cheer him, and stood there feeling sorry for him. For five years he had been remodeling—both the house and the barn—without a decent place to store tools or work on cars, trucks, or farm machinery

Wishing he didn't have to lie on such icy ground I said, "Too bad you can't get that truck in the lower level of the barn to work on it."

"Well, when the house is finally finished, *and* the barn is finally finished, that's probably when I'll have the time to build my shops—when the job is done and I hardly need them any more," he said with mock suffering.

"Look," I said, "you've been working on this place for over five years with no garage or decent shop. Why don't you design your ideal space and we'll build it somewhere. You certainly deserve it."

Immediately and with great enthusiasm he began drawing up plans. Working around the foundation of the existing barn, he came up with an L-shaped design that allowed him to build a huge, ground level addition, one story high, on the east and north sides of the existing barn. It accommodated all the spaces he needed to run the farm, store large equipment in winter, work on his truck when necessary, organize his huge collection of tools, and play with the variety of things he liked to invent and build.

When he had the space laid out, he showed me the blueprints and told me that we had two choices. We could leave his garages and shops as a single-story addition at ground level, which would be cheaper, but I would have to look out at a large expanse of flat, rubber roofing. Or, we could build a second story on top of his garages and shops, giving me a much larger main floor.

In the beginning, I thought if we made his L-shaped addition a two-story affair, it would be far too big. The equipment garage on the north end was forty-two feet by one hundred feet, and his shop, storage, and garage area on the east side would be fifty-two by forty-two! I agreed that he needed the garage, shop, and machine shed space at ground level, but what would we do with all that extra space at the main floor level? When I thought about making it a house, I worried about how I would clean such a big house. At first, I decided it had to be a one-story addition, yet I didn't want to look out the barn windows and see six thousand square feet of flat rubber roof. That would be no different than living back in the city. I changed my mind, then again, and again.

Finally, giving me a year or two to make a decision about the main floor, Jim began the process of excavation and poured foundations for the ground level before I had a chance to change my mind about his dream garage. As he laid the block, my mind went back and forth, deciding that maybe I could use some of the new space on the main floor for a bigger classroom, one that would seat twenty-five to thirty people comfortably. I had always wanted an exercise room with plenty of space to move, so that was added to the plan.

Then I decided I needed a much differently designed kitchen. This would not be a 'pretty kitchen' with flowery wallpaper, pastel colored sinks, and little canisters of white flour, sugar, coffee, and tea. This would be a 'working kitchen' designed to support food with superior nutrition. In this kitchen the large quantities of whole, organic foods we were growing could be cleaned, prepared, and eaten fresh or stored safely. It would be a place where lots of herbs could be rinsed, dried, and stored, a place where butter could be churned, chickens dressed, bread baked, or poultices made without crowding or disrupting the flow of people and life that moved through such a kitchen. It would be one in which I could expand my teaching to include classes on foods and health.

Even with a bigger classroom, a new kitchen, and an exercise room decided upon, there was still a lot of square footage that we did not know what to do with. Breaking every rule of construction design and planning by leaving this so vague and unplanned, Jim finished laying blocks and began a two-story addition.

Slowly the building went up, taking every nickel and dime we could scrape together, every minute of time and ounce of energy we had to give, and then some. We did not really have a social life; instead we had a construction company of three—Jim, myself, and Jim's dad who came out nearly every weekend to work with us.

At first we were quite excited and kept telling one another that we were making good progress... in just a "little while we'd be done with the barn," maybe by the end of the year. After several years of endless work, constant debt, and the continuous pressure to plan the next step, make one more decision in terms of concrete and stone, pipes and lumber, we were exhausted.

We began to take turns bogging down in discouragement. First Jim would lose it saying, "What is the matter with us? What ever made us start such a big project? Why did we think we could afford a building this size... It's going to cost a fortune just to turn the lights on... and the taxes... what are we doing?"

Then I would take a turn complaining, "I'm tired... I can't stand the dust and construction any more... I don't care if we ever finish this barn... Maybe we should hurry and get it done, pay someone to finish it, and sell it... I just want a quiet, simple life... We should be thinking of when we retire... what in God's name are we going to do with such a gigantic place...."

Through it all, Jim thought of the place as his garage and shops; I thought of it as my classroom. Both of us referred to it as "the barn."

Many times we had tried to quit, even *had* quit, but after only a few days of "quitting," we would start talking about this aspect, or that design, and end up right back at it. It was 1997; we had been remodeling and building for a total of ten years. Now staring at one another over a few pages of manuscript describing the main house in family business neighborhoods of the future, I was stunned at the similarity of our barn to the buildings I had seen with the little men in brown robes. Even more shocking was the fact that Jim designed it with little input from me other than an argument here and there because I wanted to spend more time writing.

It had the huge wrap-around porches and decks I had seen in the future, decks I originally balked at because of the extra cost, but which Jim insisted on because he didn't want to wash windows, clean chimneys or repair roofs from a ladder stretched two or three stories up. In his mind, the decks and porches solved this problem nicely.

The excess space we had not known what to do with became five individual bedroom suites, each with their own bath and private entrance. So far there were six bedrooms, five offices, eight bathrooms, two kitchens, an exercise and meditation room, a large classroom/living room, a medium-sized conference area, a sitting room used for reading or watching television, a laundry, my sewing room, even a central area we referred to as 'the commons' because it was used for everything—living space, teaching space, meeting space, relaxation space. The lower level housed another large office, the various shops for woodworking, machine repair, and electronics, a very large storage area for tractors and other farm equipment, a glassed in solar garden, and a combination boiler room/mudroom/mail delivery room.

Various factors influenced the final design. Jim's insistence that we build a private suite for his father... my insistence that we have a room for my mother if she needed it... grown children who moved back home, all had led to the spacious bedroom suites. My small business of teaching, personal consulting, and massage... my love of herbs, gardens, and homemade food... my understanding of what it took to stay healthy... were we already setting up the foundations for a main house and didn't even know it?

The shocking realization that our remodeled 'barn' fit the description of the main houses the little men had shown me brought immediate distress. How had this happened? How was I going to write about my visits with the little men and maintain an air of objective detachment yet hide this white elephant of a building? What had we done? More importantly, what were we really doing here with this farm? For the first time, I faced the possibility that perhaps the little men had affected my life. Still, I denied it.

Several nights later I was teaching a class and heard myself repeating some bit of information I had seen while with the little men, yet I did not mention them or their visits. When class was over, I sat in the dimly lit classroom drinking a cup of bedtime tea and thinking about what I'd done. I presented some piece of information that originally came from the little men as if it were *my* information, *my* perspective on life.

With the clarity that sometimes comes in the middle of the night, I could see that my whole life reflected what I had learned from the little men. I could deny it, of course, but anyone looking objectively at the situation could easily see the influence. We had built a flexible and fairly self-sufficient life in harmony with the earth, and although we might have had other reasons for what we were doing, we couldn't hide the presence of what certainly looked like a main house and a small but working family business.

Clearly, we had divided our time and energy between the world that currently existed, and a world that we could depend on if nations disintegrated or starvation spread. We had worked long, sometimes grueling hours, and yet we had loved it.

As if heeding the old wisdom, "Give to Caesar the things that are Caesar's..." we had planted one foot in the world of governments, tax collectors, money, and corporations, while the other was planted firmly in family and the land. Our first step toward an extended family began when my daughter and her three children came back from Germany to live and work on the farm. For six years, three generations had been working here; four generations if you counted Jim's dad for three days every week.

After a few years, we took the children out of public schools in order to teach them at home and were pleased at the overall improvement in attitudes, cooperation, responsibility, and personal creativity.

Since that one small garden back in 1981, I had continued to grow food wherever I could and now maintained a one-acre garden and orchard here on the farm. My initial experience with chamomile, peppermint, and parsley had expanded to over forty culinary herbs and almost as many medicinals, which I picked, dried, and used regularly.

In our two vineyards totaling about 14 acres altogether, we raised Concord grapes under contract to Welch Foods. By stages, we had abandoned chemical fertilizers and poisons, learning a variety of organic techniques for coaxing a crop out of the land. Because of its low cost and ability to produce food with superior nutrition, we eventually settled on Bio-Dynamic farming practices which involved specific composting procedures and herbal sprays to combat disease.

Interested in fresh eggs and getting my hands on good, rich chicken manure I bought some chickens. When the chicken population went to ninety hens and then one hundred fifty, I scratched up my guts and learned to kill and dress a few the way my Grandma had always done, an experience that deepened my appreciation for the life and gifts given by those animals that fed us. A secondary reward was the astounding difference in taste and tenderness compared to commercially grown chicken. We sold the extra eggs at a health food store in Kalamazoo where their exquisite taste and shocking orange yolks earned them constant demand and the description "those delicious eggs with the fluorescent orange yolks."

Our success and delight in owning chickens accustomed us to taking care of animals daily, and this, plus my desire for more manure, convinced us to buy a cow. When Gladys gave birth to a calf three days after we brought her home, everyone learned to milk her. When she produced over three gallons a day, we made yogurt, then a variety of cheeses, then butter and ice cream. The milk we couldn't use was sprayed as an organic nutrient in the vineyards, returning it to the earth.

As everyone in the family drank the fresh, whole, unpasteurized milk, problems with milk allergies disappeared along with the allergy "shiners" under our grandchildren's eyes. Mucous dried up, skin grew clear and soft, hair and fingernails became strong, thick and shiny. When the milk began to dry up, we walked Gladys down the road to meet the local bull and start the cycle all over again. In the meantime, we added geese, then ducks, turkeys, a goat, and honeybees to our collection of animals, learning to care for them, accept their gifts, and live with their idiosyncrasies.

We put up a greenhouse and were rewarded with a variety of lettuces and greens that grew continuously for over a year. We planted a number of small fruits and feasted on a delicious and continuous supply of berries which we ate fresh, froze, or made into jams, jellies, and syrups. Harvesting grapes from our vineyard, I learned to steam extract juice, make vinegars, and even homemade wines, which turned out to be a simple process resulting in potent, tasty wine without pesticides or preservatives.

For years I had made homemade bread simply because I enjoyed it. Now we bought wheat, oats, rye, or spelt from local organic farmers, ground it into flour, and made it into bread immediately, before the natural vitamin E and wheat oils could turn rancid. All of nature's bran and fiber was included and those who came to visit us remarked endlessly on how wonderful the bread was, and how powerful its ability to clean out their large intestine!

Gradually I became interested in collecting seeds and noticed a big improvement in germination and growth rates for those seeds that had grown and reproduced here for a year or two. Seed collecting had become one of my small passions.

Once my arthritis was gone, I took on other healing challenges in my family, tackling things like asthma and chronic bronchitis, ear, nose, and throat infections including those that were strep-based. I learned to heal kidney and bladder infections, staphylococcus infections, candida, gallstone trouble, and a host of other things we used to run to the doctor for. The victory over the staphylococcus infection was particularly sweet, as the battle had been a pitched one that finally broke through my reluctance to believe a staph infection could be healed without antibiotics. When it was over, I realized how far we had come in our efforts to manage our own healing. Chemical medicines and surgeries were there if we needed an emergency rescue, but we had learned to handle the majority of everyday illnesses, and even some serious diseases.

Because of Jim's personal interests, we had continuously upgraded our computers and computer skills. We investigated alternative sources of energy, and put in back-up heating systems. His insistence on saving energy had resulted in a barn that had 6" walls with several layers of super-insulation. Because it was so common for our electricity to go off unexpectedly for four or five hours at a time, he installed a back-up electrical system along with low-voltage emergency lighting. Without electricity we were out of water, so we put in a 4" well that would allow us to install a hand pump in the same well-pipe as the electric pump, guaranteeing access to water even if the back-up system died, although we would have to pump it by hand outside and then haul it inside.

Throughout all this designing and building, raising and teaching of children and grandchildren, the continuous deepening of our connection to the land, and the ongoing expansion of the skills of self-sufficiency, each of us continued to work full time. Jim maintained his more-than-full-time job at Ameritech, and I continued to nurse the "family business" by teaching my classes, maintaining a small personal consulting practice, writing, occasionally lecturing at one of the local colleges, and selling fresh vegetables and eggs.

We paid taxes, managed our vineyards well enough to deliver a crop of grapes to Welch each year, and kept our financial heads above water, sometimes barely, while serving as a private lending and welfare institution for our children now and then.

We didn't drive expensive cars, wear expensive clothes, or take fancy vacations. We didn't keep up with the latest fads, didn't see the latest movies, and sometimes weeks or even months would go by without radio or television.

Family members still in the city asked why we bothered to grow our own food or deal with chickens when we could just go to any store and buy whatever we needed. It was the same with my herbs, bread baking, and wine. When we bought our cow, they acted as if we had gone over the edge. They could not understand how we could tie ourselves and our life to the milk schedules of a cow, and did not see that they had tied themselves and their lives to the schedules of a corporation. They did their best to convince us that it was dangerous to drink raw milk, or that we shouldn't be drinking whole milk with all that butterfat, and they didn't notice the difference in our slim, youthful bodies, high energy, and good health.

Friends discouraged me when I took up the study of naturopathic medicine, pointing out that I did not have enough time in my day to do something like go back to school, that Michigan did not recognize naturopathic healing anyway, and therefore I would not make enough money at it to make it worthwhile.

When we stopped long enough to watch our twenty-year-old television set and look at what was happening in the world outside the farm, we worried about the potential for wars that seemed forever imminent. The rest of the time we wondered how people could spend so much time doing things that seemed either meaningless or unfulfilling to them. We loved what we were doing.

Co-workers and acquaintances talked enthusiastically about their football and baseball games, complained about the cost of putting their parents in nursing homes, lost sleep over the behavior of their teenagers or their ADHD children, and suffered from a host of physical, mental, and emotional aches.

When we spoke just as enthusiastically about building our barn, collecting seeds, healing with clay, experiments with "living water," or the benefits of home schooling, they looked at us as if we were from another planet. When we mentioned that they ought to look at their diet if they wanted to be healthy, they said they didn't have time. Yet when people came out to help us work on the building for a weekend, we learned quickly that no one we knew, not even the people half our age, had the mental energy, strength and flexibility, or physical stamina that we took for granted.

From where I stood, too many people were letting something outside themselves determine what had value and what was worth doing. They weren't doing what they loved to do. Repeatedly I observed people making decisions based on money alone, the criteria being "whatever is cheapest."

Through the years of personal consulting and counseling, I had frequently traced people's lives backward into their past lives, and sometimes ahead into their future. This process taught me a good deal about how people planned and carried out a life, as well as insight into how lifetimes unfolded. At last, I was not afraid to look out at the world and see what was happening there. Moreover, what I saw was that much of what the little men had shown me was unfolding in the world. I could see the outcomes we were headed toward. How could we *not* see what was happening?

Only a year ago the government had been shut down for months because Congress had not had time to put budgets together for approval. Huge mergers were taking place among the multi-nationals, swallowing up small and intermediate businesses as if they were so much plankton. The weather was doing strange, extreme things. On a news report I saw the exact scene that I had watched years earlier with the little men, bodies floating in an African river, their blood spilled everywhere by machine guns and machetes.

My involvement with the vineyards on the farm finally led to my understanding of the comments of the little men that 'just when we needed to get the most from our soils, we would get the least.' We had been systematically destroying the soil for many years with chemical sprays and fertilizers. Poor quality soils produced poor quality nutrition, which in turn produced poor quality people with lower physical, mental, and emotional functioning. Millions were suffering the effects of serious degeneration of the physical system. Various organs and limbs were slightly deformed and didn't work right, the endocrine system often malfunctioned, metabolism was poor and unbalanced, digestion sluggish, bone structures were thin and cheapened. Cholesterol plastered the insides of veins and arteries in an effort to strengthen the walls of the circulatory system. The ingestion of sugar, preservatives, and pesticides compounded the problems and clouded the real issue, which was the absence of high quality nutrition.

I could see that poor health and starvation of millions was possible. If people got hungry, they would be irritable, and how easy it would be for a hungry, irritable population to ignore government as well as traditional rituals of law and order! Irritable, malnourished people were much more likely to start fighting and wars.

I was still sitting in my darkened classroom when the clock began striking midnight and all the veils slid to the side. There, side-by-side in perfect harmony, were the teachings of the little men and the structures and activities of my life. With great clarity I saw that the perspectives taught by the little men were now my perspectives, their teaching was my teaching. And whether you called it intuition, common sense, maturity, the rekindling of human development, or the re-establishment of inner authority, over the intervening years I had learned to see, think, and do for myself what I thought was important. So had Jim. We supported one another in this and worked actively to nurture one another's personal development. I was teaching it to others, had been teaching it for years.

In the dark silence that surrounded me that midnight, I could no longer deny that the little men had affected me or my view of the world. I could *not* see how the government was going to survive. I *was* afraid business would come to power. I was certain lots of people were heading toward starvation, and at that point, it did not even strike me as impossible that the Earth might roll over or shift her position.

Once more, just as I had sixteen years ago, I slipped out of the net of my safe and routine reality, falling breathlessly through an empty space, gripped by the same terror that had seized me long ago when the national umbrella under which I had so securely moved through The Everyday had momentarily disappeared. This time I was propelled by the realization that my whole life had been seriously affected by what the little men had shown me and I was moving into the future they outlined. 📖

23 📖

TRANSFORMATIONS...

IN the weeks that followed, I began questioning every aspect of my life. Was I foolishly struggling to maintain two vastly different worlds, building a life of old-fashioned self-sufficiency while the rest of the world was moving into a sleek, sophisticated virtual future? When I looked at the future, was I seeing what the little men wanted me to see, or what *I* wanted to see? Was there any difference any more? Did I trust what I saw? What did other people see when they looked at the future. Had they written anything about what they saw? Suddenly the advice of my editing friends made sense. Perhaps it was a good idea to read what others had written in case what I had to say was wildly, ridiculously different.

Over the next few weeks I read nearly a dozen books whose themes were the future. Helen Wambach and Chet Snow had hypnotized thousands of people and asked them to go into the first century of the new millennium. Consistently, they reported a much smaller population on earth. In fact, about 95% of the population was gone. In addition to great financial difficulties, they reported that something awful, something devastating, had occurred in the natural world. Technology was still around, food was highly valued, and many people were living in seriously altered arrangements that sounded a lot like the families and family business neighborhoods I had seen. [8]

The writings of the ancient seers among the Hopi Indians warned their descendants against relying on supermarkets for food, or depending on wages to buy needed things, for "there will be suffering when the white man's world collapses." They sounded like the little men in brown robes when they advised that at the beginning of each new year, there should be a ritual ceremony in which we sat down and looked into the future of the coming year so that we would be prepared for everything that would happen. More than anything, they called for becoming self-sufficient in ways that maintained the harmony of the world, and respected natural laws. This reminded me of the little men's insistence that there were laws we knew nothing about, and that we needed to choose an alignment before we would be given any further secrets. [9]

The Mayans were sophisticated astronomers and devised a system of calendars that recorded the cyclical shifting of the sun's magnetic field so they could be ready for the havoc created by this shifting. In their book, *The Mayan Prophecies*, Adrian Gilbert and Maurice Cotterell reported, "When the sun's magnetic field shifts direction, it tends to twist the Earth off its axis. The tilting Earth is subjected to earthquakes, floods, conflagrations, and volcanic eruptions. The sun's magnetic field shifts five times every long cosmic cycle. This would seem to be the reason that the Mayans and others believed that the Earth has been destroyed four times in the past, and that destruction at the beginning of the 21st century in this, the fifth age of the sun, will follow in the same way." [10]

After reading *Bold New World* [11] by William Knoke, I thought briefly about writing to ask if he had also been visited by the little men in brown robes! Starting with what he called the Placeless Society, a society in which every physical location was connected to every other location on the planet via the evolution of the global network, he neatly outlined the future. His list of outdated concepts and structures included nations and their artificial borders. He predicted the collapse of these along with national corporations and multinational corporations. He stated categorically that the idea of retail stores and malls would collapse and disappear,

---

[8] See *Mass Dreams of the Future* by Chet Snow, Ph.D. published by Deep Forest Press in 1989.

[9] From *The Hopi Survival Kit* by Thomas E. Mails, published by Welcome Rain, 1997.

[10] *The Mayan Prophecies* by Adrian G. Gilbert and Maurice M. Cotterell, published by Element Books, 1995.

[11] *Bold New World* by William Knoke, published by Kodansha International in 1996.

that stock markets as we know them would become extinct, and that people would begin to trade directly with one another across the planet, unhampered by such things as national barriers, or import and export rules.

He noted that the nuclear family would disintegrate and be replaced with other forms of family, that educational institutions would disappear as the global network made it possible for the entire world to be a classroom without walls, and that we needed *self governance* not *government*. He calmly discussed the coming shakeout among the huge multinationals, predicted that naturalists would come up against industrialists, spiritualists would go against capitalists, that government would be replaced by "self-determination" and that there would be a serious need for an entirely new set of ethics, values, and morals.

When I had finished reading Knoke's book, I nearly decided to abandon the manuscript regarding the little men. Knoke had said it all just as clearly as "the Robes" and I did not see any reason to repeat what had already been written. However, when I realized that none of the other accounts of the future offered the unique "teaching approach" or the wonderful combination of depth, detail, and encouragement toward creative action that the little men had presented, I decided to go ahead with the project.

As it turned out, what I had seen was *not* wildly contradictory! Other writers or seers had forecast many of the same kinds of events. Compared to the grim collection of doomsday predictions in John Hogan's *The Millennium Book of Prophecy*, the pictures the little men presented seemed almost ho-hum.

In the end, I was not sure whether I should be pleased that the visions of other writers matched the pictures shown by the little men; or depressed, because they had seen the same miseries and suffering which lent weight to the possibilities of what we were headed for.

Entering more deeply into self-confrontation, I asked myself why I had ignored what I'd seen for so long. All sorts of excuses presented themselves. I was "waiting for proof," or thinking that by ignoring such a future it wouldn't happen. For years I denied what I was, and how I was, in the hope that all the intuitions, visions, and knowings would go away so I could return to the way I'd once been, the precious illusion of an "ordinary woman." But when all the excuses were discarded, the truth that I wrestled with, ran from, or tried to deny was my unwillingness to witness the pain, suffering, or death I had seen on such a large scale.

I could handle a sick aunt, or a dying friend. These were one-at-a-time situations and bad enough. But the suffering I had seen with the little men was massive, culture-wide, and the sense of confusion and pain had been almost more than I could bear. I did not want to watch family, friends, or even strangers suffering, starving, dying. During the times the little men had immersed me in the future, I felt helpless in the face of such massive need.

True to my own inner tradition of maintaining balance in the face of overwhelming subjective or intuitive information, I swung round to logic and reason, examining the situation through this set of lenses. Was it *possible* that we could be headed for such difficulties? Yes, I had to admit it was. Was it *likely* we would end up in such difficulties? In all truth, I had to say yes, unless we immediately cut population and made attempts to heal the earth and become more self-sufficient. Was it *possible* the earth could shift? Yes, logically I had to admit it was. Was it *likely* the earth would shift? The odds were miniscule that it would happen in my lifetime, especially when the brief span of my lifetime was cast against the background of time as measured by the births and deaths of stars and galaxies.

Yet, what if it did shift... what would such an event mean? Other than the obvious chaos, would it mean that we were doomed or God was punishing us? Logically, I had to assume that if the planet did roll or shift, the fact that humanity might suffer had less to do with beliefs that God was punishing us than with the fact that the earth had cycles of her own, things that she did regularly and naturally in the processes of her own existence as a planet.

Even if we corrected our ways and adopted flexible lifestyles, we could not say "Okay, we are safe now, this or that catastrophe won't happen." That was a childish attitude of "I'll be good if you'll be nice." If catastrophe occurred and millions died, it would be more the result of our failure to pay attention to the signs that earth was giving us, and to the sorts of things planets experienced in the course of their lives. We had long ignored the place where we lived as unimportant, of no consequence, and had not kept up our end of the relationship with Earth. Since all relationships demand attention or they fall apart, we might have to learn a few tough lessons.

Now I examined the shifts and devastation from the point of view of what I had learned about my own visions of earthquakes, planet shifts, and devastation back in 1981-82. What if the Earth remained perfectly calm and quiet, and the earthquakes that had long been predicted by many seers were symbolic of the utter loss of stability in the life that we had created here? Were the visions of earthquakes a symbolic representation of a shake-up in the industrial structures and job-oriented routines of The Everyday? Was our sense of security going to be shaken up?

Was "the pole shift" a one-hundred-eighty degree shift in the way we saw the world and our place in it? Was it a shift toward waking up to the massive problems we had created by destroying our soil, food, water, air, and the web of life? Did it symbolize a shift in the kind of work we would have to do to produce our own food, clothing, shelter, education, transportation, or communication instead of going to the store, the school, or public utilities to buy these?

Might the "devastation" mean the emotional devastation of the demise of nations, democratic governments, and the institutions that framed contemporary life? Might it mean the disappearance of many of the things that had become symbols of the good life... the loss of possessions, conveniences, or titles that led us to believe we were successful, special, and protected from things like hunger, cold, or unplanned, unannounced change?

I pondered the sorts of events that could trigger the loss of stability and certainly there were many. Wars, financial difficulties, lack of food, not enough water, extreme weather, poor health had all been mentioned by the little men. As I sifted through the many possible causes, the words of the little men came floating back, "...there will be many who will be entering the consciousness of the Christ mind..." and ever so slowly a new thought took shape.

What if "the shift" was a shift of consciousness? For years the organized churches of the world had been predicting a "second coming of Christ." What if "the planetary pole shift" that had long been predicted for the planet at the turn of this century *was* the "second coming of Christ" and a major spiritual awakening? Were we going to swing from a material pole to a spiritual pole?

Some people were expecting a new Jesus to appear, some even expected the old Jesus to return. Very few understood that the term "Christ" referred to a kind of consciousness, that Jesus had entered and maintained that kind of consciousness, and that was why he was called "The Christ." The actual definition of the word meant "the anointed one" and was used to describe an individual who had discovered the sacred "*I Am*" within the Self. This led to an unleashing of the "true Self" and the development of dignity and responsibility, of beauty and creativity, of meaning and purpose, of natural leadership and inner authority. A Christ was someone bearing healing, acting with a sense of justice, awakening others to their own true, unique Self. [12]

Now things began to click. Perhaps the second coming of Christ was not destined to occur in one individual who would go about preaching, raising the dead, and turning water into wine. This second coming of Christ was already occurring and destined to be completed in millions of us. There wouldn't be just one lone Christ. This time we would all be transformed, we would all be responsible, we would all come to recognize the true Self that was hidden in each of us, and there would be a blossoming of inner authority, personal responsibility, beauty, and creativity.

For a moment I was elated, filled with excitement about what people could accomplish with the power of such consciousness. We could have a new Golden Age! Drifting back through time, I reflected on the awakening of kundalini and resulting transformations in my own consciousness years earlier, with its trials, confusions, and difficulties. Abruptly the elation collapsed. Like a stone my stomach dropped and rolled away. Oh my god, what if the world was facing the same process I had gone through?

Most people thought of spiritual transformation as a vague change of attitude involving religion or some kind of benevolent attitude. I *knew* that it involved physical, mental, and emotional changes at very deep levels. The awakening of consciousness brought intense pressure to bear on your entire life. It affected physical health, sexual experience, careers, money, personal relationships, life-style, hobbies, and the ability to carry out The Everyday routines. It opened awareness, changed belief systems, altered expectations, values, ethics, and morals.

Spiritual transformation not only changed your entire material life, it changed mental life, altering perception, opening many psychic abilities and a respect for all of life. These changes necessitated the integration of a whole new language so you could express what you were experiencing. It also created the need for an array of behaviors appropriate to the new sensitivity toward others, be they people, animals, or members of the plant family.

A full shift of consciousness[13] could be triggered by many factors ranging from a deep encounter with nature to a powerful sexual

---

[12] *The Coming of The Cosmic Christ* by Matthew Fox, published by Harper San Francisco, a division of Harper Collins Publishers, New York, NY. 1988.

[13] A full opening of consciousness is known in the East as the "awakening of kundalini", and in the West as the "manifestation of grace." Generally misunderstood and overlooked, it is often misdiagnosed as a psychological disorder.

experience, from winning at something that had been long sought, to a look or a touch. It could be set in motion by transcendent music, a meditation, or something else altogether. Even if it was only a momentary experience, the awakening process would begin.

Once begun, it was often relentless, proceeding according to its own ancient laws of unfolding. The conformity that pushed people to follow cultural and social dictates shifted inexorably, sometimes dramatically, as personal understanding of the Self deepened, and new goals arose. As the little men once said, spiritual transformation was the transformation of *meaning* in your life. When old activities lost their meaning they were abandoned, creating the freedom to pursue new activities in line with a growing sense of purpose and inner authority.

As the new sense of purpose took hold, you could become almost dysfunctional in the old reality within a matter of months. Pursuit of new goals, new paths of interest, new ways of self-expression, along with a search for validation and support of this new Self, became the central organizing principle of life. Joseph Campbell had quite accurately called it "The Hero's Journey" because the inner battles surrounding the need to honor your own unfolding Self were fierce and required heroic strength and will.

These heroic battles arose because the deepest assumptions about how life should be organized and how you should spend your time usually conflicted with current spouses, friends, family, and the daily habits that characterized your physical existence. The new views conflicted with old routines of going to work to bring in the money needed for food, shelter, car payments, and other necessities. Usually your whole life was embedded in these old routines, thus the whole life ended up in conflict.

When these old ways no longer allowed you to express the meaning of your life, when they no longer represented how you wanted to spend your time and energy, they were often let go of, sometimes too quickly. If new structures and routines for supplying yourself with food, shelter, warmth, health, transportation, companions, education, and other comforts had not yet been created, chaos occurred.

Those working their way through an awakening of consciousness encountered great difficulty for a while because entry into the "Christ-mind" was not an issue involving a little religious fluff. It moved people toward an entirely new worldview as well as a new psychological and emotional framework for both thought and action. It literally shifted bio-chemical, neurological, and electromagnetic functioning, which not only tipped over the applecart of The Everyday, it reconnected people to the world of nature and the greater circles of culture in changing ways. The result was a new foundation for greatly expanded perception and feeling, both of which stood in marked contrast to the world that had seemed "normal" before the awakening.

📖

As the old predictions of earthquakes and pole shifts intersected with a second coming of Christ, and these were placed alongside my awareness of how difficult a spiritual awakening could be, my insides began to churn. How far could a large population go in the throes of spiritual transformation before things got really rough? What would millions of people do if they were not getting up, showering, and going to work everyday? If people were not going to work, how would they make their house payments? The entire population could not be evicted... could they? Should I try to help? Maybe I should just keep quiet. After all, I was prepared. Then memories of the agony I had felt when I saw the amount of suffering in the world would flood me. If I was the only one prepared, what good would that do? I couldn't feed myself and ignore them, and I couldn't feed the whole world with 14 acres of grapes and some home-made bread.

I was struggling with these issues, when I received an invitation to co-host several afternoon seminars whose topic was the coming "earth changes." On the day of the first seminar I arrived to find a room full of people, male and female, of all ages, and all very interested in the pre-dicted changes. Some had seen small visions of the changes, some had received messages from spirit guides or deceased relatives, others had read of them, seen them on TV, or heard things from friends and were becom-ing concerned.

As the day progressed, it became clear to me that everyone—without exception—was hoping the changes would actually occur! Curious, I questioned them to get a better picture of why they hoped such changes would come to pass. Their reasons were varied. Some wanted a way out of the rigid careers they were locked into, several had chosen careers in the field of alternative health or alternative business and felt they would never get the recognition or financial security they wanted as long as the "old boy system" was in power. Some felt the poisoning of the earth had to stop somehow and nothing less than the hand of God could accomplish such a huge and daunting task. Others reported that something vague and undefined was out of balance and needed correction. Some just felt in their bones that something needed to change, a few were bored and sensed that something momentous was going to happen, and one or two were steeped in religious righteousness and felt that the Apocalypse was near.

They seemed to be waiting for the earth to roll over so they wouldn't have to do the work of rebuilding themselves or their culture. They talked as if a shift of the planet would selectively and neatly erase big government, big business, big medicine, or big education, and leave them free to do what they wanted.

Toward the end of the day I asked the question, "So if you all, in one way or another, want or expect these changes to happen, what have you done to get ready for the new life you envision?"

There was a long silence; no one had made any attempt to think clearly about what these changes might mean in a practical sense. Everyone wanted change, but no one was ready to take responsibility for making it happen. They were waiting for something to happen and hoped that when it did, things would change for the better and the problems of our current culture would disappear.

My next question, "How would you feel if none of the changes we have discussed today happened at all and everything went on the way it is?" caused every face to fall in disappointment. Clearly, they were hoping something would happen.

Finally I said, "What if nothing changes unless you make it happen? What if the changes we've all heard about are not changes imposed from the outside, but rather changes that must come from inside you? What if the first change is a change of consciousness?"

The silence in the room was pulsing with discomfort and dismay. Everyone wanted change, yet wanted someone or something else to decide what had to be done, as well as do the actual work. They wanted to wake up one morning to a whole new world.

In the end my suggestion was that each individual go home and survey their lives with a realistic eye, answering a few important questions such as, "What do you know about growing or preserving food? Where would you get seeds? How many herbs are you familiar with and can recognize on sight? How much do you know about healing yourself without fancy drugs or surgeries? How many trees grow around your house to make it comfortable if you were without air conditioning for a time? Do you have any back-up systems for heat, lights, and water? How much do you know about other energy sources and technologies? What do you know about building or repairing a home or other shelter? If you had to retrofit your home to accommodate a much more self-sufficient lifestyle, where would you begin? In fact, what does self-sufficiency mean to you? Would you have the supplies or the skills to live in a self-sufficient manner? Who do you know that has weaving and sewing skills? How would you cook or bake without gas stoves or electricity? Who do you know that can make dishes, pans, and bakeware? When is the last time you were out in nature for any length of time? Could you make bricks, lumber, or thatch if you had to? Do you have a computer at home and are you familiar with the Internet? How many hours of physical work can you do at a time and for how many days in a row? How much thought have you given to the possibility that you might have to combine skills and resources with several other families? Who would you be most comfortable living with? Who do you think might be able to live with you?"

At the end of the day, I went home a changed woman. I knew that there were going to be changes because people wanted them desperately. Whether they came from the outside and turned our personal lives upside down, or came from our insides and turned the outer world upside down remained to be seen. As for myself, the gift given to me over the day was the realization that I had started the changes in my own life and had come a long way. All I needed to do was believe that we could continue those changes in a reasonable, sensible, creative way that connected us ever more deeply to the Earth. 📖

EPILOGUE...

IN light of all that has happened in me and in my life since the first awakening of kundalini, it seems clear to me that every area of my life has been transformed from the way I started out as a child. Not overnight, but still, slowly, immeasurably transformed. Of course, every adult is a transformed child, but most children have a sense of *how they are* deep inside and carry that sense into adulthood. I do not have that sense of continuity with childhood. Instead, I have the memory of being someone who did not know how to love or care, and of watching that former self die when the awakening of kundalini introduced me to a deeper Self and oneness with all that is.

Kundalini is the full awakening of consciousness and such an awakening leads inexorably to an entirely new view of reality and the world. For me, this has been most obvious in three major areas: the realm of people and personal relationships; the realm of plants, animals, and nature; and the realm of society and what makes sense in the world in terms of governing ourselves, education, work, health, and the things that truly bring joy to life.

People themselves have taught me about people. My relationship with plants, trees, the elves, and other small creatures that live on our farm taught me about plants, animals, and nature. And it was the little men in brown robes who taught me how to look at the world and society much differently.

Do I have any sure explanations of them and their visits? Not really. I have met at least two other people who have had encounters with a group of little men in brown robes, and this was somewhat reassuring. I have answered the question "Why me?" to at least some extent. It was because kundalini removes the limits and boundaries of perception. As for the little men, there are many beings in the universe of realities who make it their business to be helpful whenever they can. The little men in brown robes were drawn to my need, and set about teaching me to adjust my perception in ways that were in alignment with our ongoing evolution.

Their tutoring has become more powerful with each passing year and I am confident enough to say there are a few things I am certain of. One, I am absolutely certain that human evolution is built in and we will see more and more signs of advanced ability in one another as time goes by. Two, I am certain we are at a turning point and I would like it to stay a turning point and not become a flashpoint. Three, I see signs all over the culture that others are also building the infrastructures based around the concept of the family business neighborhoods. They may not realize what they are doing, but they are doing it. And last, I have chosen to align with life and creating.

📖

Legend has it that there was once a place called Atlantis with great wisdom, power, and extraordinary technologies. Part of the legend says that they became highly developed because of their respect for the Law of One, and when they turned away from this law, they were eventually destroyed by their technology.

While the story of Atlantis may or may not be true, it is obvious that there *is* a place called America. This place has great power, we have developed some extraordinary technologies, and because we do not recognize or honor our oneness with nature, we will likely be destroyed by our technology. It is not necessarily the technology of war that will bring us down, it is the technology of The Everyday... the technologies of creating artificial food by means of chemical processing, or an agriculture which destroys soil, weakens plants, and kills insects, birds, animals, and eventually people. Our demise is hidden in the technologies that allow us to keep warm with fuels that pollute the air, cover up disease with false medicines, build fancy houses that invade the territory and destroy the lives of innumerable Others in nature. It is in the technologies that allow us to waste water, use precious resources to manufacture useless trinkets, travel endlessly back and forth across the land leaving poisonous trails, or maintain our belief in mass production—whether of cars, clothes, or human beings.

Perhaps someday there will be a legend about America. Our descendants, if we have any, will look back in time and tell stories of how grand we were before our destruction. Perhaps they will say, "They mistakenly believed they had to conquer nature rather than learn to master the physical nature of themselves. They believed they were the only important beings on the planet and mistakenly cleared the land, killed the trees, poisoned the animals and insects. By capturing the water and forcing it into pipes, sewers, and tanks, they strangled the living spirit of the water and lost the powerful energies it brought them. By dumping billions of tons of waste into they air they choked themselves. By manufacturing fake food, and eating it they weakened their body/mind systems, made themselves tired and lazy, and reduced their creative abilities. Soon it became a land of wage slaves, with a slave mentality, and when the time came to make powerful, creative decisions they could not decide anything and succumbed to their own weak natures and ignorance.

Or perhaps, if we can transform ourselves and our lives, there will someday be a legend in the universe about a small planet named Earth that produced powerful, loving beings. Maybe our descendants will look back in time and tell teaching stories of how we struggled to learn and grow, working hard to correct our mistakes, until we finally emerged from the dark ages into the light of full consciousness. Perhaps they will discuss with awe how we freed ourselves from slavery and began to follow our hearts. Maybe they will draw courage from the way we recovered our inner authority, aligned ourselves with life, and tapped the deeper secrets of the universe.

I now believe that any transformation we make must begin with consciously choosing an alignment—either creating or destroying—and being willing to shoulder your inner authority then take your place in the re-creation and management of our world.

Assuming that you would choose to align yourself with life, and to participate in managing our world, what statement would you add to a World Document of Ethics? 📖

Index

About The Author

Penny Kelly is the owner, with her husband, of Lily Hill Farm & Learning Center in the southwest corner of Michigan where she writes and teaches an annual series of classes in *Developing and Using Intuition*, *Organic Gardening*, and *Getting Well Again Naturally*. She also does nutritional consultations, maintains a large spiritual counseling practice, and raises organic vegetables and fruits.

Penny holds a degree in Humanistic Studies from Wayne State University, a degree in Naturopathic Medicine from Clayton College of Natural Health, and is currently working toward her Ph.D. in nutrition from the American Holistic College of Nutrition.

Robes is book number three in the Transformation Trilogy, the first being *The Evolving Human*, and the second being *The Elves of Lily Hill Farm*. She has also written a fourth book, *From The Soil To The Stomach*, which focuses on the connection between the Earth and your health. Penny is currently at work on a 2-volume set with Dr. William Levengood titled *Consciousness and Energy*, due out in 2006.

Printed in the United States
109807LV00005B/104/A